BREAD
MATTERS

BREAD MATTERS

THE STATE OF MODERN BREAD AND A DEFINITIVE GUIDE TO BAKING YOUR OWN

ANDREW WHITLEY

FOURTH ESTATE · London

First published in Great Britain in 2006 by
Fourth Estate
An imprint of HarperCollins*Publishers*
77–85 Fulham Palace Road
London W6 8JB
www.4thestate.co.uk

Copyright © Andrew Whitley 2006
Photographs by Jeff Cottenden
Illustrations by Richard Bravery

1

A catalogue record for this book is
available from the British Library

ISBN-13 0-00-978-720374-1
ISBN-10 0-00-720374-8

Set in Granjon with Lubalin Graph by
Rowland Phototypesetting Ltd, Bury St Edmunds, Suffolk

Printed in Italy by L.E.G.O. Spa
on Cyclus Offset, a 100% recycled paper

To Veronica

CONTENTS

ACKNOWLEDGEMENTS

This book would not have been possible without the help of many people, notably the many bakers in the UK, France and Russia from whom I have learned.

Louise Haines kindly asked me to write the book and showed a commitment beyond the call of editorial duty by attending two of my courses. My understanding of some of the science of nutrition and baking was enlarged by Margaret Rayman, John Lewis, Stan Cauvain, Christian Rémésy and Frédérique Batifoulier. Kirsten Fischer-Lindahl shared her enthusiasm for good bread and helped greatly by supplying and interpreting research material. Lynda Brown, Gill and Greg Evans and Victoria Fisher gave generous advice and Jane Middleton helped bring clarity to the text. Jeff Cottenden's photographs and Julian Humphries' design completed the picture. I am grateful to all of them.

Special thanks to Veronica Burke for her patient support and enthusiastic tasting of some of the work in progress.

INTRODUCTION

This book, as befits its theme, has been fermenting for quite a while. I started the Village Bakery in Melmerby in 1976, when the growing evidence that man could not live by white industrial bread alone was still being ridiculed by the scientific and medical establishments. At that time, none of the bakeries in nearby Penrith made a wholemeal loaf because there was 'no demand for it'. All my first bread was wholemeal, made with flour stoneground at the local watermill. Partly to reassure myself that I wasn't completely mad, I wrote a short history of bread on display boards to hang on the walls of our teashop. So began an attempt to understand why people have often chosen, or been forced, to eat bread that was not very good for them and how this might be changed now that we were discovering so much about the role of good food in public health.

Towards the end of the 1980s the upsurge of apparent allergy and intolerance to the main ingredients of bread presented me with a baking challenge. I had to go back to the first principles of fermentation to make loaves without wheat, gluten or baker's yeast. It began to dawn on me that industrial bread might be making increasing numbers of people unwell because it was made too quickly. Since then, what little research has been done in this area has suggested that the longer bread is fermented, the more digestible and nutritious it gets.

I hope that something of the same effect can be detected in this book, in which I have tried to pass on the baking knowledge accumulated over 30 years. I have done so not only because making your own bread is one of the most satisfying things you can do but because, as the first chapters reveal, much of what you get in the shops should probably be avoided.

CHAPTER ONE
WHAT'S THE MATTER WITH MODERN BREAD?

'A technological triumph factory bread may be. Taste it has none. Should it be called bread?'
ELIZABETH DAVID,
English Bread and Yeast Cookery
(Allen Lane, 1977)

A very British loaf affair

Britons consume about eight million loaves a day plus countless rolls, sandwiches, pizzas and croissants. The baking industry is a model of industrial efficiency and British bread is amongst the lowest priced in Europe. Yet if you ask a Continental visitor what they think of living here, likely as not they will mention the lack of good bread.

We ourselves laugh at 'cotton wool' bread and put up with tasteless, mass-produced rolls in restaurants, canteens and takeaways. The better-off are tempted by 'healthy' loaves fortified with the latest fashionable nutrients, while the poor make do with bread sold primarily on price. If we care about bread, we have a funny way of showing it.

Behind the impressive production figures and the advertising hype of new product launches lies a revealing statistic. We eat less than half as much bread as we did 45 years ago. Well before fads like the low-carbohydrate Atkins diet, people were abandoning bread, and not only because they could afford other foods.

The startling possibility is that British consumers, without their knowledge, have been taking part in a flawed experiment. Back in the early 1960s, the national loaf was fundamentally redesigned. The flour and yeast were changed and a combination of intense energy and additives completely displaced time in the maturing of dough. Almost all our bread has been made this way for nearly half a century. It is white and light and stays soft for days. It is made largely with home-grown wheat and it is cheap. For increasing numbers of people, however, it is inedible.

This book uncovers what goes into the making of a modern loaf and charts the changes that the industry would rather we ignored. As technology finds ever more ingenious ways to adulterate our bread, so science is revealing the havoc this may be causing to public health. Recent research suggests that we urgently need to rethink the way we make bread.

If you are dismayed at the covert corruption of our daily food, you may agree with me that bread matters too much to be left to the industrial bakers. More and more people are taking control over their lives and health by making their own bread. If you are one of them, or would like to be, the second part of this book contains all you need to know in order to make your own bread, with real taste and integrity, bread you can trust and believe in.

Gut feelings

Why would hundreds of thousands of people stop eating bread and eliminate wheat from their diet? Cynics would say that the emergence of private allergy clinics and self-diagnosis by mail order might have something to do with it. For its part, much of the medical profession remains sniffy about the connection between diet and wellbeing. Yet scientific studies do show a surprisingly widespread sensitivity to wheat. This can take an extreme form known as coeliac disease, which is a serious reaction to gliadin, one of the gluten-forming proteins present mostly in wheat but also in smaller amounts in rye, barley and oats. Coeliac disease has a genetic component and, according to the Coeliac Society, may affect as many as one in 100 people in the UK. In his book *The Complete Guide to Food Allergy and Intolerance* (Bloomsbury, 1998, with L. Gamlin), leading allergy expert Professor Jonathan Brostoff describes coeliacs as 'casualties of the slow adaptation process between the human race and wheat.'

It seems that sensitivity to gluten and wheat is like an iceberg. The visible part is composed of coeliacs whose condition is diagnosed by well-established tests and whose only treatment is a complete avoidance of gluten. Below the surface is a much larger group of people who have a sensitivity to wheat with varying degrees of severity, from mild discomfort when consuming bread to a condition known as 'wheat-dependent exercise-induced anaphylaxis'[1].

The strange thing is how recent all this is. Coeliac disease was first diagnosed in the 1950s, but widespread wheat intolerance emerged less than 20 years ago. At almost the same time, people started talking about an invasive strain of yeast called *Candida albicans*, which caused joint pain and digestive discomfort.

For a baker, this came as quite a shock. For 13 years or so I had been selling a range of wheat breads raised with yeast without once hearing about wheat or yeast intolerance or allergy. Suddenly people started ringing up asking for breads made without wheat or baker's yeast – on the face of it, something of a tall order, given that the remaining ingredients of bread are just salt and water. Luckily, I was just developing a sourdough rye bread that contained no wheat and was raised using a spontaneous fermentation (lasting about 24 hours) of 'wild' yeasts present in the flour. Customers tried it and found that their digestive problems were eased. That was the first in a long line of products made without wheat for a market that had appeared from nowhere. Call it anecdotal (the word opponents use when your argument rattles them), but the evidence was clear: more and more people were buying products specifically because they didn't contain wheat, or industrial yeast, or both. The bread on offer in the shops seemed to be making them ill.

Respect

British industrial bread commands little respect. This isn't surprising when it is promoted with such mixed messages. Some loaves, described as having 'premium' qualities, seem barely distinguishable from others being sold at less than the price of a postage stamp. 'Healthy-eating' brands, adorned with images of nature and vitality, make detailed claims about the virtues of this or that added nutrient. But the big bakers keep quiet about nutrition when pushing their 'standard' loaves, which still account for over half of the market and are sold on price alone.

You might think that keeping prices down would be a good way to increase sales. But with bread, low cost and low quality have become so intertwined that conventional economics are turned on their head.

'The Irish bread industry is driven by spread sheets and low prices,' commented Derek O'Brien, head of the National Bakery School in Dublin,

in 2004. 'We produce some of the least expensive bread in Europe. But the result? Our bread consumption is one of the lowest in Europe. This is an appalling situation, particularly for the remaining number of smaller bakers, because their future is to a great extent dictated by the industrial baker.'

Many small bakers in the UK would recognise this situation. When low cost becomes *below* cost, an unseemly race to the bottom is inevitable. In the late 1990s I was told by the chief bakery buyer of one of Britain's leading supermarkets that the cost of reducing the price of a standard 800g loaf of white sliced bread from 17p to 7p (in line with her main competitor) would be £400,000 a week – a sum that might have been better invested in promoting good food. Two of the main bakeries supplying the cheapest 'value' bread went spectacularly bust in 2004–5. Since then, the remaining large bakers have had some success in moving away from low-cost bread and even the supermarkets seem to have realised that loss-leading with something as vital as bread does them little credit. But it will take more than clever branding or a little soya, linseed and omega-3 to dispel the prevailing image of British bread culture as one dominated by pap.

If that seems a harsh judgement, take a look at what actually goes into your daily bread.

This is your loaf

In 1961 the British Baking Industries Research Association in Chorleywood, Hertfordshire, devised a breadmaking method using lower-protein wheat, an assortment of additives and high-speed mixing. Over 80 per cent of all UK bread is now made using this method and most of the rest uses a process called 'activated dough development' (ADD), which involves a similar range of additives. So, apart from a tiny percentage of bread, this is what we eat today.

The Chorleywood Bread Process (CBP) produces bread of phenomenal volume and lightness, with great labour efficiency and at low apparent cost. It isn't promoted by name. You won't see it mentioned on any labels. But you can't miss it. From the clammy sides of your chilled wedge sandwich to the flabby roll astride every franchised burger, the stuff is there, with a soft, squishy texture that lasts for many days until the preservatives can hold back the mould no longer. If bread forms a ball that sticks to the roof of your mouth as you chew, thank the Chorleywood Bread Process – but don't dwell on what it will shortly be doing to your guts.

This is Britain's bread: a technological marvel combining production efficiency with a compelling appeal to the lowest common denominator of taste. It is the very embodiment of the modern age.

Below is a breakdown of a typical Chorleywood Bread Process loaf[2]. Only the first four ingredients in the table – flour, water, salt and yeast – are essential to make bread. In fact, even yeast (as an added ingredient) is unnecessary for breads made with natural leavens or sourdoughs. Bread made with these three or four simple ingredients was the basis of my bakery business for 25 years. So it is reasonable to ask: are all those other ingredients necessary? And, if not, what are they doing in our bread?

Read on and judge for yourself.

Ingredient	What does it do?	What's the problem?
FLOUR	Source of carbohydrate, protein, fat, minerals, vitamins and other micronutrients (depending on the degree of refinement of the flour).	See Chapter 2 for depletion of micronutrients in refined (white) flour.
WATER	Necessary to make flour into dough.	
SALT	Adds flavour; strengthens gluten network in the dough; aids keeping quality of bread (as a water attractant and a partial mould inhibitor).	Under pressure from the Food Standards Agency and others, the bread industry is gradually reducing levels of salt in bread.

WHAT'S THE MATTER WITH MODERN BREAD?

Ingredient	What does it do?	What's the problem?
YEAST	Aerates bread, makes it light in texture and may contribute to flavour.	Excessive use may lead to digestive problems.
FAT	Hard fats improve loaf volume, crumb softness and keeping quality. Hydrogenated fats have commonly been used, though plant bakers are phasing them out, possibly replacing them with 'fractionated' fats, which don't contain or produce transfats, which have been associated with heart disease.	Not essential in traditional breadmaking, though often used. Hard to do without some fat in CBP.
FLOUR TREATMENT AGENT	L-ascorbic acid (E300). Can be added to flour by the miller or at the baking stage. Acts as an oxidant, which helps retain gas in the dough, making the loaf rise more. Not permitted in wholemeal flour, but permitted in wholemeal bread.	No nutritional benefit to the consumer (because degraded by the heat of baking). Increased loaf volume may give false impression of value.
BLEACH	Chlorine dioxide gas to make flour whiter, used by millers for decades until banned in the UK in 1999. Flour from other countries, e.g. the USA, may be bleached.	No nutritional benefit to the consumer. Chlorine is a potent biocide and greenhouse gas.

Ingredient	What does it do?	What's the problem?
REDUCING AGENT	L-cysteine hydrochloride (E920). Cysteine is a naturally occurring amino acid. Used in baking to create stretchier doughs, especially for burger buns and French sticks.	No intended nutritional benefit, though also sold as a supplement. May be derived from animal hair and feathers.
SOYA FLOUR	Widely used in bread 'improvers'. Has a bleaching effect on flour, assists 'machinability' of dough and volume and softness of bread. Enables more water to be added to the dough mix.	Increasingly likely to be derived from genetically modified soya beans.
EMULSIFIERS	Widely used in bread 'improvers' to control the size of gas bubbles, to enable the dough to hold more gas and therefore grow bigger, to make the crumb softer, and to reduce the rate of staling. These are the main emulsifiers used: • Diacetylated tartaric acid esters of mono- and diglycerides of fatty acids (DATEM, DATA esters) – mainly for loaf volume and crumb softness. • Sodium steoryl-2-lactylate (SSL) – often used in sweet products like buns and doughnuts to increase volume and softness.	No nutritional benefit to the consumer. Soya lecithin may be derived from GM soya. Increased loaf volume may give misleading impression of value and post-baking softness may be confused with 'freshness'.

Ingredient	What does it do?	What's the problem?
EMULSIFIERS *Cont.*	• Glycerol mono-stearate (GMS) – mainly used for its effect in keeping bread soft for longer after baking. • Lecithins – naturally occurring, mainly derived from soya. Used in crusty breads (e.g. baguettes) to improve volume and crust formation.	
PRESERVATIVES	Calcium propionate widely used. Vinegar (acetic acid) is also used, though less effective. Preservatives are only necessary for prolonged shelf life. Home freezing is a chemical-free alternative.	No nutritional benefit to consumer. Calcium propionate can cause 'off' flavours if over-used and may be a carcinogen.

ENZYMES	Came to the rescue of industrial breadmakers when additives like azodicarbonamide and potassium bromate were banned. Bread enzymes fall into various categories and have varied functions in breadmaking:
	• Amylase – usually alpha-amylase from cereal, fungal or bacterial sources or glucoamylase from fungal sources. Amylase assists production of maltose (fermentable sugar) from starch
		No nutritional benefit to the consumer.
		   No requirement to be included on ingredient declarations, because they are currently treated as 'processing aids'. Even if EU law is amended, the single word 'enzymes' will be all that is required on labels, leaving consumers in the dark about the origin of the particular enzymes used (see page 14).
		   Often produced by genetic

Ingredient	What does it do?	What's the problem?
ENZYMES *Cont.*	in the flour. Used to increase loaf volume, give better crust colour and delay crumb firming associated with ageing. • Maltogenic amylase – usually from a genetically modified bacterial source (*Bacillus stearothermophilus*). Delays the rate of staling of baked bread. • Oxidase – works on flour protein by oxidation (therefore replacing chemical oxidants), which increases dough strength and elasticity. Usually seen as glucose oxidase or lipoxygenase. • Protease – usually derived from fungal sources *Aspergillus niger* and *A. oryzae*. Makes strong wheats more 'machineable'. Also used in production of very soft rolls. • Peptidase – from fungal sources, mainly used to release yeast nutrients from protein, enhancing crust flavour and colour. • Lipase – breaks fat down into compounds including mono- and diglycerides, so can replace the chemical emulsifiers of this	engineering, though this is unlikely to be stated on consumer product labels. Use of phospholipase derived from pig pancreas would be unacceptable to vegetarians and some religious groups, but there is no requirement to declare enzymes, let alone their source. Some enzymes are potential allergens, notably alpha-amylase. Bakery workers can become sensitised to enzymes from bread improvers. Amylase can retain some of its potency as an allergen in the crust of loaves after baking. Transglutaminase may act upon gliadin proteins in dough to generate the epitope associated with coeliac disease (see page 15).

Ingredient	What does it do?	What's the problem?
ENZYMES *Cont.*	type (see above). Main function is to keep bread soft for longer after baking. • Phospholipase – mainly used to modify the effectiveness of the emulsifier lecithin (see above). May be derived from the pancreas of pigs. • Hemicellulase – usually from fungal sources, though small amounts of hemicellulase occur naturally in wheat flour. Used to increase loaf volume and crumb structure and also to increase dough 'tolerance' to, as one source puts it, 'physical abuse during processing'. • Xylanase – recently developed class of enzymes from fungal or GM bacterial sources, designed to increase loaf volume, especially in lower-protein flours. • Transglutaminase – recently developed enzyme used in bread, pastry and croissants to make dough more plastic.	

If you are unnerved by all the chemical names, you may be assured that the ingredients and additives listed above have received appropriate regulatory approval. Assured, but not reassured. The same could have been said 20 or 50 years ago, when the list would have contained chemicals that have since been banned. Safety assurance has a short shelf life. The development of modern emulsifiers, and especially of the newer bakery enzymes, was given considerable impetus by the withdrawal of the oxidising 'improver' potassium bromate, which after many years' use was discovered to have carcinogenic potential (it is still used in some countries)[3].

Moreover, there is a wider concern that makes it hard to accept today's scientific consensus on food additives. New chemicals are evaluated on a primarily toxicological basis: feed a great deal of your chosen substance to laboratory rats for a limited period and, if they don't keel over and die, it can be presumed safe for humans. However rigorous, such procedures clearly do not catch the effects of long-term low-level exposure to novel compounds or altered processes, not to mention the 'cocktail' effect of combinations of active agents too numerous or unpredictable to model in the laboratory.

Enzymes and the great 'processing aid' scam

Enzymes are modern baking's big secret. A loophole classifies them as 'processing aids', which need not be declared on product labels. Additives, on the other hand, must be listed in the ingredients panel. Not surprisingly, most people have no idea that their bread contains added enzymes.

An enzyme is a protein that speeds up a metabolic reaction. Enzymes are extracted from plant, animal, fungal and bacterial sources. Chymosin, for example, is the enzyme used to curdle milk for cheese making. It is either derived from rennet from a calf's stomach or synthesised by genetic engineering. As you can see from the table above, a whole host of enzymes is used in baking. Their status as processing aids is based on the assumption that they are 'used up' in the production process and are therefore not really present in the final product. This is a deception that allows the food industry to manipulate what we eat without telling us. In their own trade literature, enzyme manufacturers extol the 'thermo-stability' of this or that product – in other words its ability to have a lasting effect on the baked bread.

Manufacturers have developed enzymes with two main objectives: to make dough hold more gas (making lighter bread) and to make bread stay softer for longer after baking. As the table shows, many bakery enzymes are derived from substances that are not part of a normal human diet. Even if such enzymes are chemically the same as some of those naturally found in flour or bread dough, they are added in larger amounts than would ever be encountered in ordinary bread.

And now the safety of bakery enzymes has been radically challenged by the discovery that the enzyme transglutaminase, used to make dough stretchier in croissants and some breads, may turn part of the wheat protein toxic to people with severe gluten intolerance[4]. This development is important because it suggests that adding enzymes to bread dough may have unintended and damaging consequences. Surely no one can seriously suggest that bakery enzymes should be omitted from bread labels.

I think we should be suspicious of bakery enzymes for four additional reasons:

- Enzymes can be allergens and should be identified on labels in the same way as the major allergen groups.
- Failure to label enzymes prevents people making informed ethical choices about what they eat.
- There is a fundamental dishonesty in treating enzymes as though they had no effect on baked bread when this is patently why they are used.
- Judgements about ingredients should take into account the whole food; an enzyme may be harmless in itself but may be used to make an undesirable product.

Allergens

People have a right to know not just what is in their food but how it has been made. Some people need to know what is – or may be – in processed food because consuming the wrong thing may make them ill. Many food labels now contain advice designed to warn consumers not just about the actual content of the product in question but also about the possibility of contamination by potential allergens from the production environment.

But here's a puzzle. Some allergens (peanuts, sesame seeds, gluten, lactose etc) have celebrity status, rightly, because of their potential for serious harm. Others, while known to specialists and sufferers, never make the charts. Amylase is one. Alpha-amylase is an enzyme naturally present in wheat in amounts that vary with variety and growing and harvesting conditions. Millers routinely add it to flour to make a more consistent product. It is also present in some compound bread 'improvers'.

Amylases are known to cause allergic reactions in some people[5]. There is an occupational health risk to bakery workers if enzymes get into the atmosphere, where they are breathed in and can cause asthma. But recent research has shown that up to 20 per cent of the allergenicity of fungal alpha-amylase can survive in the crusts of bread[6] (perhaps we should revise the old adage about eating up your crusts; they may do more than make your hair curl). So, while amylase allergy is clearly not an issue on a level with nuts or gluten, it exists and may be exacerbated by the addition of fungal amylases to flour and bread.

Ethical choices

It is not just a question of potential physical discomfort (or worse). As the controversy over genetically modified organisms (GMOs) in the late 1990s demonstrated, the way food is produced is of growing concern to many people – from the biological integrity of seeds, through farmers' rights and animal welfare, to the impact on the physical and social environment. In other words, people may make moral judgments about provenance and production methods, even if these appear to have only a marginal bearing on the nature of the actual food they ingest.

For the food enzyme industry, all of nature is a chemistry set. No organisms are too exotic or repulsive to be investigated for possible active agents. As can be seen in the table above, the dough that goes into a loaf of standard factory bread may contain the strangest stuff – a reducing agent derived from animal hair or feathers, or enzymes from the pancreas of a pig. It may come as something of a shock to a Muslim or a Jew or a vegetarian that their daily bread is produced using animal by-products. It is possible that little or nothing of the original substance survives the baking process. But that isn't the point. Bread has been made using an ingredient or process that some people find offensive. If you don't know what's gone into your bread – in the fullest sense of those words – how can you exercise any meaningful choice over whether to eat it or not?

'Choice', of course, is the mantra intoned by private business to promote product proliferation and by government to justify the intrusion of free-market economics into social provision. It is ironic therefore, that in their reluctance to declare what really goes into bread industrial bakers *inhibit* the exercise of informed choice and the regulatory authorities connive with a labelling regime that is geared more to commercial convenience than to true transparency.

Dishonest claims

We are entitled to ask why there is no requirement to tell people exactly what enzymes are put into our daily bread. European law is under review and may require processing aids to be treated like additives and declared on labels, but the new rule will not require bakers to give any more detail than the single word 'enzymes'. What earthly good is that to consumers? Does it tell them that the enzyme added is alpha-amylase, to which some people are allergic? Does it alert them to the fact that the enzymes in question may include transglutaminase, which can turn wheat protein toxic for people sensitised to gluten? No, it does not.

In other words, we will move from the current state of total secrecy to one of bogus transparency where the information divulged is completely inadequate; it will be transparent only in the sense that you will be able to see right through to the information void on the other side. You don't have to be a conspiracy theorist to wonder whether there's something they don't want us to know.

Cumulative effects

It is perfectly possible that a particular enzyme is 'harmless' in isolation, in terms of both toxicity and its functional effect in specific doughs, but the process in which it is a small element may produce bread with raised allergenicity or diminished nutritional status and ultimately, therefore, less healthy people. The challenge to industrial bakers is twofold:

- Can they be sure that all bakery enzymes are safe?
- Does their use produce the best possible bread?

On safety, the transglutaminase issue suggests that we need a more searching regulatory process and a considerably more precautionary approach.

On quality, it all depends how the word is defined. Rather than trade insults across the barricades of personal preference, it is worth asking what the makers of bread with added enzymes are actually trying to achieve: a saleable product or good food? Enzymes are used not for any nutritional benefit to the consumer, but to make it easier to produce bread on an industrial scale, to maximise loaf volume, to soften crumb texture and to maintain that softness for as long as possible. The net result is often a loaf of degraded nutritive value.

So there it is: your standard British loaf, made with all sorts of things you didn't know were in it. Do people increasingly find modern bread not to their taste because of all these additives and 'processing aids'? Perhaps. But the changes in bread since the 1960s go deeper. They affect almost every aspect of how it is made. Each change may have had its own logic at the time but together they have left us with bread that may be fundamentally flawed.

How our bread has changed

The great achievement of modern industrial baking was to make a superficially attractive loaf using a high proportion of home-grown wheat. This provided a market for British cereal farmers and saved the bakers the tariffs on imported – mostly Canadian – flour. But to turn British wheat into the kind of bread that most people appeared to want, new methods were required:

- Wheat hybrids were bred to take advantage of intensive chemical agriculture and to produce flour that suited industrial baking methods.
- Millers separated the whole wheat more completely into its constituent parts, ground the flour finer and added enzymes to make it more consistent.
- To make the dough rise quickly, bakers massively increased the amount of yeast.
- Time was squeezed out of the baking process, and with it not just flavour but vital nutritional benefits.
- Freshness was redefined and artificially induced by means of additives, some undeclared.

A technological and commercial triumph turned out to be a nutritional own-goal.

Wheat

At the end of the Second World War, explosives manufacturers experienced a distinct decline in sales. If not exactly beating bombs into ploughshares, they found a ready outlet for their chemicals in the intensive agriculture that was seen as the only way to feed rapidly growing urban populations. Grain varieties were bred to respond to heavy applications of soluble nitrogen, potash and phosphorus fertilisers. But such a regime produces flabby straw that falls over in wind or rain. So wheats with short straw were developed.

Once hooked on soluble chemicals, the new varieties showed signs of succumbing more than before to fungal and pest attack. So new strains were bred for built-in resistance. Shorter stem length means less canopy to suppress weeds, meaning the new varieties also had to be able to thrive in the presence of herbicides. The millers wanted their say, too, so the breeding programme was tweaked to produce wheats with proteins more suitable for bread baking. And each year, yields had to go on rising.

Yield, short straw, disease resistance, milling quality – the plant breeders have obliged. They have done so, to date, without recourse to GM technology, though that is in the wings.

What is striking in all of this – for those of us who think that farming has something to do with feeding people to keep them in good health – is that nutritional quality doesn't get a look in. No one seems to have asked whether, as variety succeeded variety with bewildering speed, wheat was getting better or worse to eat, more or less nutritious, more or less digestible. The most sophisticated science is used to analyse 'quality' differences between contenders for the UK National List of cereal varieties subject to Plant Breeders' Rights. Yet, cereal scientists, along with the big millers and bakers, act as though, nutritionally, all wheat varieties are much the same. Advances in the purely functional properties of wheat have come at the price of reductions in its nutritional quality. The precursors of modern bread wheats – einkorn, emmer and spelt – all contain more nutrients than their commercial successors. Research at the International Maize and Wheat Improvement Center in Mexico revealed that the best traditional wheat varieties had about twice the iron and zinc of popular modern varieties, and their wild relatives had another half as much again[7]. In Europe, the French National Institute for Agricultural Research has shown that the mineral content of current French wheats is 30–40 per cent below that of older varieties[8].

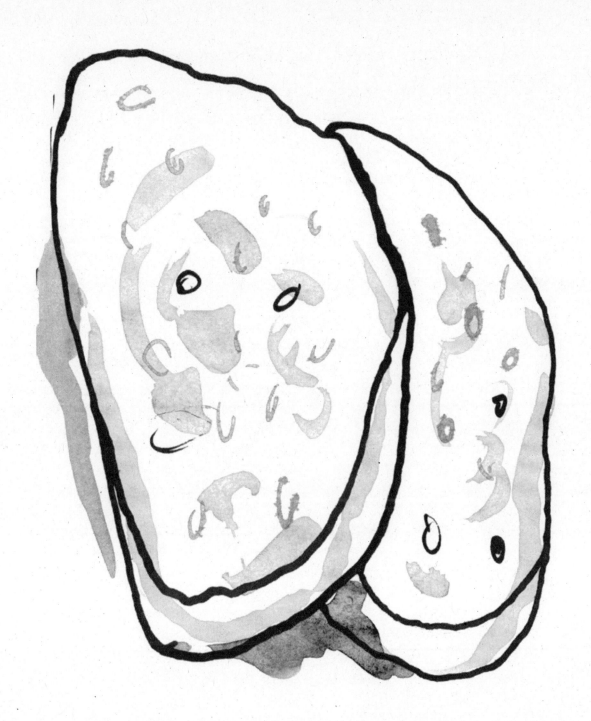

Milling methods

Before the invention of roller milling, all flour was produced by crushing wheat between revolving stones. All parts of the wheat – bran, germ and starchy endosperm – were pulverised and mixed together into what we know as wholemeal, or whole wheat, flour. If you wanted whiter flour, you had to sift the wholemeal through wire sieves or 'bolting cloths' made from cotton, linen or silk. The roller-milling system, deployed from 1870 onwards, was quite different. It passed the wheat between pairs of steel cylinders, which gradually stripped the layers off the grain, sifting the material thus produced into a series of streams, each containing a different fraction of the flour. These could be taken off and bagged separately or recombined to make 'patent' flours for various baking purposes.

Wholemeal flour is, in theory, the entire wheat grain (minus its husk) ground into flour. In British parlance, this is flour with a 100 per cent 'extraction rate': 100 per cent of the available flour or meal has been 'extracted' from the grain. White flour has only approximately 72 per cent of the content of the wheat, the remaining 28 per cent consisting of the bran layers on the outside of the grain and the germ tucked in one end. What used to be called 'wheatmeal' was about 85 per cent extraction. 'Brown' is a generic term describing flour of about 80 per cent extraction. Most of the vitamins and minerals are in the outer bran layers of wheat. In white flour milling, these are mostly sold for animal feed.

Wheat sold as breadmaking flour is more valuable in monetary terms to the miller than the residues that go to the animals. When it comes to nutritional value, however, the reverse is true. The table below shows what happens when whole wheat is milled to white flour[9]:

Vitamin and mineral loss during the refining of whole wheat to 70 per cent extraction white flour

Nutrient	Loss
Thiamine (B_1)	77%
Riboflavin (B_2)	80%
Niacin (nicotinic acid)	81%
Pyridoxine (B_6)	72%
Pantothenic acid	50%
Vitamin E	86%
Calcium	60%
Phosphorus	71%
Magnesium	84%
Potassium	77%
Sodium	78%
Chromium	40%
Manganese	86%
Iron	76%
Cobalt	89%
Zinc	78%
Copper	68%
Selenium	16%
Molybdenum	48%

The only word to describe bread made with such flour is 'depleted'.

Whereas stone milling and sieving/bolting had generally produced a white flour consisting of 75–80 per cent of the original wheat, roller milling reduced this to 70–73 per cent. The visible effect was to produce a whiter flour with fewer flecks of bran in it. Far more important, however, was the reduction in the roller-milled flour of several important nutrients, including calcium, iron and B vitamins, which the stones had formerly dispersed throughout the flour. Removing the germ, which contains virtually all the valuable vitamin E of the wheat, was a nutritional disaster but a great benefit to the millers. The wheat germ oil tended to oxidise and go rancid within a few weeks. Without it, white flour could last for several months – exactly what was needed as milling companies became larger, with ever-longer distribution chains along the country's fast-expanding network of railways and roads. Not for the last time, nutritional integrity was a casualty of the commercial need for 'shelf life'. Some of the vitamin E, incidentally, goes to the supplement industry, which is happy to sell it back to us in capsules at many times what it might have cost us if we simply ate bread made with stoneground wholemeal flour.

In a French study in 2005, stoneground organic flour was shown to have 50 per cent more magnesium and 46 per cent more zinc than roller-milled non-organic flour[10]. This effect, it should be explained, was observed not in wholemeal but in flour milled to a finer extraction rate of around 80–85 per cent. Many people consume too little magnesium and the role of zinc in good health is well established. It would not be unreasonable to expect the benefits of organic growing (see page 43) and stone milling to apply similarly to other important micronutrients in flour.

The intriguing question is whether modern roller mills could be adapted to deliver flour with the same nutritional integrity as stoneground. It is hard to believe that the technological ingenuity would be lacking. But commercial will is quite another matter. The track record of the big milling concerns does not suggest a major commitment to the nutritional quality of their flour.

WHEAT

Milling technology is currently focused on the functional effects to be had from producing ever finer fractions of flour.

In 1941 nutritional scientists persuaded the government to force a reluctant milling industry to add calcium to its white flour. Three other nutrients (iron, vitamin B_1 and nicotinic acid) were added in 1953 – although in lower amounts than would be found in wholemeal flour. All the other deficiencies and differences between stoneground and roller-milled and wholemeal and white flours listed above remain.

Official advice does now stress the importance of whole grain cereals in the diet. However, almost all the 'whole' wheat flour produced today is from roller mills. In other words, it is reassembled from the separated fractions of flour but without the crucial wheat germ oil, on the grounds that replacing it would shorten the flour's shelf life. Perhaps such flour should be labelled 'reconstituted semi-whole wheat flour' to alert consumers to the fact that it does not contain all the elements of the original grain.

Yeast

Ever since our ancestors thousands of years ago noticed that a flour and water paste begins to aerate if left for some hours, people in wheat- and rye-growing areas have eaten leavened bread. During fermentation, naturally occurring enzymes break carbohydrates down into sugars on which yeasts feed, producing carbon dioxide (the gas that raises the bread) and alcohol. This process was fully understood only after Louis Pasteur's discovery in 1857 of the micro-organisms involved. It eventually became possible to identify and culture pure strains of yeast that gave fast and predictable results for bread-makers. Of the 160 or so known strains of yeast, the one commonly used for baker's yeast is *Saccharomyces cerevisiae*. Other strains are involved in natural leavens and sourdoughs.

Before the development of commercial yeast in the late nineteenth century, bakers had to make their own, either with a 'wild' sourdough culture or by making a 'barm', which may have been seeded with yeast residue from a brewery. Either way, the process took time because the number of viable yeast cells in a sourdough or barm was relatively small. When commercial yeast became available, it contained much larger populations of cells and worked quickly. But it was expensive, and the thrifty baker could make it go further by using a small quantity in a preliminary 'sponge' consisting of a proportion of the flour and water to be used in the bread. This was allowed to ferment for 12 to 24 hours: given warmth, water and food, the yeast cells multiplied. On the following day, fresh flour and water (and occasionally some fat) would be added to make the final dough.

Even when commercial yeast became accessible to all bakers in the twentieth century, the 'sponge-and-dough' method remained a favoured way of breadmaking. In a typical overnight recipe from John Kirkland's famous 1907 manual, *The Modern Baker, Confectioner and Caterer*, the yeast quantity is less than 0.1 per cent of the final dough weight. According to *The Master Bakers' Book of Breadmaking* (National Association of Master Bakers, 1996), the Chorleywood Bread Process needs 2.38 per cent yeast for Vienna bread and rolls. In other words, over 23 times as much initial yeast as in Kirkland's sponge-and-dough bread. Even compared with the fastest pre-War doughs, the Chorleywood Bread Process uses over three and a half times as much yeast.

If, after several decades in which most bread has been made with increased amounts of yeast, significant numbers of people develop an intolerance or allergy to yeast, it seems reasonable to ask whether there is a link. And there is another thing. Yeast, like the other raw materials of baking, has changed. It, too, needed a makeover if it was to be up to the task of Chorleywood baking. According to a manual for professional bakers, *Baking Problems Solved* (Stanley Cauvain and Linda Young, Woodhead Publishing Ltd, 2001):

'When the CBP was introduced in the 1960s the type of baker's yeast then used was unable to provide carbon dioxide gas in the critical early stages of baking and it became necessary for the yeast strain to be changed. Though the precise nature of the changes is not public knowledge it undoubtedly was related to the enzyme activity within the yeast cell.'

There's an ominous note in that second sentence: the precise nature of the yeast used to make our national bread is 'not public knowledge'. This was the 1960s – long (we thought) before the creeping capture of science by private business and certainly a good 20 years before the first emergence of genetic engineering.

About time, too

For almost all of mankind's baking history, bread had taken a long time to rise. Bakers' barms or sourdoughs contained relatively sparse populations of mixed strains of 'wild' yeasts. Whatever they were and wherever they came from, the one thing they had in common was that they worked slowly. The whole process from starter dough to finished product could take 24 hours or more. Single varieties of the most active strains of yeast appeared in the late nineteenth century and made faster fermentation possible. Though convenient, this was an expensive commercial option and most bakers eked out their yeast by using the sponge-and-dough method described above.

As the price of yeast came down and productivity pressures grew, fermentation times shortened. With the invention of the Chorleywood Bread Process, the goal of 'instant' dough became attainable. With new machinery, ingenious chemistry and a terrific blast of (ever so slightly modified) yeast, bread needed no fermentation at all.

It was good for business, of course, and the manufacturer's costs could be contained or reduced. Everyone could now afford the whitest, softest bread they had ever known, though, curiously, consumption kept on falling.

Research has recently revealed that making yeasted breads quickly may not leave time for important changes to take place. For example, fermenting dough for six hours as opposed to 30 minutes removes around 80 per cent of a potentially carcinogenic substance called acrylamide that is found in bread crusts[11], and long yeast fermentations conserve the highest levels of B vitamins in dough (48 per cent of vitamin B_1 is lost in rapidly made white bread)[12].

Freshness

Traditional bakers know that the longer you ferment your dough, the better the bread keeps. Time invested in the making is repaid in the eating. Modern bakers and retailers have destroyed this elegant balance. They have stolen time from the production process, a theft they try to disguise in contradictory ways. In the case of standard sliced and wrapped bread, they use additives to keep the crumb soft (or 'fresh', as they would say) for a week or more. With the unwrapped bread, on the other hand, time is distorted in a rather different way.

Supermarkets and their industrial bakery suppliers have robbed 'freshness' of all meaning. One loaf, unwrapped and apparently 'freshly' baked on the premises, has in fact been made and probably baked elsewhere days or weeks before. Another loaf, baked elsewhere, has been laced with undeclared and unspecified enzymes – a kind of baking Botox – so that its soft, cloying texture remains in an unchanging caricature of freshness, day after depressing day.

To reclaim freshness – word and concept – from the self-serving interests that have hijacked it, two things are necessary: to agree a definition of 'fresh' that accords with the best evidence of our senses, and to conquer the unnecessary fear of what happens as freshness wanes. In the case of bread, 'fresh' can surely mean only one thing – recently baked (for the first and only time). I have some ideas about enjoying bread as it ages in the final chapter of this book.

So modern baking is schizophrenic about time, now wanting to reduce it to nothing, now trying to extend it indefinitely. And it is also in two minds about its raw materials, torn between the desire to remove things that get in the way and the impulse to add things that will make the bread easier (for machine production), bigger, softer, cheaper, longer lasting or more apparently healthy. Baking technologists just can't leave well alone. There's always some functional advantage to be pursued, some marginal value to be prised from dumb nature, as if the human race had never quite mastered this business of bread.

We have evolved an industrial breadmaking system that, in a variety of ways we can no longer ignore, produces bread that more and more people cannot and should not eat. Some would say that the pappy texture and bland flavour of Chorleywood Process bread are reason enough to consign it to the compost heap of food history. However, these qualities are ultimately matters of personal preference. The use of additives, on the other hand, especially those whose provenance or purpose is not apparent to the consumer, raises serious questions of accountability and trust. Above all, the baking industry must respond to the growing body of research that is charting the profound unhealthiness of making bread quickly.

From wheat to finished loaf, industrial baking needs to be reconstructed from first principles, of which the most important is a proper respect for time.

CHAPTER TWO

DOES IT REALLY MATTER WHAT BREAD WE EAT?

'I know that
"man cannot live on bread alone".
I say, let us get the bread right.'
DAVID SCOTT,
Selected Poems
(Bloodaxe, 1998)

Mixed messages

The food industry argument goes like this. Thanks to modern agriculture and technology, we all have more than enough to eat these days; everyone can afford a variety of foods from which they derive reasonable nutrition; if this or that food is less than perfect, it doesn't make any real difference. We should enjoy the unparalleled choices now open to us and stop criticising the food industry.

According to this view, it doesn't matter if industrial bread is nutritionally depleted because any missing nutrients are available in other foods. The words 'in the context of a balanced diet ...' are often used to justify questionable products. The large food processing groups and multiple retailers in the UK give public support to healthy eating policies but only in so far as they are not prevented from marketing pretty much any edible substance they choose. Their general strategy is to avoid discussing the particular nutritional profile of any one product. A healthy diet, they insist, results from a combination of food choices, but don't blame us if legitimate promotion of our brands results in over-consumption of nutritionally depleted products. That's down to individual choice. The *balanced* bit of the diet, the message seems to be, can be provided by some other sucker.

Notice how the tune changes, however, when food companies are promoting their special (perhaps a bit more profitable) ranges, all promising 'wellbeing' from a 'lifestyle' involving 'healthy eating'. Now the particular, ingredient-specific attributes of this or that product are highlighted: its low-fat, low glycaemic index or high-fibre status, perhaps, or the presence of prebiotics, probiotics or obscure additives that 'have been linked to heart health'.

Whenever I see an advertisement for a new 'healthy-eating' addition to a product range, I itch to ask the obvious question: if all the qualities with which you have so generously endowed this new line are as vital for my health as you imply, why are your ordinary ranges not as good?

So what are they recommending: nutritionally enhanced products or a balanced diet?

The 'whole diet' approach to nutrition is useful because it takes account of the variety of foods that people actually consume. It recognises that we do not (and, in my view, should not) see foods solely as bundles of nutrients. After all, food performs many functions additional to mere survival – as a source of comfort, celebration, indulgence and sensual pleasure, for example. But whole diets are composed of individual food types and products and in healthy people the good is balanced with the less good. Limitations of information, money or access mean that some people struggle to achieve this balance. For them, it is crucial that basic foods are as wholesome as possible because they cannot or do not consume the range of foods that contain a satisfactory spectrum of nutrients.

According to the government's 2002–3 National Food Survey, 99 per cent of UK households eat bread. It forms about 9 per cent (by weight) of the average diet. But low-income families eat more than twice as much white bread and 25 per cent less wholemeal than high-income families. For some people, bread amounts to as much as 20 per cent of their diet. It matters that this bread is good. But the cheapest, most basic British bread, the standard white sliced loaf that accounts for about half of the market, is also the least nutritious. It contains smaller quantities of several important minerals and vitamins than plain wholemeal bread. This leads to another problem. Most people in the UK get enough nutrients, though certain population groups are low in iron and magnesium and almost everyone consumes less fibre than recommended. But the *density* of everyday foods is important: the fewer nutrients a food has in it, the more portions we have to eat to get what our bodies need. Poor-quality basic foods are programmed for over-consumption. Is it any wonder that obesity is on the rise?

The industrial bakers give out very mixed messages. They promote all bread as being healthy. When challenged to explain how loaves whose nutrient profiles differ considerably can be equally good, they say that the public demands cheap white bread and that it is absolutely fine in the context of a balanced diet. They then promote their speciality breads on the basis that they provide the very things that are glaringly absent in the standard stuff.

By emphasising the low cost, convenience and neutral taste of its primary offering – the white sliced loaf – the bread industry has pandered to a public that knows what it likes and is resistant to change. Why would anyone change, if they were constantly assured that all bread, whatever its type and content, is 'good'?

Who decides?

The baking industry argues that it is embracing the 'health agenda' with new, more nutritious products and that a wide choice of breads is now available to everyone. But to make real choices, you have to have enough information and you need to know how to evaluate it. The ingredients list is where you look if you want to know exactly what is in a product. Even if you understand all the terms used on a bread label, you may still be in the dark – for instance, if added enzymes were used to make the bread but are not declared on the label, with details of their origin and effect. By not stating in clear and simple language how their product is made, industrial bakers make it difficult for ordinary people to judge whether their bread is good to eat.

The basis of choice is effectively controlled by the industry. And, in the tart estimate of academic nutritionist Professor Marion Nestle, 'nutrition becomes a factor in corporate thinking only when it can help sell food' (*Food Politics: How the Food Industry Influences Nutrition and Health*, University of California Press, 2003). There is a long history of industry reluctance to make good the deficiencies of white bread. The millers and bakers fought tooth and nail against the scientific consensus in the 1930s that roller milling had removed so many nutrients from flour that many people, especially the poor, were subsisting on considerably less than was physiologically required. Then, as now, they sidestepped the lamentable quality of their basic product and agreed to 'fortify' white flour with a small number of minerals and vitamins derived from synthetic sources.

Fortification has now become 'nutrification' – an approach to food described by one apologist as 'the most rapidly applied, the most flexible, and the most socially acceptable intervention method of changing the intake of nutrients without a vast educational effort and without changing the current food patterns of a given population'. Industry, having fought against it, now loves it because it leaves the structure and direction of food processing untouched. Any new nutritional problems can be solved by recourse to its increasingly sophisticated chemistry set and a whole new commercial opportunity has emerged to 'add value' by creating 'functional foods'.

Adding relatively large amounts of synthetic nutrients to basic foodstuffs is scientifically primitive because it must assume that everyone will eat roughly the same amount of fortified food to ensure the right nutrient intake across the whole population. But what if some people already consume a diet naturally rich in nutrients? Are they to be warned off these new foods in case they unwittingly overdose on something?

There is, in fact, a real risk of over-consumption of individual micro-nutrients. Marion Nestle estimates that industry-initiated additions of iron to the food supply may well be contributing to haemochromatosis (caused by too much iron), which affects at least a million adult Americans. In the case of folic acid, fortification of all flour (as is done in the USA) can lead to a problem, especially with elderly people, in which excessive intake of folate complicates the diagnosis of vitamin B_{12} deficiency. Too much added calcium is implicated in prostate cancer[1] and a recent study links high intake of both iron and calcium with lung cancer[2].

The mandatory addition of folic acid to flour has so far been rejected in the UK, but the government's Scientific Advisory Committee on Nutrition now wants to see it implemented. The millers are happy to oblige, so long as the government picks up the tab. So we are faced with the unedifying spectacle of a milling industry that removes more than half the folate from wheat asking to be paid to put it back again in synthetic form. Nice work if you can get it.

The baking industry is keen on the principle of nutrification because it opens up rich new seams of product development and added value. Breads are now appearing enriched with extra calcium and iron, oestrogen from soya, omega-3 essential fatty acids from linseed and extra fibre from oats, peas or more exotic sources. Such additional ingredients may be of benefit to some consumers but they constitute only a fraction of the nutrients essential to human health, which can be readily obtained from whole grains, fruits and vegetables. And in any case, I cannot help thinking that the baking industry's historical, and continuing, investment in low-cost white bread makes it an unconvincing advocate of dietary improvement.

As science has confirmed the dietary importance of whole grains, the baking industry has sought ever more ingenious ways to engineer their benefits into breads that have the same bland flavour and ease of production as standard white bread, though with a healthier margin of profit. A charitable observer might regard this as 'doing good by stealth', and there can be no denying that any replacement of missing nutrients is good. It is good, particularly, because by focusing on health, however partially, it acknowledges that your choice of bread does matter.

However, any such positive message is undermined in several ways. The industry is still reluctant to state clearly and unambiguously what goes into standard white bread and the extent to which it is nutritionally inferior to less processed alternatives. The strategy of nutrification takes power away from the consumer: the miller, baker or additive formulator controls the quantity and mix of extra nutrients in a loaf – with the result that people whose consumption patterns deviate from the average may end up with an inappropriate intake.

But all this tinkering with added ingredients conceals a much more fundamental reason why your choice of bread matters a great deal.

The slow route to health

Industrial bread is made far too fast.

Old-time bakers knew that if you left dough to ferment for a long time in the right conditions, 'acids' would 'ripen' your mix and produce a moister crumb and better keeping quality, as well as that indefinable bread flavour. In Germany, Poland and Russia especially, the cultivation of lactic and acetic acids in traditional sourdough fermentation was valued for the flavour and digestibility of the local (mainly rye) breads.

Most of us are rather amazed that mixing flour, yeast and water produces dough that rises and can be baked into light-textured bread. But this is only half the story. While yeast turns sugars released from the flour by enzymes into carbon dioxide and alcohol, lactic acid bacteria are also at work. If yeast is the exuberant entrepreneur of dough expansion, lactic acid bacteria are the thrifty housekeepers. Not only do they not compete with yeast directly for food, relying on different sugars for their sustenance, but they coexist in a more active way. Lactic acid bacteria use amino acids and peptides generated by yeasts and in turn enable the yeasts to produce more carbon dioxide, as well as making gluten more elastic. These modest functional effects are disdained in the high-tech world of chemical additives and bread improvers. But lactic acid bacteria can do much more than make stretchier dough. They can transform this dough into healthy food by:

- Enhancing the nutritional properties of bread.
- Making nutrients more 'bioavailable'.
- Counteracting certain 'anti-nutrients' in flour.
- Lowering its glycaemic index.
- Controlling potential spoilage organisms.
- Neutralising the parts of gluten that are harmful to people with coeliac disease and other wheat allergies.

Industrial breadmaking does not allow sufficient time for lactic acid bacteria to develop in the dough.

Nutritional enhancement and bioavailability

More and more research is demonstrating the remarkable power of lactic acid bacteria, not just to control potentially harmful substances but also to enhance beneficial ones. For instance, sourdough rye bread has larger quantities of the antioxidant pronyl-L-lysine than breads made with an ordinary yeast fermentation[3].

Sourdough fermentation has also been shown to more than double levels of folate, as well as enhancing levels of several other micronutrients and antioxidants[4]. Baking bread using the long sourdough process may make minerals, especially magnesium, iron and zinc, more available to the body[5].

Counteracting anti-nutrients

Lactic acid bacteria play a part in neutralising substances in wheat flour that can limit nutrient availability to human consumers. The bran layers on the outside of the wheat grain contain important sources of minerals such as potassium, magnesium, iron and zinc, but the bran also contains considerable amounts of phytic acid, which inhibits the absorption of these valuable minerals and trace elements. Mineral deficiencies are widely reported in developing countries and even in France a survey revealed that 72 per cent of men and 77 per cent of women had magnesium intakes below the dietary guidelines. Wholemeal bread is one of the best sources of magnesium (it has three times as much as white bread) but much of this remains inaccessible unless the phytic acid (phytate) is neutralised. A recent French study demonstrated that the action of lactic acid bacteria in sourdough fermentations improves the nutritional quality of wheat bread by reducing the amount of phytate. Simple fermentation with yeast produced less than half the quantity of soluble (available) magnesium at the end of a four-hour period compared with the sourdough[6].

All this raises serious questions about the bioavailability of important nutrients in fast systems such as the Chorleywood Bread Process. The industrial bakers are showing renewed interest in wholegrain cereals for their 'healthy eating' ranges. It looks as though their ultra-fast doughs will be unable to deliver all the expected (and aggressively advertised) nutritional goodies.

Glycaemic response

The production of acids by lactic acid bacteria can lower the glycaemic response (the speed at which food raises blood glucose levels) to sourdough bread. This is of potentially greater significance than any glycaemic effect attributable to the difference in fibre content between wholemeal and white breads. In view of the enormous public health implications of obesity and diabetes, a natural way of reducing the glycaemic index of bread should be of great interest to responsible bakers.

Spoilage

In addition to their many other properties, lactic acid bacteria generate antimicrobial substances, or 'bacteriocins', that play an important role in food safety[7]. 'Rope' is the name given to the spoilage, caused by strains of *Bacillus* bacteria, that occurs in bread, usually in warm, humid weather. The word 'ropy' comes from this condition, and eating ropy bread can make people ill[8]. Rope is kept at bay in modern baking by strict hygiene, temperature control and ultimately with chemical preservatives such as calcium propionate, which may be a carcinogen. But according to recent studies, lactic acid bacteria typically found in wheat and rye sourdoughs are capable of destroying the *Bacillus* species responsible[9]. So, long-fermented breads are much less likely to suffer from rope. Furthermore, the lactic and acetic acids that build up as the lactic acid bacteria work act as a natural preservative (in the sense of mould inhibitor) and thus obviate the need for chemicals.

Removal of harmful agents

The most interesting recent research, with considerable implications for making our daily bread wholesome again, has shown that lactic acid bacteria are capable of de-activating the very substances that cause wheat allergy and coeliac disease.

In 2002 Italian scientists demonstrated for the first time that selected sourdough lactic acid bacteria could neutralise some of the wheat gliadin that attacks the intestinal mucosa of coeliacs[10]. In 2004 a Japanese study showed how the lactic fermentation of soy sauce completely removes any allergens from wheat, which is one of its two main ingredients[11]. This is no mean feat, since other studies have proved that the particular parts of the wheat gliadin that harm humans are hardly affected at all by stomach enzymes and very acidic gastric and duodenal fluids[12]. It seems to be the unique property of certain lactic acid bacteria that, given time, they can knock out some other-wise impervious elements that make wheat unpalatable for so many people.

But these are test-tube studies. What do they mean for the bread we eat – or can't eat?

Most remarkably, the Italians made a bread with 30 per cent wheat flour (plus oats, millet and buckwheat) and fermented the dough with selected sourdough lactobacilli. It took 24 hours to hydrolyse almost completely the wheat gliadins and the '33-mer peptide, the most potent inducer of gut-derived human T-cell lines' (the things that do the damage) in coeliac patients. They made a similar bread raised with baker's yeast, and fed samples of both to coeliacs in a double-blind acute challenge. Thirteen out of 17 patients showed a marked alteration of intestinal permeability (popularly known as 'leaky gut') after eating the yeast-raised bread. But the same 13 patients, when fed the sourdough bread, showed no significant reaction: remarkably, coeliacs had eaten bread with wheat in it with no ill effects. (The remaining four did not respond to gluten in either of the breads.) The authors of the experiment conclude, rather modestly, that bread made using selected lactobacilli and

41

a long fermentation time 'is a novel tool for decreasing the level of gluten intolerance in humans'[13].

Currently, the only treatment for coeliac disease is a lifetime abstention from gluten. This experiment is a ray of hope for coeliacs. It suggests that everyone should be able to eat wheat and rye bread *if we get the bread-making right*. What's more, it may point to how cereal intolerance is not so much a matter of genetic chance as a consequence of the reckless application of scientific knowledge in the service of private gain rather than public health.

Slow is beautiful

There was a time when almost all breadmaking involved lactic acid bacteria and a long fermentation time. Before modern yeasts were isolated, most bread was fermented with what we would now call a sourdough and it would have taken many hours to rise. It is an intriguing possibility that, even if the wheats our forefathers cultivated contained the same potentially harmful gliadins as modern varieties, they were largely neutralised by the lactic acid bacteria that bakers couldn't help developing in their doughs.

Coeliac disease was identified only in the 1950s. In its severest form, it is a seriously debilitating condition unless treated by total avoidance of gluten. If such a disease had existed from our earliest wheat-eating days, is it not likely that sufferers, not knowing the cause or not having enough other food to eat, would have fared rather badly in the evolutionary stakes? Yet it seems that a good many of their genes have survived. A more plausible explanation might be that it was a combination of changes in wheat itself and a move to fast fermentation using commercial yeast and little or no natural lactic acid bacteria that rendered bread indigestible to certain individuals who may, granted, have had some genetic predisposition against gluten.

Could there be a connection between the Irish tradition of making bread without any fermentation at all (it is aerated with bicarbonate of soda) and the high incidence of coeliac disease in that country?

Whatever the outcome of detailed research into the exact mechanisms of cereal intolerance, it is abundantly clear that we have evolved an industrial breadmaking system that, in a variety of ways we can no longer ignore, produces bread that more and more people cannot and should not eat.

Quality, wholeness, health

When we choose a loaf of bread, we are not simply choosing a shape, a flavour or even the method that was used to make it. We can also choose how its basic ingredient is grown. We can opt for bread made with organic flour, milled from wheat grown in soil kept fertile by compost, crop rotation and green manures in a system that minimises the use of synthetic chemical biocides. Or we can choose flour from conventional wheat production, which uses energy-intensive chemical fertilisers, herbicides and pesticides to maximise grain yield and milling quality.

I grew up in a village with a 'glebe' – a piece of land adjacent to the church, which was originally part of the vicar's benefice. The word comes from the Latin *gleba* or *glæba*, meaning earth or soil. From this comes the old English *hlaf*, or loaf. The Russian for bread is *khlyeb*. Old German was *laib*. And so on – because bread comes from the soil, is of the soil. The fertility of the glebe gives rise to grain, the staging post between soil and bread. Bread's roots are in the soil.

In bread we gain access to the vitality of the seed, a vitality that surely extends beyond mere bodily function to include what George Stapledon called 'its ability to enliven'[14]. For this and other reasons, it seems to me that the quality of our food, and therefore of our life, is inextricably linked with the condition of the few inches of 'the delicate organism known as soil', beneath which 'is a planet as lifeless as the moon' (as Jacks and Whyte put it in their 1939 book, *The Rape of the Earth: A World Survey of Soil Erosion*). In the words of Robert McCarrison, whose comparative research into the diets of the Hunzas in Northwest India and the urban poor of Bombay in the 1920s and 1930s helped establish the link between food, soil and health:

'[Natural foods], when properly combined in the diet, supply all the food essentials, known and unknown, discovered and undiscovered, needed for normal nutrition, provided they are produced on soil which is not impoverished, for if they be proceeds of impoverished soil, their quality will be poor and the health of those who eat them, man and his domestic animals, will suffer accordingly.'[15]

Thanks to advances in molecular biology and genetics, we know that the expression of genes in wheat differs markedly depending on whether the grain has been grown organically or with synthetic nitrogen fertiliser[16]. Further research may tell us whether organic flour is more or less palatable than non-organic, particularly in relation to the gliadin proteins that are responsible for wheat allergy and intolerance.

To my way of thinking, there is a deep sympathy between organic agriculture and slow breadmaking. In both, the natural world is not an enemy, to be bludgeoned into submission by an arsenal of chemical weaponry. It is, rather, one element in a web of life that sustains us all. The prudent farmer seeks to understand natural processes and to work with them, appreciating that the world we inhabit tends in the long run to reward perseverance and restraint and to punish exploitation and shortcuts. In organic agriculture the transmission of nutrients – of life – depends on the creation and maintenance of the right conditions in which millions of tiny unseen agents (bacteria, fungi and protozoa) can work most effectively. It is a project requiring patience, observation, humility and some compromise between productivity and permanence. By comparison, the chemical model of fertility has all the subtlety of an intravenous injection: a small number of active ingredients, chosen for their immediate effectiveness, are delivered by the most direct route to the heart of the organism. The equivalent in baking is to rely on additives rather than time to produce the changes in dough that make it fit to eat.

The scientific and agricultural establishments have tried hard to play down any evidence of the superior quality of organic food. Such evidence is not plentiful, largely because not many people are gathering it: less than 2 per cent of the UK's agricultural research and development budget in 2000 was allocated to organics. But a review of all the available and valid research conducted by the Soil Association in 2001 did conclude that 'eating organically grown food is likely to improve one's intake of minerals, vitamin C and antioxidant secondary nutrients while reducing exposure to potentially harmful pesticide residues, nitrates, GMOs and artificial additives used in food processing.'[17] Earlier I cited evidence that a combination of organic growing and stone milling significantly increases the available minerals in bread flour and that modern plant breeding has produced varieties that are poorer in certain nutrients than their forebears.

The work of gathering such evidence is painstaking and important. But it does seem to me that for an individual to put off any action on the source of his or her food ingredients until some sort of 'conclusive' proof is available is, in fact, deeply irrational. If the notion that healthy soil gives rise to healthy plants (and therefore animals and people) is so threatening to today's orthodoxy, try turning it on its head: would you expect the kind of depleted, unhealthy soil more typical of intensive agriculture to produce healthy food? If not, then it is simply good sense to seek to produce the healthiest soil possible and to choose food that has grown in it.

For me, it is a matter not of mysticism but of observation that wholeness (which is the precursor, through its ancient variant *wholth*, of our word *health*) is the outcome of a process in which many elements interact in complicated and changing patterns. It demonstrably consists of more than the sum of its constituent parts and is diminished by separation, rupture or reduction. Health is not a static condition, but one that requires us to engage intelligently with our surroundings, enlarging our understanding by patient observation and experiment. Collaboration, coexistence, sufficiency – these are the watchwords; not exploitation, domination, maximisation.

The kind of breadmaking that I advocate is in harmony with this 'organic' approach – not just in the provenance of the raw materials but in expecting the healthiest outcome from processes in which we temper technological enthusiasm with a little humility.

Take, eat …

There is another reason why it matters what bread we eat. Our choice of bread is symbolic, in the sense that it reflects something more profound than the mere desire to be filled.

I am intrigued by the transformation that is central to leavened bread. The process by which dough changes in response to kneading, expands slowly through yeast fermentation and then is fixed in a new form in the oven has a mysterious quality even to those who know the science. The mystery lies not in the fact that we cannot predict the outcome when we assemble the necessary ingredients, although some variability is always likely in non-industrial baking. What is, I contend, endlessly mysterious is the fact of the transformation itself. Perhaps when we participate in that transformation, when the result is, reliably, bread, we cannot help feeling a humility born in part of a sense that we are not the only agent in the process.

It is not hard, therefore, to see why bread has acquired symbolic significance. Bread *is* life, in the sense that without food the body dies. But bread also *represents* life because it is the result of an indefinitely renewable cycle involving the birth, reproduction and death of the organisms within it (yeasts, bacteria, etc).

Much of the symbolism around bread involves sharing. From the derivation of our word 'com*pan*ion' (someone with whom we share bread) to the words in the Christian Eucharist, the material simplicity of bread as food is constantly suggestive of its involvement in friendship, hope and transformation.

What can we do?

So it does matter what bread we eat. But how do we get hold of the good stuff? And what is the good stuff?

To 'get the bread right', in David Scott's phrase, requires baking methods using flours with plenty of their original goodness left in and fermentation over periods long enough to make as many nutrients as possible available to the consumer. And the bread must taste great, too.

Clearly the origin of the raw materials comes into it, but the most important questions to ask when choosing bread are:

- Has the dough been fermented for long enough?
- Have any additives been used?
- How much yeast has been used?
- Does it contain any added enzymes?

The answers to these questions (if you can get them out of the manufacturer) will largely determine whether the bread is industrial or artisan, made quickly with chemicals or slowly with skill. Unfortunately, appearances can be deceptive and labels opaque, so some detective work may be required. But some simple tests can be applied. For example, if a loaf looks big and airy but tastes insipid and seems curiously unsatisfying, it has probably been engineered more for volume than for integrity; or, if the texture of a loaf does not gradually change as the days pass, if it seems to stay uniformly soft for several days, it has almost certainly got 'crumb-softening' enzymes in it.

People are already asking these questions and voting with their feet. If British bread is ever to rise above the status of culinary doormat, we need honesty about ingredients (all of them), clarity about nutrition, and a desire to educate public taste about the relationship between time, flavour and health. To restore trust in bread and reverse its long-term sales decline, the industrial bakers need to clean up their act. Below are some modest suggestions for how to do this, based on the growing body of evidence that the way most modern bread is produced is a nutritional and digestive shambles.

1. All bread additives and enzymes should be labelled in sufficient detail for consumers to be able to tell what they are and where they have come from.

2. No new bakery enzymes should be approved until research establishes whether any of the enzymes currently in use has the same kind of toxic potential as was recently identified in transglutaminase.
3. Much more research should be conducted to compare the digestibility and nutrient availability of fast-made and long-fermented breads.
4. Roller-mills should use all the constituents of the wheat grain in their reconstituted wholemeal flour or should indicate clearly what has been removed and why.
5. Roller-milling procedures should be adapted to produce white and other low extraction-rate flours with at least as high a nutrient profile as stone-milled flours with the same extraction rate.
6. Baseline standards of important micronutrients should be established for wheat (and other cereal) breeding programmes, with the aim of gradually restoring (and in time exceeding) levels found in older varieties. Breeding (and farming) methods should also aim to produce grain with as little of the harmful gliadin protein as possible.

The aim of these measures is simple: to make all bread (white, wholemeal and in between) as good as it can be. If the milling and baking industries adopted them, they would no longer need to hide behind obscure labelling, devious marketing and defensive public relations.

For the consumer not prepared to wait for this happy day, there are two options: seek out an artisan baker or bake your own bread.

A world away from Chorleywood, in villages and industrial estates, farm shops, delis and food halls, selling at farmers' markets or on the internet, a new breed of artisan bakers is using skill not scale, time not trickery, to reach an increasing number of customers attracted by the openness and integrity of real baking. Here are no additives, enzymes and high-speed doughs – just good ingredients, often organic and local, transformed with patience and effort into loaves full of life.

Although the number of new artisan bakeries has grown significantly in the past ten years, they still account for only a tiny percentage of British bread. But

I sense a growing interest in 'slow' bread, both from consumers and from the steadily increasing numbers of people who want to learn real baking. Even as the supermarkets' in-store 'bakeries' (many of which simply reheat bread made elsewhere) struggle to retain staff, my 'Baking for a Living' courses are over-subscribed, often by people drawn to bread and fermentation from comfortable but unfulfilling professional careers. Home bakers, whether they use traditional methods or bread machines, like to decide for themselves what goes into their bread and how it is made. If you are one of them, or would like to be, what follows will tell you all you need to know to do it well.

CHAPTER THREE
TAKING CONTROL

'Making bread strikes a mysteriously
prehistoric chord somewhere inside us ...
alongside the mental satisfaction, you
discover new and different gastronomic
pleasures that enrich you and those
around you.'

LIONEL POILÂNE,
Guide de l'amateur de pain
(Editions Robert Laffont, 1981)

Time to choose

British bread is a nutritional, culinary, social and environmental mess – made from aggressively hybridised wheat that is grown in soils of diminishing natural fertility, sprayed with toxins to counter pests and diseases, milled in a way that robs it of the best part of its nutrients, fortified with just two minerals and two vitamins in a vain attempt to make good the damage, and made into bread using a cocktail of functional additives and a super-fast fermentation (based on greatly increased amounts of yeast), which inhibits assimilation of some of the remaining nutrients while causing digestive discomfort to many consumers.

There are some signs of a renaissance of small-scale artisan baking. However, the whole 'craft' bakery sector accounts for only 6 per cent of UK bread so, unless something changes, most people will have to put up with bread from the industrial plant bakers or the supermarket in-store bakeries for a long time to come, perhaps for ever.

The concentration of commercial power into ever bigger corporate units is often presented as being necessary to keep prices down and enlarge consumer choice. And on the face of it, the consumer has never been offered so many choices before. Scores of brands and hundreds of ranges compete for shelf space and seem to cater for every conceivable preference. But are these real choices?

The world's seeds and plant breeding programmes are dominated by a handful of global corporations, as is the trade in key food commodities. Four supermarket chains account for the majority of retail sales in the UK. Yes, these companies compete against one another. But they do so from within a single monolithic view of how the world should feed itself. Standardisation in the name of 'efficiency' and cost reduction has led to increasing dependence on just a few varieties of key crops and methods of processing. Over 80 per cent of British bread is made by the ultra-fast, additive-dependent Chorleywood Bread Process. Much of the rest, particularly in the supermarkets' in-store bakeries, uses a similar range of chemical and enzyme additives in the process known as activated dough development. For most consumers, 'choice' between breads is meaningless because they are all made in essentially the same way.

Meanwhile, advertising keeps alive the illusion of choice. It emphasises minor differences between brands or varieties and keeps very quiet indeed about what really goes into, or is left out of, our daily bread.

Not surprisingly, disappointment with the bland character of over-processed food is fuelling a growing outrage at the food industry's lack of transparency and cynical exploitation of farmers, process workers and consumers. People are realising that the undoubted convenience of processed food comes at the expense of any sense of control over our most basic nourishment. If the food industry won't tell us what is really in our food, how can we make sensible choices, let alone feel that we are doing the right thing for the health of ourselves and our families?

It is time to take matters into our own hands. One way of fighting back is to refuse to buy foods produced in ways we find unacceptable. Making bread at home enables us to take control of a significant part of our diet by choosing exactly what goes into it. But if this control is to be real, we must first define what wholesome, nutritious and digestible bread really is. Simply to imitate commercial loaves is to accept the industrial food agenda.

My aim is to show that making good bread is not difficult.

One step at a time

Many people think that baking bread takes too long. It is true that to make a well-fermented loaf takes quite a while. But it doesn't need to take much of *your* time – i.e. time that you may not have or feel you cannot spare. Breadmaking is a sequence of relatively short actions interspersed with periods of waiting. Here are the stages involved in making a simple loaf and the amount of time that each takes:

Action	Minutes taken
Weighing ingredients	5
Mixing and kneading	10–15
Dividing and moulding	5–10
Putting into oven and taking out	5
Washing up utensils	5
Total	**30–40**

So all it takes is half an hour or so of your time. This can be spread over 4, 12 or 24 hours, depending on the method you use and the other demands on your time.

The important point is that a pressured lifestyle doesn't have to entail rushed bread. Forget the claims of bread machines that promise a loaf in little more than an hour. If fermentation is involved, for reasons of nutrition and flavour that only the slow baker can appreciate, the longer the better.

The simple life

There is only a handful of basic breadmaking methods. Don't be misled by books that boast prodigious numbers of recipes; many will be no more than small variations on a theme. Be inspired by new ideas by all means, but do not be intimidated by the apparent size of the task ahead. Baking is easy once you understand what is happening at the heart of it.

'When there is a conscious sensuous pleasure in the work itself, it is done by artists,' wrote William Morris[1]. 'Artisans' do not reject the appropriate use of machines but they decline to be dominated by them. They gain satisfaction from intimate contact with the materials of their trade and from direct involvement in the whole process from flour to baked loaf. The feel of soft, warm dough under the hands, the sight of an oven well set with loaves, the beguiling smell of baking bread, the satisfying sound of crackling crusts – all these can be yours when you make your own bread.

One of the reasons breadmaking is so satisfying is that it provides a balance between variation and repetition. The human body seems to need both the stimulation of different tasks and the mental relaxation produced by rhythmic repetition. Hand breadmaking has it all.

Breadmaking machines

I am often asked (in a 'lighting the blue touch paper' sort of spirit) what I think of domestic bread machines. There are certainly a lot of them in circulation – or gathering dust, perhaps. An insurance firm that commissions an annual survey of the least-used household gadgets reported in 2004 that 7.4 million people in the UK own a bread machine but never use it[2]. What a shame. They could make serious inroads into the eight million large loaves sold each day. And, believe it or not, apart from producing delicious bread with no additives, this might be better for the environment. A well-known miller has calculated that, taking into account the whole process from bakery to shop to consumer, factory bread uses more energy than bread made in a domestic machine. If this is so, it throws interesting light on the whole notion of industrial 'efficiency'.

After some initial scepticism, I have realised that automatic bread-makers have introduced millions of people to the pleasure of home-made bread. And if at first all the control seems to be in the hands of the machine, users soon discover how to adjust the settings to achieve the results they want. I know one pillar of the wholefood establishment (he also owns a small bakery) who produces wonderful sourdough bread in his domestic breadmaker.

Many a bread journey has begun with one of these machines, a journey to discover how fermentation works and how time, taste and texture are connected. It is often a journey of liberation: as you understand more about the ingredients, you leave behind the programmed settings and risk the 'sensuous pleasure' of the process. In my experience, it is a journey that never really ends.

So let's begin. You don't need to acquire an expensive array of equipment before you start. But there are some essential tools – both mental and physical – that will be needed along the way. First and foremost, it helps to approach the task in the right frame of mind:

- **Be patient**
  If nothing seems to be happening to your dough, it doesn't mean that something won't eventually happen.
- **Watch and learn**
  Notice what happens and when; don't change more than one variable at a time.
- **Empathise**
  You are working with living organisms (yeasts and bacteria); do as you would be done by – keep them warm and nourished.
- **Take it easy**
  You are making bread to eat, not taking part in a competition, so don't judge or be judged solely on appearances.

Tools and equipment

Bowls

I prefer stainless-steel or polypropylene bowls because they are lighter and won't break. However, earthenware and glass are better insulators. Wood, too, keeps dough warm and is making a comeback as a food contact material after it was found to harbour fewer microbes than some of the synthetic alternatives.

Polythene bags

These have many uses, e.g. covering bowls of dough and rising loaves, because they retain moisture and prevent a skin forming on the surface of the dough. They can be washed and re-used, unlike the ghastly 'oiled cling film'.

Scales

The best kind to get are electronic ones with a 'tare' facility (which resets the display to zero) and ideally with 1 gram or 2 gram steps. Otherwise, balance scales are fine, but you will have to rely on teaspoons and fractions thereof for small quantities of spice, dried yeast or salt, which is bound to be a bit risky until you are confident enough to judge these things by eye.

Measuring jugs

I use jugs (either glass or polypropylene) more for pouring than for measuring because they are never very accurate. Since one millilitre of water conveniently weighs one gram, it is easier to weigh liquids than to measure them, particularly for small amounts. This is where the electronic scales come into their own. Just zero the display and weigh your liquid on top of the other ingredients.

Thermometer

A thermometer is useful for checking liquid and dough temperatures until you can judge them by hand. The best is a digital probe – a stainless-steel rod that you can poke into dough or dip into liquids. It should have a read-out with a temperature range of −20°C to +150°C or thereabouts.

Worktop

Wood is the warmest surface and therefore kindest to typical bread doughs, but it can take more effort to clean if the dough gets into the grain. Laminated worktops are fine, though possibly less able to resist scratching from scrapers. Marble and stone, being naturally cold, are best for pastry and croissants.

Scraper

A plastic scraper is one of the most useful tools to have around. It can be used for dividing dough, folding and stretching wet Italian doughs, getting dough off your hands, cleaning the worktop and so on. Bakers also use the 'Scotch' scraper, which is a stainless-steel rectangle with a wooden or plastic handle. If you use only one, get a flexible plastic scraper with two slightly rounded corners, which make cleaning bowls out much easier.

Knife

A sharp knife or razor blade is useful for marking or 'slashing' dough before baking. The blade needs to be very sharp and not serrated, otherwise it will drag on the dough and make an unsightly cut. A 10cm scalloped blade is best.

Baking tins

A good baking tin is a lasting friend. They come in various shapes, sizes and finishes. Although 'small' tins are supposed to hold 1lb (454g) of dough and 'large' tins 2lb (900g), they vary in size considerably – and in any case, not all types of dough expand to the same extent. I find many domestic tins rather shallow and wide and the resulting loaves can be unflattering to look at. Unless you have particular requirements such as a desired size of slice, try to find tins that are tall, narrow and deep.

I would avoid older-type non-stick finishes because they eventually break up and can leave pieces embedded in the loaf crust. There are some new non-stick finishes based on silicone rubber that are effective. Best of all is a glass-like finish, which is baked on to the tin like stove enamel. This is very durable so long as you do not dig loaves out of the tin with a knife – but you shouldn't need to because this finish is reliably non-stick. In general, the heavier the metal, the more evenly the heat will be conducted to the loaf inside and the less chance of the tin distorting in the heat of the oven.

Try to avoid washing baking tins, especially plain metal ones, because repeated greasing and baking can build up a natural sheen, which makes it less likely that dough will stick. If you do need to clean tins, wipe them with a soft, wet cloth and no detergent.

Baking trays

Try to get trays that exactly fit (either alone or two side by side) your oven shelf dimensions. Go for the thickest-gauge metal available. Thin steel or aluminium trays may be cheap but they have an annoying habit of buckling as they heat up, and the sudden movement can cause the collapse of rolls or loaves whose structure has not yet 'set'.

Proving baskets and cloths

Proving dough in a basket or cloth is the traditional Continental way of handling dough destined to be baked on the sole (or bottom) of a brick oven, or that is too sloppy to prove as a freestanding loaf without flowing into a puddle. It is an example of adaptation to the quality of the gluten in local wheats, which tended to be soft and extensible rather than strong and elastic. Great lightness and a very open structure are possible with such dough, but only if it can be held in a reasonably coherent shape before being fixed by the heat of baking.

Proving baskets

Known as *pannetons* in French and *Brotformen* in German, these are commercially available but rather expensive. The French type consists of a wicker basket with a linen liner stitched inside. The German ones, most often associated with rye bread, are round or oblong and made from bent willow cane or wood pulp; they are not lined with fabric, so the dough takes on the ribbed profile of the basket. Both types of basket must be dusted with flour to prevent the dough sticking. They are not generally washed between uses and gradually acquire more of a non-stick character.

You can make your own proving basket using a piece of linen or thick, unbleached calico and a cheap wicker basket. Do not be tempted to use a tea towel unless it is made of fairly thick linen. It is important that the fabric has an open weave, so that air can penetrate to conduct moisture from the surface of the dough. For this reason, light cotton and muslin are not suitable. Nor is a plastic or steel bowl, because moisture from the warm dough will condense on the surface and make the dough stick to the fabric. In an attempt to save money, I once bought a load of plastic basins to make my own proving baskets when demand for the bakery's French Country Bread began to rocket. I drilled dozens of holes in the basins to create an air flow to the dough, but it still tended to stick to the liner fabric. You may notice the same effect if you try to make a proving basket out of a plastic colander and a tea towel.

Cloths

Known as *couches* in French, linen cloths, well rubbed with flour, can be rucked up into channels to allow long loaves such as baguettes to prove. The channels are pushed fairly close to each other so that the dough pieces can only expand vertically. When ready, they are gently rolled on to a peel (see below), from which they are slid on to the oven sole. If using cloths, take care to make the channels tall enough to contain the dough: it can be frustrating if a piece of dough rises over the top of the channel and sticks to its neighbour.

Peels

A peel is a flat, shovel-like tool, usually on the end of a long shaft, used by bakers to slide risen dough pieces into the oven to bake directly on the bricks or tiles that form the 'sole', or bottom, of the baking chamber. A 'slip' is a long, narrow peel from which several small rolls or a baguette can be slid sideways on to the oven bottom. If you have some sort of ceramic baking surface

in your oven (see below), you will need to improvise a peel, preferably with enough of a handle to ensure you do not burn your hands on the oven as you slide the bread in. A piece of stiff cardboard will do, though there is always a risk of it bending under the weight of a large, moist piece of dough. Some people use the removable flat metal base from a cake tin. Hardboard or plywood can be cut by anyone with basic skills into the characteristic spade-like shape. Quite a few companies now sell 'pizza peels', which work equally well for bread. Whatever you use, dust your peel with rice flour, maize (corn) meal or semolina to stop the dough sticking to it. These flours provide more

63

'non-stick' effect than ordinary wheat flour but if you don't have any of them to hand use wholemeal wheat flour rather than white: the branny bits give a reasonably slippery surface.

Ovens

Most domestic ovens, whether gas, electric, fan assisted or solid fuel, will bake bread quite adequately. But, not surprisingly, some are better than others. Understanding the way bread bakes will help you adjust your oven's settings to best effect and perhaps compensate for, or at least forgive, its little foibles.

The big issue when baking bread is whether you do it with applied or retained heat. Most domestic ovens, including the Aga type of range, consist of a steel chamber that is heated by applied energy from a flame, element or furnace. A thermostat controls the flow of heat according to the chosen setting. Once the oven is up to the desired temperature, the flow of heat is reduced. However, the temperature in the oven may have to fall by as much as 30°C before the thermostat calls for renewed heat, so the item being baked is subjected to a constantly oscillating temperature. Cast-iron ranges have more thermal mass built into them than normal domestic ovens and should hold a more even temperature.

The principle of the brick oven is that a mass of masonry retains the energy imparted by the wood (or gas or oil) fire and then radiates, convects and conducts it to the baked object with almost complete evenness. This produces a 'solid' bake, where the heat seems to penetrate the bread quicker and more consistently than in applied-heat ovens. Bread that bakes quicker, provided it is baked fully, will retain more internal moisture and so keep a little better, as well as tasting more succulent.

The best aspect of baking in a masonry oven is being able to place the dough directly on to the hot stone. This gives it a terrific thermal kick up the pants and helps to lift the sagging circumference of a freestanding loaf. You can achieve this effect in a conventional domestic oven by using a 'pizza stone' or a large unglazed quarry tile. Heat the stone up with the oven and then tip or slide the risen loaf or pizza on to it. You may need to improvise some sort of peel (see above). For the more ambitious retained-heat baker, a company in the USA sells complete ceramic liners designed to fit inside standard domestic ovens (see page 354).

Know your oven

The knobs and dials on domestic ovens are notoriously unreliable. Even where they indicate a precise temperature rather than a rough guide or a regulo number, you should regard the setting as approximate. It can be useful to check your oven's actual heat with a separate oven thermometer, trying it in various places to see whether there is an even temperature throughout. But all that is really required is to know what setting gives a cool, moderate or hot oven. Remember that a fan delivers an extra 10–20°C of effective heat, so if you have it on (or are stuck with it) use settings slightly lower than you might expect.

In my recipes I try not to be too precise with oven temperatures. This is partly because of the variability just mentioned but mainly because if you understand roughly what heat a loaf requires (e.g. pretty hot for a big, wet, rye sourdough, moderate for an enriched sweet bread), you won't go far wrong; common sense and a watchful eye will give better results than sticking religiously to a supposedly precise setting.

A note on measures

I recommend accurate measuring when you tackle a recipe for the first time; this makes it easier to see the effect of later adjustments. Once you have more of a feel for the relationship between ingredients and how dough looks and behaves, you can take a more relaxed approach – though it always pays to be careful with salt, spice and baker's yeast.

I prefer to use metric measurements. In home baking, quite small quantities of ingredients are used. The Imperial system is unsuited to this because many of the most sensitive ingredients in baking, such as salt, yeast and spice, are required in tiny fractions of its basic unit, the ounce (28.35g). The result is chaos, with three unsatisfactory alternatives being deployed for the measurement of small quantities. For example, 5g is the amount of salt that I suggest for around a kilo of basic bread dough. This can be expressed as, very roughly:

- one-fifth of an ounce – but who has a one-fifth weight for their scales?
- '0.2oz' – which mixes decimals with an essentially non-decimal system.
- one teaspoon – which abandons the Imperial system altogether and relies on your having a plastic measure of exactly the right size or taking your chances with whatever small spoon comes to hand.

The US system of measuring in cups, while handy for simple cake making, is completely unsuited to measuring small quantities of breadmaking ingredients. A recent serious American baking book for professionals and keen amateurs actually asks home bakers to measure amounts such as '3.2oz (⅞ cup)'. Need I say more?

The metric system avoids all this nonsense and has the added advantage that recipes can be scaled up or down with ease using basic mental arithmetic (or a calculator). A set of electronic scales accurate to 1 gram is a very useful tool.

Bakers' percentages

I may offend the baking fraternity by also rejecting the system known as 'bakers' percentages'. This bizarre throwback seems to me to defy logic as much as language by treating the flour quantity in any recipe as 100 per cent and relating other ingredients to that. A typical bread recipe might have 100 per cent flour, 65 per cent water, 1.5 per cent salt and 1.25 per cent yeast, making the *total* 167.75 'per cent'. If you want to know how much salt there is in a recipe expressed in this way, you cannot go by the stated figure (1.5 per cent) because it tells you only what percentage the salt is of the flour (in this example, salt is in fact 0.89 per cent of the dough). Bakers' percentages are usually justified in terms of assisting with the scaling up or down of a recipe. But with metric measurements nothing could be easier.

Eggs

I show eggs in terms of grams, which allows for greater accuracy in view of the considerable variation in egg sizes. One large egg weighs (without the shell) about 50g and most of the recipes involving egg therefore use multiples of 50g.

Liquids

I express all liquids in grams rather than millilitres because it is often easier to measure small quantities by weight (measuring jugs being rather inaccurate and dependent on the angle at which you hold them). When adding oil to a recipe, unless the method recommends otherwise, it is handy to pour it straight from the bottle into the bowl with the flour and salt, having reset the scales to zero: this saves dirtying another utensil and can be more accurate. One millilitre of water weighs one gram, so you can either weigh or measure, as you prefer. Oil weighs slightly less than water (which is why it floats on it) so some inaccuracy can creep in if you treat one millilitre as one gram, but this is hardly significant in small quantities.

Scaling up recipes

Most ingredient quantities can be scaled up or down pro rata. There are two main exceptions. More yeast is generally used in small doughs to compensate for the fact that, in typical kitchen conditions, they lose heat quite quickly, whereas large volumes of dough conserve and even stimulate heat gain. As a rough rule of thumb, yeast should be reduced by one-third for doughs between 2 kilos and 10 kilos and by half beyond that. The recipes in this book generally recommend less yeast than usual, so some experimentation may be required. Do bear in mind that slower fermentation with less yeast almost always results in bread with better flavour, texture and keeping quality.

Substituting flours

Unless there is a stated reason for not doing so, white wheat flour can be replaced by wholemeal or vice versa in any of the recipes. Some adjustment of the liquid may be necessary because the bran in wholemeal flour can, with time, absorb a considerable amount of moisture. Doughs with a high proportion of wholemeal will not expand to quite the same volume as those made with white flour.

Water temperature

To determine the temperature of water for breadmaking, use the following formula:

2 × desired dough temperature *minus* actual flour temperature *equals* required water temperature

Example:
Desired dough temperature is 27°C; flour temperature is likely to be around 20°C in summer and, in extreme circumstances, 6°C in winter.

Summer:
2 × 27 = 54 – 20 = 34°C

Winter:
2 × 27 = 54 – 6 = 48°C

Conversion tables

In some instances the conversions given below have been rounded to produce more friendly numbers. If you need to be super-accurate, use the conversion factors given (and a calculator).

Weight
g = gram; kg = kilogram

To covert ounces (oz) to grams (g), multiply by 28.35
To convert grams to ounces, multiply by 0.035 (or divide by 28.35)

Imperial	Metric	Metric	Imperial
¼oz	7g	5g	⅕oz
½oz	14g	10g	⅓oz
¾oz	21g	15g	½oz
1oz	28g	20g	¾oz
1½oz	43g	25g	⅞oz
2oz	57g	30g	1oz
3oz	85g	35g	1¼oz
4oz	113g	40g	1½oz
5oz	142g	50g	1¾oz
6oz	170g	60g	2oz
7oz	198g	65g	2¼oz
8oz	227g	70g	2½oz
9oz	255g	75g	2⅔oz
10oz	283g	80g	2¾oz
11oz	312g	85g	3oz
12oz	340g	90g	3¼oz
13oz	369g	95g	3⅓oz

Imperial	Metric	Metric	Imperial
14oz	397g	100g	3½oz
15oz	425g	150g	5oz
16oz (1lb)	454g	200g	7oz
1¼lb	567g	250g	9oz
1½lb	680g	300g	10½oz
1¾lb	794g	400g	14oz
2lb	907g	500g	17½oz
3lb	1.36kg	1kg	2¼lb
4lb	1.81kg	2kg	4½lb
5lb	2.27kg	3kg	6½lb

Volume

fl oz = fluid ounce; tsp = teaspoon; tbsp = tablespoon; ml = millilitre

To covert fluid ounces to millilitres, multiply by 28.35
To convert millilitres to fluid ounces, multiply by 0.035 (or divide by 28.35)

Metric	Imperial
5ml	1 tsp
15ml	1 tbsp
30ml	1fl oz
50ml	1¾fl oz
100ml	3½fl oz
110ml	4fl oz
140ml	5fl oz (¼ pint)
200ml	7fl oz
250ml	9fl oz
300ml	10fl oz (½ pint)
350ml	12fl oz
400ml	14fl oz
450ml	16fl oz
500ml	18fl oz
568ml	20fl oz (1 pint)
600ml	21fl oz
700ml	25fl oz
800ml	28fl oz
900ml	32fl oz
1 litre	35fl oz
1.14 litres	40fl oz (1 quart)
2 litres	70fl oz
4.54 litres	160fl oz (1 gallon)
5 litres	176fl oz

Temperature

To covert Fahrenheit to Celsius, subtract 32 and multiply by 0.555
To convert Celsius to Fahrenheit, multiply by 1.8 and add 32

°C	°F	Gas Mark	Description
0	32		
5	41		
10	50		
15	59		
20	68		
25	77		
30	86		
35	95		
40	104		
50	122		
75	167		
100	212	¼	Very cool
120	250	½	
135	275	1	Cool
150	300	2	
160	320	3	Warm
180	350	4	Moderate
190	375	5	
200	390	6	Fairly hot
210	410		
220	430	7	Hot
230	445	8	Very hot
240	465		
250	480	9	Very hot
260	500		

CHAPTER FOUR

THE ESSENTIAL INGREDIENTS

'To sustain man's strength as it was
intended, bread must be made of sound
and pure ingredients; and no economy can
be more false or mistaken in its character
than that which seeks to cheapen it by any
admixture of materials which are not so.'

ELIZA ACTON,
The English Bread Book
(Longman, 1857)

One of the beauties of bread is that it can be made with so few ingredients. Flour and water alone, treated in the right way, are sufficient. The following run-down of the essentials is not meant to be an exhaustive treatise but a practical guide. It is useful, but not essential, to read this before starting on the recipes.

Wheat flour

Flour is produced from a large number of wheat varieties, grown in different soils and climates (for other grains, see below). Millers select and blend different varieties and batches of grain to create flours for all purposes, from biscuits and cakes to bread and pasta. Unfortunately, there is no international classification system for flour, so it can be hard to grasp the different properties and uses denoted by a bewildering array of names and descriptions.

In order to make a judgement about the nutritional quality and likely baking performance of a flour, the home baker needs answers to the following questions:

- How was it milled? Stoneground for better retention of nutrients, or roller-milled?
- What is its 'extraction rate' – i.e. how brown is it?
- What is its protein content? What sort of a dough will it make? Strong and tight or soft and extensible?

If a flour has been stoneground, this will almost always be advertised on the bag since it is, rightly, deemed to be an advantage and therefore a selling point. The other two issues are more complicated.

Extraction rate

Extraction rate is the term used in the UK to denote the amount of the original grain left in the flour. Milling between stones gives a flour with all the constituents of the original grain mixed together: the mill has 'extracted' 100 per cent of the grain. This is known as a high extraction rate flour. To make white flour, the mill strips and sifts out the germ and the bran layers on the outside of the wheat grain which together constitute about 28 per cent of the grain, leaving a '72 per cent' extraction flour. There are various grades in between: brown flour has some of the bran and germ replaced to take it back to about 80 per cent of the original grain.

The problem for the home baker is that, apart from '100 per cent wholemeal', extraction rate is rarely mentioned on flour bags in so many words. Indeed, words like 'brown' and 'mixed grain' actually confuse the issue, perhaps sounding a bit nearer to 'whole' than they really are.

Here are some typical UK flours with their approximate extraction rates and other details:

British flour types

Description	Extraction rate	Protein	Notes
Stoneground strong wholemeal	100%	12–14%	Designed for breadmaking
Stoneground wholemeal	100%	9–11%	Suitable for cakes, pastry and some breads
Strong wholemeal	±95%	12–14%	Roller-milled; for bread
Strong white (or extra strong)	72–75%	12–15%	For bread

Description	Extraction rate	Protein	Notes
Plain white	72–75%	9–11%	Mainly for cakes and biscuits but can be used for Italian-type breads
Brown	80%	12–14%	Not to be confused with wholemeal
'Wheatmeal'	85%	12–14%	Not now a legal term
Malted grain or 'Malthouse'	80–85%	11–13%	A mixture of brown flour and sometimes rye flour with malted flakes of wheat, rye or barley and non-diastatic (not enzyme-active) malt flour

Self-raising flours are usually lower-protein flours (white, wholemeal or brown) with added baking powder. They are designed for making cakes and scones.

Incidentally, 'wholewheat' is the term Americans use for wholemeal. It is specific to wheat, of course; the British wholemeal can be applied to any grain, hence wholemeal rye flour, wholemeal buckwheat flour. Latterly the term 'wholegrain' has emerged as an alternative. Thus 'wholegrain wheat flour' is the same as what the British call 'wholemeal wheat flour'. If you find this confusing, wait until you see industrial millers and bakers touting products made with 'white wholegrain flour'. It is already happening, in defiance of language if not of nutritional good sense. The flour thus named claims to be milled from a variety of 'white' (light-coloured) American wheat using a process that grinds the bran so finely that it becomes invisible. Expect a revelation in due course that rather less than 100 per cent of the wheat grain ends up in this 'wholegrain' flour.

The flour classification system used on the Continent is based on 'ash content', a measurement of the minerals left when all the other constituents of flour are burned. The lower the number, the lower the mineral content, reflecting the degree of refinement of the flour, and therefore of its loss of nutritional value (the lower the ash content, the less nutritious the flour).

Continental flour classification

French	Italian	German	Extraction rate	Ash content
	Type 00	Type 405	50%	0.4%
Type 45			60–70%	<0.5%
	Type 0	Type 550	72%	0.5–0.6%
Type 55			75%	0.5–0.6%
Type 65	Type 1		80%	0.62–0.65%
Type 80	Type 2	Type 812	85%	0.75–0.9%
Type 110		Type 1200	88–90%	1–1.2%
Type 150			95%	1.4%
		Type 1740	95%	1.7%

The problem with the Continental system is that, while it tells you a good deal about the presence or absence of the branny parts of the grain, which contain all the minerals, it says nothing about the protein content of the flour. Which is a pity, because for bread baking, much depends on the quantity and quality of flour protein.

Protein

Protein is important because of its relationship to gluten. The more protein there is in a wheat, the more gluten there will be in a dough made from it.

The terms 'hard' and 'soft' are often used to differentiate between types of wheat. They reflect the physical character of the grains and have become associated with their baking properties. Hard wheats are generally high in protein and have flinty grains that do not break up easily. Soft wheats are lower in protein, with grains that are plump and quite easily crushed.

Durum wheat, despite the etymological link, is not the same as hard wheat. It is a distinctly different variety of the *Triticum* species (*Triticum turgidum L. var. durum*), which is used mainly in pasta manufacture. Durum wheat is high in protein and has the particular quality that its endosperm, the floury material in the middle of the grain, does not immediately reduce to a powder when milled. It holds together in granular lumps called semolina. This can be further milled to a fine flour, but is often used as it comes. Pasta types such as spaghetti and macaroni are extruded – i.e. a stiff dough is forced through nozzles and comes out in the form of tubes. For this process to work, the dough must not be springy or elastic, otherwise it would simply compress in a rubbery mass and block the nozzles. The semolina from durum wheat produces a coherent but not very stretchy dough, which can be extruded and which holds together well afterwards. Rather surprisingly in view of its coarse texture, semolina can also be used to make bread.

The two components of wheat protein that concern the baker are gliadin and glutenin, which together form gluten, the grey-brown web of stretchy material that traps the carbon dioxide gas produced by yeast fermentation and so enables dough to increase in volume. There is an absolute correlation between protein quantity and loaf volume: the higher the flour protein percentage, the greater the potential loaf volume. However, this is where things get a little complicated.

Glutens vary according to their extensibility (how far they will stretch without breaking) and their elasticity (their propensity to spring back when stretched). For most baking purposes, the ideal dough is one that stretches easily, stretches a long way without breaking and doesn't shrink back. To get maximum volume in a loaf, the gluten matrix must be capable of stretching ever wider (and therefore thinner) without rupturing and letting the fermentation gases escape. Its ability to do this depends partly on the variety and origin of the wheat and partly on the way the baker manages the development of the dough.

As far as the innate properties of the wheat are concerned, hard varieties, often associated with growing conditions in continental climates such as

North America, Australia, Ukraine, generally produce 'strong' gluten, which holds together well as it stretches, but can be very elastic, with a marked tendency to shrink back. By contrast, the soft wheats of England and France tend to produce gluten that will stretch a long way but can rupture easily and has relatively little elasticity. Flours made from such wheats are often called 'weak'.

I hope that it is becoming clear that flour quality should not be seen in simple hierarchical terms, as if hard/strong is always better than soft/weak. If this were true, we should presumably not envy France its traditional *pain de campagne*, nor Italy its focaccia, both examples of flattish breads with an open, holey crumb – the product of precisely the kind of gluten formed from locally adapted varieties of wheat.

Most British flours are milled from blends of UK and imported (often Canadian) wheat and are designed to produce a typically British loaf – very aerated with a close, even texture and, heaven forbid, no holes. However, they may well have too much protein, or too strong and elastic a protein, to produce the best results in open-textured Continental styles of bread. The obvious solution, if you are aiming for authenticity, would be to seek out specialist flours milled abroad, always remembering that you will probably be buying flour milled to a certain style rather than from the wheat of the nation concerned. However, such flours are not widely available, though some British mills do supply their own blends of flour for ciabatta and the like.

One alternative would be to mix a strong flour with a lower-protein 'plain' flour or one that does not have the word 'strong' in its title. Check on the nutrition information panel to establish the approximate protein percentage. Another possibility is to try flour from a small British watermill or windmill. Often these mill organic wheat and, since they have limited grain storage space, their flour is not usually blended; in other words, it is milled from single batches of wheat, which can often be traced to a specific field on the farm. These small mills almost always use stones for grinding and so preserve the maximum amount of nutrients in the flour, and they are unlikely to throw in any additives such as amylase enzymes. The one drawback (if it is a drawback) of single varieties is their unpredictability: one batch may be superb, another rather less so.

The summers of 1975 and 1976 were warm and dry and the English Maris Widgeon wheat with which I started serious baking was strong and sweet. It was only when we hit the wet harvest of 1977 that I had any real inkling of the pitfalls of using local wheat. Suddenly, my loaves were shrinking in volume and occasionally they even had holes just under the crust. At that time almost all my bread was baked in tins; ciabatta and rustic French styles were a decade away. So the weak, sloppy gluten of those British flours could not be put to good use in holey flat breads. I had to sharpen my skills to ensure that the bread held together.

English wheat

'Today on his table he has the best wholegrain bread I have ever tasted, baked by his wife. The good miller, he said, milled the whole grain palatably, hygienically and digestibly from fresh wheat locally grown. But it would not keep (good things to eat seldom do). The modernised millers imported the dry Canadian wheats, which will store and travel, standardised the moisture content and extracted the offals with the germ to be resold. Big business sprang out of lifeless bread.'

H. J. MASSINGHAM, *The Wisdom of the Fields* (Collins, 1945)

Flavour

It is striking that in professional manuals and domestic baking books alike, there is rarely, if ever, a mention of the flavour of flour. True, many factors contribute to the flavour of a baked loaf, not least the length and method of fermentation. But flour is by far the largest component of bread, and since much bread is made with white flour, which is intrinsically pretty tasteless, one might have thought that some attention would be paid to the differences in flavour between various wheat varieties. It seems, however, that the average British consumer rather favours blandness. Some years ago a large independent bakery firm did some trials with a sourdough system for making standard white sliced loaves, but did not adopt the new method when taste panels reported that the bread had 'too much flavour'.

For those home bakers who *do* want to make the best-tasting bread, I recommend British wheat every time. It goes without saying that I mean good, organically grown British wheat. Any wheat grown in a cold, sunless summer, harvested too late and needing to be dried mechanically is unlikely to taste wonderful. But there is something about the conditions in the better kind of British summer that, combined with the right soil and a suitable wheat variety, can produce flour that tastes superb. And I do mean British, not just English. Some of the highest-protein wheat in Britain has been grown on the Black Isle (north of Inverness), whose microclimate and extended summer day-length must be partly responsible[1]. I hope that the work currently being done in various European countries to develop wheat varieties more suited to organic systems will not forget to include flavour as a key criterion.

Volume

It often seems that the only measure of flour quality that counts is loaf volume. In addition to the remarks about flavour above, I would point out that there is an inverse correlation between volume and nutritional value. The more white flour there is in a dough, the more gluten and hence the bigger the aggregate volume of all the fermentation gases trapped in the dough structure. The bran layers and the wheat germ, where almost all the minerals and micronutrients reside, are not capable of holding gas: they act as a dead weight which must be 'carried' by the gluten structure. So any dough with an appreciable amount of bran and germ (e.g. made with a flour of 85 per cent extraction or higher) cannot be expected to expand to the volume of its all-white counterpart. The same applies to dough enriched with other ingredients such as seeds, nuts, fruits, vegetables and spices: all will tend to depress loaf volume. But so what? Let's have a little less stress on structural engineering and a little more on flavour and nutrition. Bread is food, after all.

Bread machine mixes

Not so long ago, the market for home-baking flours was in steep decline. Then came automatic breadmakers and an opportunity for mills to 'add value' by presenting what they had formerly sold as 'flour' as 'bread machine mix'. Sometimes it is just a matter of new packaging, but the mixes may include some additional ingredients. Things such as nuts and seeds are obvious and will be easily visible. But 'improving' additives, such as vitamin C and alpha-amylase enzymes, may be there too – presumably to help ensure that the machine produces a perfect result every time, 'untouched by human hand', as they used to say. Many big mills routinely add amylase to the flours they supply to bakeries. It is an enzyme that occurs naturally in wheat and its role in breadmaking is to convert starch granules into maltose, which can then be fermented by baker's yeast to produce the carbon dioxide gas that expands the dough. Some wheats do not have enough natural alpha-amylase and so the miller adds extra; most commercial amylases are now derived by genetic engineering from fungi such as *Aspergillus oryzae*.

The presence of additives, hidden or declared, in mixes for bread machines may not be to everyone's liking. The idea that this way of making bread requires a special mix suggests just another attempt to create a dependent consumer – whereas surely the whole point of making your own bread is to enjoy some independence from the increasingly monolithic food system. Those who share this view can be reassured that it is perfectly possible to make good bread in a bread machine using ordinary flour, yeast, salt and water.

Other flours and grains

Rye

Of the other flours of interest to bakers, rye is probably the most important. Once widely grown in Britain, its use declined from the seventeenth century as agricultural improvements made wheat growing easier and the public love affair with white wheat bread took hold. Rye prospers in poorer soils and colder climates than wheat and is still widely grown in northeastern Europe and northern Russia. With the recent emergence of wheat intolerances, rye bread has gained some popularity in the UK but it is still very much a minority taste. Rye flour does contain gluten, so it is unsuitable for people with coeliac disease, but there is less of it than in wheat flour. Rye gluten can trap fermentation gases but it is much weaker than wheat gluten, so pure rye bread will not rise so much. Rye is rich in pentosans, components of non-starch polysaccharides or dietary fibre; they are mainly soluble and have a blood-cholesterol-lowering effect.

From the baker's point of view, pentosans contribute to rye flour's ability to absorb a great deal of water. Indeed, a pure rye dough must be made wet or the resulting bread will be like concrete. Rye flour is alkaline and bland-tasting, so if you use it to make ordinary bread you are likely to get an insipid brick. This is why rye and sourdough are so often linked. Sourdough – a spontaneous fermentation of yeasts and bacteria found in the flour itself, which produces lactic and acetic acids – is essential for rye bread because:

- It creates flavour from a bland flour.
- The acids counteract excessive enzyme activity in the dough, which can make it collapse during baking.
- Acidity in the baked loaf helps it to keep for longer.

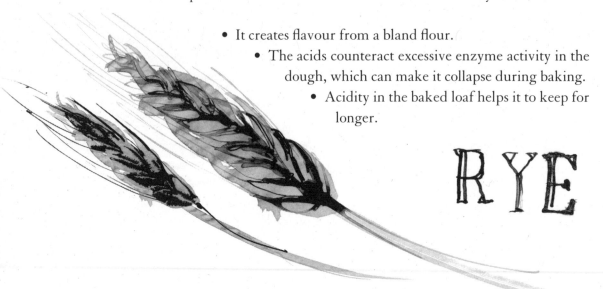

RYE

The acid flavour of sourdough rye bread can be a bit of a shock to the English palate, but it grows on you. It is an essential accompaniment to strong flavours, such as smoked fish or ripe cheese.

Barley

'For ten-o'clocks we'd have barley bannocks and a piece of Willimer Whang [a hard cheese from West Cumberland],' according to William Dodd, a farmer and local historian from Ousby Row, a couple of miles from my bakery in Melmerby. Cumberland baking was full of sweet recipes using the sugar, spices, ginger and rum that came in through the ports of Whitehaven and Maryport, the third leg of the triangular trade taking British goods to Africa and slaves to the West Indies. William Dodd's bannocks may have been made with pure barley flour, but probably included a little wheat to hold them together.

Barley was widely used for bread in the northern uplands, where poorer soils and a damp climate made wheat difficult to grow. Now it is almost exclusively used in brewing – understandable on account of its very low gluten content, but a pity from the nutritional point of view. Recent research has highlighted the fact that barley has good quantities of vitamin E and high levels of soluble fibre (beta glucans), which may have a cholesterol-lowering potential similar to oats (see below).

Barley flour can be added to a wheat dough at up to 30 per cent of the total flour weight without major changes in dough quality. When baked, it has a pronounced sweetness and a suggestion of maltiness. This effect can be multiplied if the barley flour is cooked with some water before being added to the dough: gelatinisation triggers the enzymic conversion of starch to maltose (as indeed it does with all flours). I learned this from the recipe for Tibetan barley bread in my first baking guide, the

inimitable *Tassajara Bread Book* by Edward
Espe Brown (Shambala Publications, 1970).

The advantages of barley flour to the
home baker are that:

- It is suitable for a wheat-free diet.
- It adds a sweet, slightly malty flavour to bread.
- It is digestible and nutritious.

Oats

The gluten status of oats is still a matter of some controversy.
Although the quantity of gluten in oats was always known to be
small, they were traditionally off-limits to coeliacs (people with a serious
gluten intolerance). Then several studies, particularly in Finland, showed that
oats could be tolerated without harm by most coeliac adults and children.
However, there is not complete unanimity in the scientific community and
the current position of the UK Coeliac Society is that 'moderate amounts of
oats may be consumed by most coeliacs without risk', but that severe coeliacs
should avoid them[2].

One further reason for coeliacs being suspicious of oats is that they are
often processed in factories that also handle wheat and may be inadvertently
cross-contaminated.

Nutritionally, oats are unquestionably a valuable cereal and therefore a
good addition to mixed grain breads. Lacking any effective gluten, they will
contribute to flavour and texture but not to volume or aeration. However, the
high natural oil content of oats can contribute to a softening of the crumb. An
addition of less than 10 per cent oat flour or meal can give an impression of
extra lightness even if, objectively, the loaf volume remains pretty much the
same. Oat fibre, or oat bran, is available in some wholefood shops and can
be used in the dough or for dipping or dusting the whole loaf. Similarly, oat
flakes (preferably rolled oats or 'jumbo' oats, which have been less processed

than porridge oats) make a striking addition to the dough; if used to decorate the crust, they benefit from being exposed to a toasting effect, which really brings out their flavour.

Spelt

One of the 'covered' wheats – i.e. those whose husk does not fall off during threshing – spelt is the best-known 'alternative' source of flour, particularly for people who feel they cannot tolerate standard wheat. Science does not support the theory that spelt is 'better' because it is an ancient precursor of wheat, untainted by intensive plant breeding. However, there is no doubt that many people find spelt easier to digest and this is surely reason enough to give it a try. It is generally higher in protein than common wheat, with the proviso that protein levels for all types of wheat are dependent on cropping conditions.

Spelt flour is available usually as wholemeal, though a white version is now beginning to appear. It looks and performs much like ordinary wheat flour, though it tends to have a slightly weaker gluten than the strongest breadmaking wheats. It can have a bitter aftertaste, which may be simply a consequence of oxidation in flour that has been stored for too long. Wholemeal spelt has lively populations of natural yeasts and bacteria and produces a vigorous sourdough culture in a shorter time than ordinary wheat flour.

Kamut

Considered to be an ancient relative of durum wheat, Kamut is the registered tradename for a cereal derived from 36 grains, mailed by an American airman in Egypt to his father in Montana in the 1950s. Its production is always organic and is controlled by the Quinn family. Kamut is generally higher in protein than wheat but with poorer-quality gluten. Like spelt, it can often be tolerated by people with sensitivities to modern wheats, lending support to the proposition that plant breeders, in their striving to improve yield and gluten quality, have overlooked nutritional quality and palatability.

Einkorn and emmer

These two ancient precursors of wheat seem to be enjoying something of a revival, particularly in Germany. If you get the chance, you may be interested to try making bread with grains that are not very different from those eaten by our Paleolithic ancestors as long as 18,000 years ago[3]. Einkorn is the older one, and there is some evidence that it is not toxic to people with coeliac disease. Emmer became the dominant wheat throughout the Near and Far East, Europe and North Africa from 10,000 to 4,000 BC, when the 'naked' wheats (i.e. those in which the husk separates from the kernel during threshing) began to take over. Emmer remains an important crop in Ethiopia and some is grown in India and Italy. Both einkorn and emmer are significantly higher in overall protein than modern wheat and have a good flavour. They have a slightly sticky gluten and produce loaves of smaller volume than modern flours.

Grains and flours suitable for gluten-free baking are discussed in Chapter 12.

Water

For most practical purposes, any normal mains water supply will be fine for baking, with no perceptible differences between hard and soft water areas. At the extremes, very hard (alkaline, with a high calcium content) water may tend to reduce the rate of yeast fermentation and tighten the gluten in a dough, whereas very soft water may produce a stickier result. But unless you move between areas with widely differing water types, you will probably not notice any particular effect – or rather you will get used to working with what you have got. The one exception to this is in the production of natural leavens and sourdoughs. Some domestic supplies are quite heavily chlorinated and, since chlorine kills almost all bacteria (that's why it's there), it is advisable to filter your mains water or use still spring water from bottles, particularly in the early stages of starting a natural fermentation. Leaving mains water in a bucket or jug overnight removes most of the chlorine.

Yeast

Yeast is what makes dough rise. By feeding on simple sugars obtained from the flour, it produces carbon dioxide (CO_2) gas and alcohol. The gas inflates whatever gluten network has developed in the dough; most of the alcohol is evaporated at the baking stage. Baker's yeast is the term used to describe industrially produced, highly concentrated sources of yeast, which are supplied either liquid (for large bakeries), fresh or dried in various forms. Leavens or sourdoughs are cultures of naturally occurring yeasts and lactobacilli. They are dealt with in more detail in Chapter 7.

Yeast is a single-celled micro-organism belonging to the fungi family. It has a porous skin through which materials dissolved into small molecules pass to 'feed' the organism. The yeast cell releases 14 different enzymes, which help break down carbohydrates into forms that are accessible. Yeast reproduces by 'budding', or dividing into identical cells. If it becomes dry, it forms spores, which can last in the environment for a long time.

There are hundreds of genera, species and strains of yeast. Baker's yeast is *Saccharomyces cerevisiae*; the species *S. exiguus* is often found in acid leavens or sourdoughs. *Candida* is another genus of yeast. It gets a bad press through its species *C. albicans*, which, though present and harmless in up to 50 per cent of humans, can in some people produce strains that are pathogenic and cause harmful irritation of the gut and other membranes. However, *C. milleri* is one of the commonest 'wild' yeasts present in natural fermentations; it has a pronounced ability to live in stable association with the lactobacilli that are the other crucial component of sourdoughs[4].

Fermentation and reproduction are not the same thing. Yeast fermentation can take place in the absence of oxygen, hence Louis Pasteur's remark that 'fermentation is life without air'. The presence of oxygen inhibits fermentation but increases yeast reproduction. This is why yeast manufacturers blow large amounts of air through their fermenters, reducing fermentation, which generates unwanted CO_2, and encouraging the yeast to reproduce itself. In fast-made bread, there is no time for yeast reproduction to take place, which explains why much larger initial quantities are required to produce sufficient gas to expand the dough. In long fermentations, however, such as an overnight sponge (see page 126), a relatively small amount of initial yeast will reproduce itself until there are enough cells to provide the fermentative activity that aerates the dough during the final proof stage.

Apart from food in the form of sugars, yeast needs water and warmth. The optimal temperature for yeast fermentation is 25–28°C. At this temperature, water feels slightly warm to the hand. Above about 46°C and below about 10°C yeast works very slowly. It is killed at around 60°C. It follows that dough temperature and fermentation speed are closely connected – a fact that can be used both to produce better bread and to fit the whole process into the life of the home baker. It also follows that you may need to adjust yeast quantity and dough temperature to reflect the changing seasons.

Fresh yeast

This should be stored at around 5°C – the temperature of a domestic refrigerator on a fairly high setting – and used within a couple of weeks. Its gassing power progressively reduces as it gets older. If you store fresh yeast at 15°C for two weeks, it will take twice as long to prove your bread. As it ages, fresh yeast becomes crumbly and may form dark patches on its surface. It will still work in this condition, but it may lack gassing power and may also introduce by-products into the dough that have a negative effect on the strength of the gluten network[5]. As a last resort, fresh yeast can be frozen, but it turns to a runny mess on defrosting and loses a significant amount of its efficacy. Yeast is best stored in its dried form.

Dried yeast

There are two kinds of dried yeast – the traditional 'active dried' yeast, in the form of small granules, and 'instant' or 'fast-action' yeast, which looks more like fine iron filings. The latter may come already mixed with additives such as vitamin C and 'rehydration agent'. Quite why this form of yeast needs something to help it get wet (other than water) is doomed to remain a mystery for as long as the manufacturers follow that irritating food industry habit of adding ingredients with opaque or meaningless descriptions and no indication of any valid reason for their inclusion. Presumably it is a belt-and-braces measure to ensure that this kind of yeast lives up to its 'instant' name, enabling it to be chucked into the dough mix without prior dispersal in water. In fact, both fresh and traditional granular dried yeast could also be added straight to the dough mix.

Fast-action yeast is more concentrated than traditional dried yeast and both are, weight for weight, more concentrated than fresh yeast. The recipes in this book use fresh yeast but will work equally well with either of the dried versions. The rule of thumb when converting a recipe for the kind of yeast you have available is:

10g fresh yeast = 5g traditional 'active dried' yeast = 3g 'fast-action' yeast

I prefer to dissolve all yeast, including the 'fast-action' variety, in water prior to mixing, simply to ensure its complete dispersal throughout the dough. If granular dried yeast is added without being dissolved, some of it may fail to disperse if you don't knead thoroughly, and can show up as little brown specks in a dough that may not rise as well as it should. A further reason for dissolving dried yeast in water before adding it to the flour is as a check on its efficacy. If it has been hanging around in a not-very-airtight tub or opened sachet for a while, it may not be in good condition. Sprinkled into some warm water (30°C), or mixed with a little flour and water into a sponge or 'ferment', it should start to work in a few minutes. If it doesn't show any signs of life after half an hour, you should consider it moribund and start again with a new source; at least you won't have wasted a whole dough and all the effort expended in kneading it.

Organic yeast

It may come as something of a surprise to discover that the yeast used in organic bread is not necessarily organic. When organic food production in the European Union was given a legal definition in 1992, yeast was treated, like salt, as a 'non-agricultural' ingredient, and therefore fell outside the scope of the legislation. In any case, at that time there was no commercially available organic yeast. However, unlike salt, yeast production has clear connections with agriculture. Conventional, non-organic yeast is produced primarily on a substrate of non-organic sugar molasses, whereas organic yeast grows in a broth made with water and organically grown wheat flour. So for every ton of yeast produced, an acreage of land has been cultivated to produce either non-organic sugar (usually beet) or organic wheat, with all the attendant chemical fertilisers, herbicides and pesticides that are, or are not, used under the two systems. That's not all. There are huge differences in manufacturing method, with environmental implications. Non-organic yeast uses ammonia and ammonium salts as a yeast food, sulphuric acid and caustic soda as acidity regulators and cleansers, synthetic vitamins and mineral salts as processing aids, and synthetic anti-foaming agents to control the fermentation froth. As a result, every three kilos of non-organic yeast generate a kilo of polluted waste water whose disposal creates an environmental problem. By contrast, organic yeast production uses no yeast foods other than brewer's yeast, no acidity regulators and only a little organic sunflower oil to control foaming. It produces no waste water because the liquid that is squeezed out of the yeast at the end of the process is used as raw material for other products, such as drinks[6].

Organic yeast is produced in commercial quantities in a former brewery in southern Germany (I have seen the process myself) and is being used by many certified organic bakeries on the Continent. Until recently, distribution to the UK has been difficult, but both fresh and dried versions of the yeast are now available in specialist shops. The Soil Association has developed a standard for the use of organic yeast in baking and, despite an initially dismissive attitude by the UK yeast industry and the big bakers, it is likely that, in time, it will become the norm for organic bread, in line with both agricultural logic and consumer expectations.

Coeliacs and people with wheat allergies may be concerned that organic yeast is grown on a substrate of wheat flour. However, the manufacturer (Agrano) says that the wheat protein is consumed (hydrolysed) by enzymes during the process and that no gluten has been found in the finished organic yeast using the ELISA test (the industry-standard way of testing for gluten). Agrano adds that it cannot exclude the possibility that traces of gluten may exist at levels below the current limits of detection.

Sugar

Many recipes call for sugar to be added to the water in which the yeast is dissolved. It is true that 'sugar' is a yeast food, but only up to a point. When yeast has an adequate supply of sugar (in the form of maltose) derived from the flour, adding extra sucrose will not make it produce more gas. Indeed, when sugar is added at more than 5 per cent of the flour weight, it begins to have a detrimental effect on yeast activity. This explains why considerably more yeast is needed in a sugar-enriched bun dough than in a plain bread dough.

Sugar does a variety of things in the baking process, apart from its obvious sweetening effect. As a yeast stimulant in a dough to which sugar would not otherwise be added, it seems to me to be of dubious value. Modern yeast strains are bred to be extremely vigorous and probably don't need the sweet kick up the pants that may have been called for in days gone by. In *The English Bread Book* (1857), Eliza Acton has recipes using both liquid brewer's yeast and compressed 'German' yeast, which was becoming available in towns in the middle of the nineteenth century and which she noted was considerably more vigorous than the alternatives. She suggests adding a little sugar only to 'freshen or aid the fermentation of stale yeast' and doesn't include it routinely in her basic recipes. In an age when we are advised to reduce sugar consumption, omitting it from our everyday bread combines sensible practice with a modest concession to dietary correctness.

Malt

I have already referred in various places to the alpha-amylase enzymes that are present in, and often also added to, breadmaking flours. Alpha-amylase is also known as dextrinogenic amylase, or diastase, and its function is to begin the process (completed by the enzyme beta-amylase) of converting starch to maltose, a simple sugar that can be metabolised by yeast. This process is sometimes referred to as diastatic activity, and it is of interest to the baker because if it is not happening very much (due to insufficient diastase), yeast fermentation and the consequent expansion of the dough will be limited. Conversely, excessive diastatic activity can make the dough gummy, leading to the partial or complete collapse of the structure.

Malt flour can be added to dough in order to improve the conversion of starch to sugars. You might wish to do this if your normal flour seems to be giving a consistently pale crust, suggesting that there are insufficient sugars available to caramelise at the baking stage. Malt flour can be particularly useful in long-process doughs (including sourdoughs), where the length of the fermentation allows the yeasts to use up all the sugars. In the above cases, a very small amount (perhaps as little as 0.1 per cent of the flour weight) of diastatic malt flour is what you need. Non-diastatic malt flour has been heat treated to deactivate the enzymes and so has no effect on fermentation, but it does contribute a malty flavour. The same applies to liquid malt extracts: the ones you will find in wholefood shops are normally non-diastatic, while enzyme-active ones can be had from home-brewing suppliers.

Malt flour is not easy to obtain in its pure form, so the most practical solution for a home baker looking for the benefits of malt in a dough is to use a certain amount of a proprietary malted flour – the type that usually has bits of malted grain in it. Otherwise, try a home-brewing supplier or one of the specialist flour suppliers listed on pages 351–352.

Salt

Salt (sodium chloride) plays an important part in breadmaking, but don't believe those who say that it is impossible to make bread without it.

Salt performs the following functions in breadmaking:

- It affects flavour: many people in the UK (especially north of the border) dislike bread with low levels of salt. However, as with sugar in tea, it doesn't take long to get used to its absence or reduction.
- It has a strengthening effect on the gluten.
- It acts as a preservative and so extends the mould-free life of the loaf; it is also hygroscopic (it attracts water), so it may draw moisture into the loaf from the environment.
- It affects crust colour: bread with excessive salt can take on a slightly reddish hue – what bakers traditionally described as 'foxy'. If your bread has an unexpectedly pale crust, this may be a sign that you forgot the salt.

Salt inhibits yeast activity, and care should be taken to avoid direct contact between the two before mixing the dough. Once the salt is dissolved in water and is evenly spread throughout the dough, its negative effect on the yeast is minimised and its gluten-strengthening action can begin.

Sea salt, especially the coarse flaked varieties from Anglesey or the Guérande in France, retains a wider spectrum of minerals, including valuable iodine, than industrially processed rock salt. Avoid anything with 'anti-caking agent' in it. This is designed to make salt flow freely through automatic machines into processed food mixes. At home, if damp does get into your salt and make it a bit lumpy, it is not the hardest task in the world to break it up again.

With the current focus on reducing sodium in the diet in an attempt to limit heart attacks and strokes, various alternatives have appeared, usually based on potassium chloride. One that we used a great deal in the bakery is from a natural under-sea source in Iceland (see page 352): I like the fact that geo-thermal energy is used to evaporate it. Be aware, though, that potassium-based salt has to be used judiciously, otherwise it can impart a bitter taste to baked products.

Fats and oils

It is quite possible to make bread without any added fat or oil. Indeed, from a nutritional perspective, it is probably desirable to do so, partly because most of us already consume excessive amounts of fat and partly because it is known that heating even 'good' fats like olive oil beyond a certain point produces some harmful compounds. Gastronomically, there is clearly an honourable place for breads and buns enriched with fat. But, other things being equal, I would always prefer to consume any fat on my bread rather than in it. Much of the flavour of olive oil, for instance, is lost if it is baked into a ciabatta dough. Dipping freshly baked bread into a dish of murky green virgin oil is quite another matter.

If you add a modest amount of fat to an ordinary bread dough – not an 'enriched' one like a lardy cake or a brioche – it may have a small effect on keeping quality, but the main reason for including it is to improve gas retention in the dough and hence loaf volume. However, it is important to note that dough volume will be enhanced only by solid fats, not by liquid oils. The latter have a slightly depressing effect on volume.

Hydrogenated fat

Passing hydrogen gas through liquid oil has the effect of making it hard at room temperature. But it also has the undesirable effect of creating so-called trans-fatty acids, which the body cannot metabolise and which have been implicated in raised blood cholesterol levels. This means that the many margarines and spreads that include hydrogenated or partially hydrogenated fat should be avoided.

Hard fat

There is no avoiding the fact that fats that are hard at room temperature, such as butter and lard, are likely to have a high saturated fat content. But they do have the advantage of giving extra volume to bread, something that neither liquid oils nor semi-hard 'spreads' do.

The cereal chemists say that strong (high-protein) white flours require more fat than weaker ones and wholemeal flours more still. If you are going to experiment with additions of fat, the rule of thumb is that an addition of about 5g fat per kilo of flour will give maximum loaf volume, with rather more needed for wholemeal breads.

In the recipes in this book, I suggest using butter in plain English-type breads and rolls and olive oil in Italian ones. You can happily use olive oil throughout with a small, but I would say quite acceptable, sacrifice of volume.

Oils

Olive oil, especially cold-pressed extra-virgin oil, imparts a wonderful flavour to bread, subject to my remarks above about baking destroying some of it. If you can afford it, always use olive as your liquid oil in breads. Sunflower oil is not a bad alternative, especially the unrefined version, though bear in mind that this can go rancid much quicker than olive oil. Organic sunflower oils are usually 'deodorised' by a steaming process, which is preferable to chemical refining. They keep well, but have much less flavour and colour than the 'raw' variant. Of course, this may be an advantage in a delicate product where you do not want too much flavour. The same applies to soya oil, which, in its raw form, gives a distinctly beany flavour that is absent in the refined version. Walnut oil is very expensive but gives a wonderful flavour to bread and is very nutritious. Safflower oil is equally rich in polyunsaturated fatty acids but milder in flavour. I avoid unspecified 'vegetable oil' on the principle that if the manufacturers won't tell me what oils are included, they probably have something to hide.

These, then, are the essential ingredients of bread. Many other ingredients can be added to achieve particular flavours, textures or nutritional effects. I will deal with these as we go along, especially in the chapters on enriched savoury and sweet doughs.

Now we can get down to business. Determined to reject the deceptions and nutritional impoverishment of British industrial baking, armed with essential information about what goes into real bread, we can approach the basic processes of breadmaking, looking in particular at the way time can be used to build true quality into bread without unduly disrupting busy lives.

CHAPTER FIVE
STARTING FROM SCRATCH

'Every time a recipe is not strictly
followed, every time a risk is taken
with changed ingredients or proportions,
the resulting food is a creative work,
good or bad, into which humans
have put a little of themselves.'
THEODORE ZELDIN,
An Intimate History of Humanity
(Vintage, 1998)

Before describing how to make a loaf of bread, I need to get a few things off my chest.

Over the years, I have bought, read and used a good many recipe books. I have been inspired by some and I have learned from many. But as my experience has grown, I have been increasingly bothered by certain instructions that crop up repeatedly in the baking canon. They often seem to have been sprinkled over the text like holy water in a random gesture that owes more to faith than to evidence.

These instructions take various forms. There is the bald assertion, the confident claim that is completely irrelevant, or the advice so vague that it leaves the reader bemused. Many of them are handed on from book to book until they acquire all the permanence of holy writ. Of course they do no real harm. But once you see through one of these shibboleths you wonder how far you can rely on the author's other pronouncements.

Here are a few of the worst offenders.

Eight illogical instructions

Instruction	Presumed purpose	Comment
1. Make a well in the flour and pour in the yeasty water.	Even mixing of all ingredients.	Pointless, because kneading will mix everything anyway. This makes sense only if you are adding water to a pile of flour on the table.
2. Tepid, lukewarm, hand-hot, blood heat …	Description of what breadmaking water should feel like.	Imprecise terms. Water may need to be much cooler in summer and warmer in winter.
3. Knead on a floured surface.	To stop the dough sticking.	Most doughs when first mixed *should* be wet enough to stick to worktops. Kneading on a floured surface risks drying and firming the dough.

Instruction	Presumed purpose	Comment
4. Prove until the dough is within half an inch of the top of the tin.	The right moment to put the bread into the oven.	Do they know exactly what size tin you are using? There are better ways to judge when to put your loaf into the oven.
5. Put a tray of water or ice cubes in the bottom of the oven.	To make a baguette-type crust.	This is poor physics. Water (ice even more so) takes heat from the oven to turn to steam. To produce a thin crust, the steam needs to be very hot and to stay in the oven for 10 minutes. Most domestic ovens will let the steam straight out through a vent or round the door.
6. Tap the loaf on the bottom: if it sounds hollow, it is done.	To see if it is baked through.	Far too subjective – most loaves when tapped on the bottom sound 'hollow'; other signs are more helpful.
7. Start your sourdough with grapes, raisins, yoghurt, oranges, apples, etc.	To establish a natural ferment.	Most of these ingredients are completely unnecessary (though harmless). Flour and water are all you need to start a sourdough.
8. Put your sourdough starter outdoors.	To 'catch a wild yeast'.	You might catch more than you bargain for. This is based on a misconception of the location and behaviour of yeasts and lactobacilli.

My objection to these commonly found instructions is not that they are wrong, though some clearly are. It is more that they present breadmaking as a question of simply obeying orders rather than observing and understanding. Too often these apparently authoritative pronouncements confuse or miss out the vital information that enables us to understand and take control of the process. To do that, you need to know what is happening and why.

Once you have grasped the general principles, you will be able to make bread without constant reference to specific instructions. More importantly, you will be able to adjust your methods in the light of a clear understanding of what is actually going on in your dough. Breadmaking may seem to have the precision of chemistry; in fact, it has all the variability of biology, where sympathetic adaptation works better than unthinking compliance every time.

The following explanations apply to breadmaking in general. I will add more detail, as appropriate, to individual recipes in later chapters.

Joined-up baking

In the early 1990s, French artisan bakers felt so disgusted (and threatened) by the rise of frozen and reheated 'bake-off' bread that they managed to get a law passed forbidding the use of the term *boulangerie* for any establishment in which the five stages of baking were not conducted in one unbroken process.

In the UK, 'scratch' is the term for a baking operation that uses the basic elements – flour, water, yeast, salt etc – and no prepared mixes or frozen or part-baked dough.

The five stages of breadmaking

There are five stages in making a loaf of bread:

- Mixing and kneading.
- Rising or 'fermenting'.
- Shaping or 'moulding'.
- Proving.
- Baking.

In this chapter I describe what happens in each of these stages. If you would rather go straight to the recipes, you can always return to these pages to check on the details.

Mixing and kneading

In home baking, kneading is the word used to describe the action of working dough to develop a structure that will enable it to rise. But before any work can be done with the dough, the main ingredients must be combined.

Mixing

It is surprising how reluctant some ingredients can be to come together. Try, for instance, mixing fresh yeast, a small amount of flour and a rather larger quantity of water to make a sloppy 'ferment' that will allow the yeast to bubble vigorously. If you throw all the components in together, some of the flour and yeast will almost invariably form little flinty nodules that resolutely refuse to soften. To avoid lumps, dissolve the yeast in a little of the water first, make a paste with this liquid and a little of the flour, then gradually work in the remainder of the water.

Fresh yeast, stirred around in water with a finger, will dissolve in a few seconds into a brownish liquid. Dried yeast granules will take a little longer. They will float to the top and should be left for a few minutes to swell and bubble. Fast-action yeast will dissolve almost immediately.

Stir any salt or spice called for in the recipe into the flour before you add the liquid. If you are using a solid fat, such as butter or lard, there is no need to rub it in but it will disperse into the dough better if it has not come straight from the fridge.

Now add the liquid and work the ingredients together gently with your hands. Most books recommend gradually incorporating the flour with a wooden spoon. I can't see the point of dirtying another utensil. Your hands will get sticky anyway when kneading, so why delay?

WELL-WORN ADVICE

There is no need to 'make a well in the flour' for the yeasty water. Legions of home bakers have read this comfortingly precise instruction in countless recipe books and obeyed it, quite reasonably assuming that it had some purpose. But does it? After all, the ingredients are going to end up as a sticky dough, however they are mixed – by hand, with a wooden spoon or in a mixer. So why the myth of making a well?

My guess is that this is a hand-me-down from an age when bread, forming the greater part of a family's food, would be made in large quantities, even in ordinary households. According to Eliza Acton, writing in *The English Bread Book*, the bread consumption in a country clergyman's family in the middle of the nineteenth century was about five pounds of bread per person a week – equivalent to not far short of a small loaf each per day, or more than three times what the average person consumes now.

The family doughs of times gone by would almost certainly have been made not in a bowl but by heaping the flour on to a large kitchen table. As anyone who has mixed mortar knows, the only way to avoid a frenzied scraping round the yard is to make a well in the mound of dry material, gradually working in the liquid so that it cannot escape. So here is the justification for making a well. But if we mix dough in a bowl, there is no need.

Pre-soaking

Usually known by its French name, autolyse, this involves mixing the dough ingredients just until they are combined and then leaving them to rest for about half an hour, before resuming mixing/kneading.

Pre-soaking is a process of self-digestion catalysed by hydrolytic enzymes. In a bread dough, the flour proteins (glutenin and gliadin) come under the influence of enzymes as soon as they are wet. The changes that occur are similar to the kind of gluten 'development' achieved by kneading. So why not forget the kneading and leave it all to the pre-soak? Because the passive process, while useful, cannot develop gluten quality as effectively as a combination of physical and enzymic action.

Kneading

The purpose of kneading is:

- To ensure the even distribution of all the ingredients.
- To develop the dough structure.

The mechanical action of kneading, combined with the chemical reactions between the various ingredients, creates a three-dimensional gluten network from the two main protein fractions of the wheat, glutenin and gliadin. This is best visualised as a series of tiny balloons which will be inflated by the carbon dioxide gas produced by yeast fermentation. Vigorous working of the dough develops the material from which the balloons are formed. If a great deal of water is added, the structure will be very soft and, while the balloons may inflate well, they will not support much vertical lift. Conversely, a tight dough with insufficient water will prevent the full expansion of the gluten matrix, resulting in a smaller loaf.

One of the by-products of the invention of high-speed mixers for the Chorleywood Bread Process was the discovery that the rate at which energy goes into the dough significantly affects gluten development. In other words, a given amount of energy will have more effect if delivered to a dough over a shorter rather than a longer period of time. In domestic terms, this would explain why a reasonably efficient mixer will usually produce better dough than hand kneading. However strong our biceps, we cannot normally impart energy as quickly as a mechanical mixer.

MACHINE OR HAND?

Why knead by hand if a mixer does it better? There are several answers. For a start, not everyone has a mixer and it would be wrong to suggest that good bread cannot be made without one. Furthermore, only if you mix by hand will you experience the whole process of change as it occurs, and thereby develop an ability to recognise what good dough feels like. Even in modern bakery colleges, where students are prepared for the world of machines and additives, the very first assignment is usually to make bread by hand. It is also true, as many a perspiring student of mine has observed, that kneading is a good physical work-out that beats going to the gym, if only because it costs little, can be done at home and has an edible end-product.

But perhaps the most compelling reason to knead by hand if only once in your life is that bread made this way is truly yours. In using your body's energy to mix and work the dough, you are literally giving of yourself, and a loaf made like this contains and therefore expresses you in a way that cannot be said of ingredients transformed – however conveniently – by the ingenuity of distant engineers and technologists.

HAND KNEADING

This should be fun, energetic, even therapeutic. It doesn't much matter how you do it as long as you understand what the end result should be. Bear in mind the following points and you will not go far wrong:

- Don't worry about sticky hands.
- Don't add more flour until you're sure it's needed.
- Wetter is better.
- Try 'air kneading'.
- Use flour to clean your hands.
- Sticky = bad; soft = good.

DON'T WORRY ABOUT STICKY HANDS

Having mixed the ingredients together with your hands, you can start to apply more energy when no more dry bits are visible and the dough is becoming a coherent mass. Avoid the temptation to add more flour at this stage. Perhaps it is the unconscious need to make our hands feel more comfortable (or the ubiquitous injunction to 'knead on a floured surface') that propels us to the flour bowl even before the dough is fully mixed. Something in our brain tells us that our fingers shouldn't be stuck to one another, so we try to dry them off by dipping them in flour. However understandable, this reflex must be resisted.

DON'T ADD MORE FLOUR UNTIL YOU'RE SURE IT'S NEEDED

As soon as you can, get the dough out of the bowl and on to the table. Scrape the bowl clean so that you have all the dough in one lump. You cannot judge whether the dough is too wet or too dry until all the flour has been moistened and a reasonably smooth mass has formed. The action of kneading develops the gluten structure and helps the flour absorb water. This takes some time. If you add flour too soon, you risk adding too much.

WETTER IS BETTER

It is hard to describe in words or even in pictures exactly what a dough looks like when it has the correct amount of water. Flours vary considerably in their absorbency, so sticking precisely to the recipe doesn't guarantee success. Phrases like 'knead until a soft dough is formed' beg the question as to what 'soft' actually feels like to the touch. For most breads I suggest that the dough should be *a bit wetter than you think it ought to be*. Only if the dough is going to be shaped into something freestanding like a cottage loaf does it need to be firm. But a dough that is firm at the kneading stage is likely to make indifferent bread. Only a wet dough will produce that wonderful chewy, open-textured, slightly rubbery crumb that defines good bread. Home bakers usually err on the side of drier, more easily handled doughs because no one has told them that this is the way to bake bricks. No more. If the frustration of

dough sticking to your hands becomes unbearable, remember the mantra: *the wetter the better*. And anyway, soft, wet doughs are a great deal easier to knead than firm ones.

TRY 'AIR KNEADING'

There is no one correct kneading technique. The important thing is to work the dough with as much energy as possible for at least ten minutes, preferably a little longer. Any manner of squashing, stretching, turning and folding will do, so long as it subjects all the dough to vigorous stress. My favourite way of kneading, especially for soft doughs, is to stretch the entire lump horizontally between my hands held up at about chest level. By holding the dough virtually with my fingertips, I can squeeze and stretch it without it all sticking to my palms. As the dough develops and will stretch further and further without tearing, the action looks rather like playing the concertina. Air kneading has several advantages:

- You are standing upright with a straight back, not bending over the worktop.
- You can apply the energy of both hands to all the dough all the time.
- The squeezing/pulling action develops the dough efficiently.
- You get a good sense of how things are going as the dough tightens and begins to come away from your hands.

After a few minutes' work, the flour will have absorbed all the water, the gluten matrix will begin to develop and consequently the dough will begin to feel a little firmer and more stretchy.

USE FLOUR TO CLEAN YOUR HANDS

At this stage it may help to clean your fingers and palms, otherwise they simply go on sticking to the dough and prevent the formation of a more coherent mass. Put the lump of dough on the worktop and get the worst off your hands with a plastic scraper. Don't be tempted to clean your hands with water. It's a waste of time and dough, and clean damp hands will just get sticky again. Instead, dip your flat hands lightly into some flour and then rub them together firmly as if you were washing them with soap, allowing the slivers of floury dough to fall on and around your main piece. With another very light dusting of flour on your hands, you can then work all the debris into a smooth dough. In this way, you are simultaneously cleaning your hands and working a minimal amount of extra flour into the dough. The process can be repeated as often as is necessary and is certainly better than sprinkling random amounts of flour over the dough in the hope that the sticky mass will become manageable.

If, at the other extreme, the dough seems dry, tight and hard to work, it needs more water. Flatten it out as best you can and prod it firmly with your fingertips to make craters in it. Sprinkle some water into the craters and then fold the dough over on itself to prevent the water escaping. As you knead, the wetness may break through the surface, making a squelchy mess, but this will soon disappear as the water is evenly dispersed through the dough. Never be afraid to add extra water if the dough seems too tight.

STICKY = BAD; SOFT = GOOD

There is a difference between stickiness and softness. A fairly firm dough can have a sticky surface and a very soft dough can be silky and non-stick. Stickiness is an inconvenience on the way to producing a good dough and can always be managed by a judicious flick of flour at a critical moment such as moulding. But if a dough is too firm (however conveniently manageable), it will make brick-like bread: the only remedy is to soften it with extra water.

One useful gauge of dough development is to take a piece the size of a ping-pong ball and squeeze it flat between your fingers. Hold it up to a bright light and gradually tease it thinner and thinner. If it has been energetically developed, the gluten matrix will show as a kind of translucent film, milky grey in colour. Ignore the creamy-coloured starch (and, in the case of whole-meal flour, the bits of bran and wheatgerm) and see how thin you can make your 'window pane'. If the dough is not fully kneaded (or if the flour you are using is weak, i.e. with a low gluten content), the pane will tear very easily.

In a nicely developed dough, the hole formed by pushing a finger end through the pane will leave clean edges without any ragged strands.

At the end of kneading, the dough should have developed something of a silky sheen on its surface (rather easier to recognise in white bread than wholemeal). If left on an unfloured table for a moment or two it may still stick a bit. It's time for a rest, so put the dough back in the mixing bowl (or on a wet worktop – see Folding, below), cover it loosely with a polythene bag (making sure that the bag doesn't touch the dough) and keep it warm and out of draughts. Don't use the traditional 'damp cloth': evaporation causes a drop in temperature – precisely not what we want right next to our dough as it rises.

IS IT POSSIBLE TO OVER-KNEAD?

Yes, though this is much more likely during mechanical mixing than when you knead by hand. The signs of an over-mixed dough can appear quite suddenly: a structure that was smooth, silky and elastic begins to break up into a coarse, sticky mess with a 'curdled' appearance. Doughs made with significant amounts of acid-containing sponge or sourdough are more prone to over-kneading because the acids and enzymes that have built up over a long period get to work on the gluten at the same time as mechanical action is 'developing' the dough structure by aligning the gluten strands. For this reason, it is a good idea, though not essential, to add an acid sponge, leaven or sourdough not at the beginning of kneading but when the main dough has already been formed and partially developed.

Rising

The period of time after the dough has been mixed and before it is moulded into its final shape is called variously 'first rise', 'first proof' and 'bulk fermentation time'. It has three functions:

- To enable the yeast (of whatever origin) in the dough to ferment.
- To relax, soften and ripen the gluten structure, making it more able to stretch and retain optimal amounts of carbon dioxide (CO_2) gas.
- To accumulate flavour from the acids and other by-products of fermentation.

Even a short period of rising will partially achieve the first purpose, but longer is required for the other two. Temperatures, flour types and degrees of mixing vary so much that it is difficult to give hard and fast rules for fermentation time. However, you can be sure that a 'straight' dough (one with no sponge or starter) will not accumulate much in the way of flavour in less than four hours at average temperatures. This is why the use of a sponge or old dough is so useful, because it effectively transfers previously accumulated 'time' into your dough and thereby reduces the need for a long period of fermentation in bulk. There is more detail on the use of sponges and other 'preliminary' doughs on page 123.

It is more important to protect a rising dough from draughts (which may chill it unevenly and produce a dry 'skin' on parts of the surface) than it is to keep it in a particularly warm place. The warmer it is, of course, the quicker fermentation will proceed. But a long, cool fermentation may be what you want, fitting in with your schedule and accumulating extra flavour at the same time. If you have the means to control the temperature of the place where your dough ferments, 27°C is considered the optimum temperature for a straightforward yeasted bread. If you have no choice in the matter, don't worry: just remember that if your kitchen is on the cool side, things will take a little longer. Do not be tempted to warm the dough too much – for example, by putting it right above the cooker or a radiator: very warm, fast-fermenting dough is hard to handle and usually makes dry, crumbly bread.

The usual rule of thumb is to leave dough to ferment 'until it has doubled in size'. This is fine as far as it goes, although I suspect that a mathematically precise doubling in volume would seem rather a small expansion to most eyes. The important thing is not to be intimidated by such apparently explicit instructions. If a dough is fermenting fast, if the gluten has relaxed well, if it contains flavour-carrying acids from a preliminary dough of some kind, then it is perfectly all right to take it to the next stage after as little as 40 minutes or an hour. At the other extreme, if you leave it too long in bulk, the worst that can happen is that the yeast runs out of food, the gluten softens and stretches until it collapses and a pronounced acidity builds up.

In most cases, gathering the dough together and giving it a very brief press will be all that is required to prepare it for the next stage.

Knocking back

Some recipes call for the dough to be 'knocked back' in the middle of its first rise. This normally means a very brief knead (15 seconds by hand or half a dozen turns of the dough hook in a machine), which expels all the gas from the dough. The theory is that an accumulation of CO_2 begins to inhibit further fermentation. Certainly a quick reworking of the dough always results in a renewed expansion, so the yeast must like it. But there are additional benefits to be had from this action. In doughs made with relatively weak flours, when the desired result is an open-textured, Continental-style loaf, random 'knocking back' should take the form of a deliberate folding of the dough. This has some de-gassing effect, but more importantly it stretches and thins the gluten membrane, making it more likely to inflate into bigger – and more randomly shaped – bubbles.

Folding

This procedure is best suited to soft, wet doughs such as ciabatta. Leave the dough to ferment on a wet surface (covered by a bowl) and do the folding with wet hands and wet plastic scrapers. If you use flour to lubricate your hands and the worktop at this stage, it is almost inevitable that you will fold some raw flour into the dough, which may appear as 'cores' and streaks in the baked bread.

After an hour or two lying on the worktop under a bowl, your dough will probably have flowed out into a flat, but slightly puffy, disc. Imagining your dough as a flat globe, slip your scrapers (one in each hand) under the northern hemisphere, ease the dough from the table, gently stretch it away from you and then fold it back on itself so that it reaches about halfway across the body of the disc. Do this with the southern quarter and then from east and west in the same way. You will feel the gluten tightening as you stretch, so don't go too far or it will rupture. The end result will be a disc that is smaller in diameter but quite a bit thicker than before. Cover the dough with a bowl again to stop the surface drying out and skinning over. This folding action can be performed more than once, so long as the gluten is allowed to relax between times. Each fold and stretch will thin the gluten membrane and distort the shape of the balloons of gas as they inflate. Both these effects will contribute towards an open texture and an interesting crumb in the baked bread. However, there is no point using this method if you subsequently knock all the air out of the dough while shaping it. So it is best deployed with soft doughs such as *pain de campagne*, which are supported in baskets while they rise, or ciabatta, where every effort is made to preserve the gas that accumulates in the dough after mixing.

Rising may seem boring, a period of time when nothing much is happening. But every minute that you allow your dough to ferment before shaping it will set your bread further apart from the additive-laced industrial pap that is given no rise at all. Every hour of slow fermentation makes your bread more digestible and its nutrients more available. Good things are worth waiting for.

Shaping

Most dough needs to be shaped (or 'moulded') for its final rise before being baked. Shaping determines:

- The texture of the crumb.
- The profile of the loaf.

Texture and shape usually reflect the character of the flour (weak/strong, elastic/extensible) and the way the bread is going to be eaten. A loaf baked in a tin, for instance, is likely to be used to make sandwiches or toast and, in British baking at least, should have a close, even texture (and definitely no holes to let the marmalade through). To shape this sort of bread, flatten the dough out into a sausage about twice as long as the longest side of your tin. Flatten it with your knuckles and then fold it in three. Press the dough down again until it is a flattish rectangle about two-thirds the length of the tin. Roll the dough up as tightly as possible without tearing the surface and place it in the tin with the 'seam' facing down. In this way, the dough will expand evenly in the tin, giving an attractively domed top.

By contrast, gently fold and stretch a ciabatta dough as described above in order to preserve and develop the very open texture which is characteristic of this type of bread and which makes it so good for mopping up oily sauces and salads.

If rolling the dough up firmly and evenly is a knack that you have yet to master, don't worry, the worst that can happen is that your loaf will have a rather 'Continental' texture – uneven and holey – and the top may be dimpled or undulating. But does this matter if the bread is for home consumption? Its appearance doesn't alter its ability to nourish.

If, despite your best endeavours, the surface of the dough is a bit ragged, there is a simple solution: dip it in something before putting it in the tin or on the baking tray. Flour or cracked wheat, sunflower, sesame or poppy seeds, oat flakes or even nuts – all provide visual appeal and contribute to the flavour and texture of the loaf.

Most tin bread recipes for home bakers are based on the erroneous notion that there is such a thing as a standard baking tin. Originally a 'small' tin was one suited to 1lb (454g) of plain dough, with a 'large' one twice the size, and there were few variations in the shape and design available. But even that apparent standardisation overlooked the fact that a pound of white dough would expand into a much bigger loaf than a pound of wholemeal (because of the unstretchy bran and germ which constitute about 28 per cent of the

PLATE SECTION I

latter's flour weight). So a tin that adequately accommodates a given quantity of white dough is likely to leave the same amount of wholemeal looking a bit shrunken.

Nowadays there is such a variety of shapes and sizes available that you need to make a judgement based on the actual tin you are using and the amount by which you expect the dough to expand. Here is a rough guide:

Type of dough	Fill tin
White	One-third full
Wholemeal or fruited	Half full
Sourdough rye	Half to two-thirds full

If you don't want to bake your loaf in a tin, you can shape it into a cob and place it on a baking sheet instead. There is a technique, known as 'chaffing', which is used to form a piece of dough into a tight ball to prove and bake as a freestanding cob. One hand, with fingers together and held fairly rigid at the wrist, works at a tangent to the round mass of dough. A small amount of dough at the edge of the mass is repeatedly trapped between the side of the hand and the table and stretched in such a way as to create a tension around the circumference of the dough piece. The ragged edge of dough, which is pulled away from the main mass (but not separated from it), is tucked under the main body of dough and the process is repeated until a tight cob is formed. The point of doing this with one hand (and not, as it were, 'pushing' with the other to help with the formation of the cob) is that dough under tension at the circumference will be less likely to stretch and allow the dough to 'flow' out into a flat pancake. Like other aspects of breadmaking, this is a bit of a knack, but once you get the hang of it you may enjoy the rather sensuous feeling of an amorphous mass of soft dough taking firm shape under your hands.

Proving

After being moulded, dough needs time to expand. The gluten relaxes and stretches under pressure from the gas produced by yeast fermentation. This produces a lighter, more open texture in the baked loaf. Put the bread in the oven too soon and you will get a dense (and possibly underbaked) centre and a top crust that seems to be trying to part company with the rest of the loaf. Prove for too long and the yeast will run out of food and stop producing enough gas to inflate the dough; your loaf will shrink back in the oven, leaving a crumpled and sad-looking crust.

Over-proving bread is not the end of the world: no damage is done to nutritional quality and, although the texture may be a bit crumbly, the bread is perfectly edible. However, it is a pity if your loaf 'falls' at the last hurdle. There is no more dispiriting sound in baking than the resigned sigh that escapes from an over-proved loaf as it cannot bear the movement of its final journey to the oven. So it is better to err a little on the side of under-proof.

To get proof right, you need to:

- Create the right conditions.
- Judge when the dough is ready to go into the oven.

CREATING THE RIGHT CONDITIONS

If the dough surface dries out, it becomes hard and cannot stretch without tearing. This leads to reduced expansion and an unsightly leathery crust. So it is important to protect your loaf from draughts or drying air. Temperature plays a role, too: the warmer the conditions, the faster the proof. Bear in mind, however, that warm places are also likely to be dry ones and that if a loaf is proving fast it is easy to miss the precise moment when it is ready to go into the oven. Don't get hung up on creating a warm place; loaves perched above stoves or snuggled against radiators may get warm too quickly or too unevenly, and fast-proved bread can have a crumbly, cakey texture. A cooler, more even temperature may give better results. It is quite possible to prove bread in the fridge over several hours.

To keep the surface of the dough moist and stretchy during proof, you need to enclose the tin or baking tray in a large polythene bag, which will create a 'fug' and recycle any moisture evaporating from the loaf. The easiest way to make sure that the polythene doesn't stick to the dough is to blow the bag up like a balloon and seal it to keep the air in. Your warm, moist breath will bring a little extra humidity into the bag, helping to stop the dough surface from drying out and so preventing a good rise.

You can achieve the same effect with a plant propagator that has a base that can be heated and a large, clear plastic dome to create a warm, moist environment. Put the loaf tin or tray on some sort of insulating mat so that any heat from the propagator's warming cable is not so intense that it 'cooks' the bottom of the loaf. A cup of freshly boiled water placed beside the loaf will create ample humidity.

Waterproof

An original method of judging proof is given in a famous Russian cookbook and household manual from the 1860s called *A Gift to Young Housewives* by Elena Molokhovets (the equivalent of Mrs Beeton)[1].

After moulding dough made with fine flour, wrote Elena, 'you may put the loaves in a bucket of water (the temperature of a river in summer), where they will lie on the bottom until they are fully proved. When they float to the surface, put them straight in the oven. This method has the advantage that you can be relaxed about judging the time it takes for the bread to rise: when it comes to the surface, just pop it in the oven. Incidentally, if you are proving bread on the table, you can put a small test piece of dough into cold water; when it rises to the surface, you can put all your loaves into the oven.'

This dramatic illustration of the way yeast ferments in the absence of air does actually work, though in my experience, getting hold of the slippery floating dough is like catching fish with your bare hands.

JUDGING WHEN THE DOUGH IS READY TO GO INTO THE OVEN

To judge when dough is fully risen, it is necessary to educate your fingers. Of course, there are other indicators: how long has it been proving? How much has it grown? How much do I expect doughs of this type to expand? But the best arbiter is your finger pad, pressing gently on the surface of the dough, feeling how far the dough is 'fighting back'. Test a rising dough periodically during its final rise and you will notice how the resistance changes. At first, the dough feels tight and unforgiving and any impression made by your finger quickly disappears. As time goes on and the dough inflates, you feel a springiness but still a definite counter pressure, as if the dough is determined to hold your finger at bay. Nearing the limit of proof, you sense a growing fragility and the whole structure of the dough quivers slightly if moved.

Cutting

Some loaves are cut just before they are put in the oven. The purpose of cutting the top surface of a loaf is to enable it to expand further than it might be able to if left uncut. Even when sufficient humidity has been provided during proving, the dough surface always acts as a kind of skin, restraining the expansion of the middle of the loaf. If the surface is not cut, it may split randomly during baking. This can be quite attractive. However, you get two further benefits from cutting. More crust means more flavour; and cuts can be decorative, with every slight variation marking the loaf out as an individual. Certain patterns of cuts are closely associated with particular loaves – for example, baguettes and bloomers. In the days of communal ovens, people used to mark their loaves with a distinctive cut so that they knew that they would get out what they put in.

Baking

Baking turns wet dough into firm, edible bread. As the dough begins to feel the effects of oven heat, gas production by the yeast increases in speed, ending completely when the dough reaches about 55°C. The surface of the dough is heated first and begins to form a shell, but it takes much longer for the centre to get hot enough to kill the yeast, so for a time there is a continued gas pressure from the middle of the dough to the outside. This final yeast fermentation, coupled with the pressure of water in the dough turning to steam, creates 'oven spring', an increase in volume that is indicated by a moderate (and attractive) tearing of the dough at the 'shoulders' where the sides meet the top crust.

Bread goes brown on top when baked for two reasons. First, reactions (known as Maillard-type reactions) occur between amino acids and sugars in the surface dough. Second, when the temperature is above 150°C, caramelisation of the sugars begins. A pale crust is usually a sign that there was insufficient sugar left in the dough to support these reactions. This may be because the dough has been over-fermented, or because the flour itself was deficient in the enzymes necessary to convert starch into maltose (the main sugar involved). If you get pale crusts even after shortening the overall fermentation time, you can add extra enzymes naturally by using a small amount of diastatic malt (see page 94). Enriched breads such as hot cross buns and stollen, which are sweetened with added sugar, will go brown more quickly and so should be baked at a lower temperature than plain breads.

Considerable effort is expended by some home bakers to get steam into their ovens. I am not a fan of baguette-type crusts, so I do not intend to contribute to what I regard as a fruitless exercise. The theory behind steaming is as follows: if you flood the oven with super-heated steam, it condenses on the surface of the dough (the coolest thing in the oven) and forms a kind of gel with the starch. This, being initially wet, slows down the rate of crust formation but eventually dries out into a very thin and shiny layer, behind which a thicker but less crisp crust forms. The key requirement in this process is to keep the oven tightly closed and full of steam for 10 minutes – something that is impossible in domestic ovens. So most of the suggested strategies for introducing steam are doomed to failure. A certain gloss and crispness of the crust may result if you pre-heat a heavy cast-iron tray and then squirt boiling water on to it as you put your loaves into the oven, but you still have the problem that most of the steam thus generated will almost immediately seep out of the cracks round the door or up the vent.

Some ways of creating different crust colours and textures are discussed in Chapter 9.

Suffer the little children

Arriving for a holiday in a small French village some years ago, I made a beeline for the *boulangerie*. I was surprised that the bread counter was awash with rather regular-looking baguettes. I explained that I was a baker and asked to see the wood-fired oven. The owner ushered me rather sheepishly into the bakehouse and I immediately realised that his oven was cold. 'How did you bake all those?' I asked, pointing at the serried sticks. 'Oh, I buy those in frozen and bake them off in a little electric oven,' came the reply.

I made a rapid exit and sought out some genuine artisan bread in the nearby town. My children were not as po-faced as I and ripped into 'fresh' baguettes with glee. Within two days, they couldn't eat another morsel. The roofs of their mouths were red and bleeding, lacerated by the razor-sharp crusts twice-baked into those industrial baguettes.

I'm a bit of a no-pain, no-gain person myself, but I draw the line at a technology that turns daily bread into an instrument of torture.

How do I know when it is baked?

There is hardly a recipe book that doesn't suggest tapping a loaf on its bottom to check whether it is properly baked. A hollow sound is supposed to be the clue. There is nothing wrong with this, and indeed I find myself doing it instinctively: after all, a gentle pat on the bottom is a most satisfying gesture of intimacy and approval. The problem is in determining what 'hollow' really sounds like. I have come across brave attempts to qualify hollowness with words such as 'sonorous' and descriptions of the vibration patterns in a baked loaf that border on the nerdy. But, apart from experience, a little common sense is really all that is required. In addition to the obligatory tap on the bottom, I recommend the following simple checks:

- Does it look done? Check both top and bottom crusts for firmness and colour.
- How long has it been in the oven? If a large loaf looks as if it might be ready after 10 minutes, it is unlikely to be baked through. The oven may be delivering too much top heat, so try to shield the top crust with a sheet or two of baking parchment while the rest of the loaf bakes. Conversely, if it has been in the oven for 50 minutes and still looks rather pale, it may well be simply drying out: the lack of colour may be due to insufficient oven heat or a 'spent' dough without enough residual sugars to produce crust colour. Get it out before it turns to a biscuit.
- How do the 'shoulders' look and feel? The shoulder of a loaf is the point just below the top of the side where it gives way to the domed top. This is easier to see in a tin loaf, but the principle applies to freestanding loaves as well. The shoulder is often the last area of crust to firm up. Sometimes it is obvious to the eye, but you can confirm whether it is done by gently pushing a fingertip into the side of the loaf. If it feels at all fragile or squashy, it needs a bit longer in the oven.
- If your oven consistently seems to bake the top crust of a tin loaf before the sides or bottom are done, you can tip the loaf out of its tin and finish baking it on the oven rack, which will allow more direct heat to firm up the crust all round.

Preliminary yeasted doughs

Making bread from start to finish in one sequence can seem an impossible rush and you may sometimes feel that you have no alternative but to make warm dough and add extra yeast, simply to get a result in the time available. I know the feeling: nothing is worse for a commercial baker than realising that the bread won't be ready by the time the van departs or the shop opens. But if we respond to pressure by cutting corners, we end up with poor bread. Luckily, there is a way of slowing the breadmaking process down *and* making deadlines easier to meet. It involves the use of preliminary doughs, such as 'sponges' and 'ferments', which are a way of building extra time into the process to improve flavour, texture and nutritional quality. Preliminary doughs have many names and often seem complicated. In fact, they are quite easy to manage. And not only do they produce better bread, they make it easier to fit the whole activity into a busy life.

Preliminary doughs, made in advance of the main dough, have the following functions:

- Yeast reproduction.
- Flavour accumulation.
- Gluten ripening.
- Improved nutrition.

Until commercial baker's yeast became widely available at reasonable prices, it was uncommon to make a 'straight' dough, in which all the ingredients are mixed in one go. Early manufactured yeasts were expensive and hard to store without refrigeration. Before that, bakers used a barm, the froth on a fermenting malt liquor, often obtained from a brewery. Either way, they needed to spend some time growing more yeast cells so that there were enough of them to aerate the final dough.

A small quantity of yeast, mixed with a source of food (usually flour) and water and left for several hours, will multiply. Some fermentation will also take place, but provided that there is sufficient oxygen in the mix, the yeast cells will reproduce. Over a period of many hours, lactobacilli, present in the flour and water mix, will also become active, producing lactic and acetic acids, which give the dough a vinegary aroma and a slightly acid taste. The pH of the dough will gradually drop, eventually creating conditions that are more favourable to 'wild' strains of yeast rather than standard baker's yeast (*Saccharomyces cerevisiae*).

A preliminary dough that has been fermented for several hours generates a complex of enzymes and acids that have a 'ripening' effect on the gluten of the main dough, which retains more gas and so turns into a better-risen loaf.

Finally, the preliminary stages play an important part in long fermentations, not just because the result is stretchier or better-tasting dough but also because lactic acid bacteria can improve the nutritional quality of bread in the following ways:

- They lower post-prandial glucose and insulin responses in humans, thereby reducing the risk of obesity and diabetes.
- They assist in the formation of resistant starch, a type of dietary fibre.
- They increase mineral bioavailability, partly by reducing phytic acid, which stops the body absorbing minerals such as iron, calcium, zinc and magnesium.
- They neutralise the gliadin peptides in wheat flour, which are toxic to coeliacs[2].

Several names are used to describe preliminary doughs. Here are some of them, with notes about their particular function:

Pre-ferment

A general term for a part of the dough's ingredients that is fermented separately in advance.

Ferment

A thin batter containing water, yeast, a small amount of flour and sometimes a little sugar. Its purpose is to encourage yeast to begin fermenting and reproducing quickly to give it a good 'start', particularly when it is to be added to a dough containing significant amounts of fat, fruit, sugar, spice etc, which inhibit yeast activity. Some gluten 'ripening' takes place in a ferment: if it is left for long enough, it froths up and then 'falls' as the gluten is softened and over-extended. 'Ripeness' is defined as a softening of the gluten, which allows a finer and more extensible network of gas bubbles to develop.

A 'flying ferment' is one that provides a modest boost to yeast activity but is not allowed to stand long enough to froth up and fall.

Sponge

Stiffer than a ferment but slacker than a proper dough, a sponge is a mixture of flour, water and yeast that is fermented for two to 24 hours. In the traditional terminology, a 'half sponge' was one using half of the total amount of dough liquid. Half sponges and quarter sponges were most common. Depending on the length of time for which the sponge is fermented, the following changes occur:

- Soluble protein is produced, which acts as a yeast food.
- The gluten softens and becomes more extensible.
- Acids (lactic, acetic and a small amount of butyric) and esters develop, giving flavour to the sponge and subsequent dough.
- Yeast cells reproduce and increase in number.

Biga

This is the Italian term for a sponge. In some Italian recipes the biga is made very stiff and contains a large proportion of the total flour; the final dough is made by adding mostly water. The advantage of this method is that it helps control the speed of yeast fermentation and reproduction at ambient temperatures in very warm conditions.

Poolish

Despite its strange name, this is the French equivalent of the English sponge. The term is much loved by a rather earnest kind of American artisan baker.

Starter

Usually denotes an initial culture of flour, water and 'wild' yeasts and lactobacilli, either bought in or self-generated (as in sourdough starter), or a residual piece of dough or batter kept back to initiate a subsequent cycle of dough development.

Old dough

An admirably explicit English term, to be preferred to the slightly less precise French *pâte fermentée* because the English indicates that the dough has indeed been fermented for long enough to be described as 'old'. This is usually a piece of dough kept back from the previous day's baking, so it is at least 24 hours old. It contains all the dough ingredients, including any salt and fat in the recipe, which are not normally found in sponges or sourdoughs. It contains significant amounts of lactic and acetic acids and, like a sponge, conditions the gluten in the main dough as well as contributing flavour. Old dough is to be distinguished from 'acid dough', which is made specifically for the purpose of adding to a fresh dough and does not contain salt or fat. Old dough can be used at up to 20 per cent of final dough weight. The longer it is kept the more acid it becomes, and the smaller the amount that should be used in the final dough.

Leavens and sourdoughs

These are preliminary doughs based on naturally occurring yeasts and bacteria. They are dealt with in more detail in Chapter 7.

You now have a general idea of how to make good bread. Of course, I have dealt so far with general principles; I will go into more detail in the individual recipes as required.

But before actually getting your hands dirty, spare a moment to think about how you are going to time things. Good bread needs a lot of time; you probably don't have much to spare. Here are some ideas for scheduling the various stages of baking to fit in with life as we live it.

Timing it right

Two variables control the speed at which bread dough works – temperature and yeast activity (although yeast quantity and yeast activity are related, they are not the same thing). So, with a bit of planning, we can determine how quickly dough ferments by warming it up or cooling it down and by deciding how much yeast (and what kind) to use. The key variable is temperature: yeast works more quickly in warm doughs than in cool ones. Some speeding up can be achieved by increasing the amount of yeast used, but I don't recommend this. For one thing, the resulting bread may have a pronounced aftertaste of yeast, which some people dislike; for another, dough made with excessive yeast can be harder to control and may produce over-aerated, crumbly and dry-tasting bread. And even with extra yeast, if the dough is cold, it may take a long time to rise.

Before starting, you need to decide when you want to be taking your baked loaves out of the oven. Approximate timings for the five stages involved in producing bread, using various strategies, are given below.

Straight dough

A straight dough is defined as one where all the ingredients are mixed at the beginning of the process, which then proceeds with no interruptions other than the time required for each stage.

Weighing out, mixing and kneading	15 minutes
Rising	2 hours
Shaping	10 minutes
Proving	1 hour
Baking	40 minutes
Total	**4 hours 5 minutes**

These are only guidelines. Baking time, for instance, will vary from oven to oven and both rising and proving may take more or less time.

To achieve a baked loaf from scratch in three or four hours with normal quantities of yeast, a starting dough temperature of around 27°C is required, as is a reasonably warm place (say 22–27°C) for the dough to rise and prove. If you cannot provide these conditions, it doesn't matter, but remember that the whole process may take longer.

Adjusting the heat of the water is the easiest way of getting the right dough temperature. You can warm the flour but it takes much longer – and you still need to know how hot or cold the water should be. For a simple formula to determine the water temperature required, see page 68.

Many recipe books call for tepid, lukewarm or hand-hot water – without any reference to the other ingredients or the time of year. This can result in doughs that ferment too quickly in summer and appear moribund in winter. Flour taken from a cold larder in winter may be as low as 6°C. To make this into a dough at the desired temperature of 27°C requires water which, at 48°C, is a good deal hotter than a typical clothes wash.

Dissolving yeast in hot water may harm it, so use some cooler water for this purpose; it follows that you will need to make the remainder slightly warmer still in order to maintain the correct overall water temperature. Don't get too anxious about all this, though. The important thing is simply to avoid killing the yeast with hot water.

Once you've made bread a few times, you'll probably be able to adjust your water without a thermometer. But it pays to do the calculation and follow it precisely a few times, if only to appreciate how warm (or cool) water sometimes needs to be and to get to know what a dough feels like when it is made at around 27°C.

There is nothing magic about this figure. Indeed, in summer or in parts of the world where kitchen temperatures may rise to 30°C and beyond, you should start a dough at a temperature lower than 27°C in order to control the speed of fermentation, remembering that the friction of kneading as well as exposure to the heat of the surroundings can cause a significant rise in temperature. In warm bakeries in summer, ice is often used in the dough to keep the temperature down. Of course, mechanical mixing generates significant heat, which does not easily escape from a large mass of dough. The more typical problem for home bakers is to prevent heat loss from a relatively small volume of dough.

In a dough that is too warm, the yeast can work so fast that it quickly exhausts its available nourishment and stops producing the carbon dioxide gas that makes the dough rise. In extreme cases, it may 'run out of steam' before the dough has risen properly, resulting in a pale, sad-looking, undersized loaf. Bread made with hot dough tends to have a drier, more crumbly texture and to stale rapidly. And above all, fast doughs leave no time for the other, bacterial, fermentation whose by-products contribute significant flavour and nutritional value to the baked bread.

It is possible to make an adequate loaf in less than four hours. If you go as low as two hours, you are effectively making what bakers call a no-time dough – one in which the dough is given no time at all to ferment in bulk. Commercial white and brown bread have been made this way for four decades, but the process depends on the use of additives and, anyway, to help reproduce that insipid flavourlessness and cotton-wool texture is not the purpose of this book.

If the rising time is reduced to an hour and proof takes only 45 minutes, around three hours is the minimum time required to bake a traditional yeasted loaf. The process can be speeded up a little by adjusting the initial water temperature to make the dough warmer. It can also be slowed down by reducing the dough temperature.

A better 'no-time' dough?

The 'Grant Loaf' was invented in the 1940s by the redoubtable nutritionist and campaigner for unadulterated food, Doris Grant[3]. I was brought up on it. It was made with wholemeal flour, water, yeast, salt and a little Barbados sugar, honey or molasses. The secret was no kneading: you just mixed all the ingredients into a very wet dough, slurped it into a baking tin, let it rise and baked it. It was so easy that, as

Doris Grant reported in ever so slightly patronising tones, 'even husbands can make it without difficulty, and a surprising number of them do ...' Actually, it was so quick (perhaps because the sugar supercharged the yeast activity and because a wet dough ferments faster than a dry one) that it often caught my mother out. Proving on top of the Aga didn't help, of course: given half a chance, the dough would erupt over the top of the tin. For much of my childhood, I thought that all loaves were mushroom-topped.

To some extent the wet no-time dough works because of autolysis, the partial development of gluten that is achieved simply by wetting it. This a good way to make bread if you are in a hurry and like the damp, slightly cakey texture that results. But there is little chance for flavour to develop during such a quick fermentation.

Slower is better

There are advantages to extending the breadmaking process beyond the basic four hours or so. These include additional flavour, improved texture, moisture retention (hence better keeping quality) and digestibility, not to mention compatibility with a busy life. How much can a straight dough be slowed down?

In the illustration above, the dough starts life at 27°C and the whole process takes four hours. If we make a dough at 22°C, it will take twice as long for the same amount of yeast to complete a given amount of fermentation, which means that the whole process would take around seven hours, assuming that the time taken for mixing, moulding and baking remained the same. The revised water temperature calculation (assuming that the flour is still at 20°C) looks like this: 2 × 22 = 44 – 20 = 24°C. Water at this temperature doesn't feel cold – indeed some people might describe it as lukewarm – but it more or less doubles the time that it takes to bake bread. So, a thermometer is a good investment, particularly for those first attempts at breadmaking before your hands have learned the feel of a well-tempered dough.

The other way of extending fermentation time in a straight dough is by reducing the amount of yeast. It is difficult to give precise guidance because much depends on the vigour of the yeast and the temperature of the dough as it goes through the stages. But, very roughly, halving the yeast quantity will double the fermentation time. It is worth experimenting a bit, perhaps with small reductions of yeast at first, to establish the effect under your conditions. Try to use some constant measure of activity. For instance, note how much vertical rise there is for a constant amount of dough in the same container for various lengths of time.

Although a straight dough is normally begun and ended on the same day, there is no reason why, with suitable adjustments of yeast and temperature, it should not be fermented over a considerably longer period. Two examples follow.

Overnight first rise

This might suit someone who wants to give their bread a good, long rise for reasons of flavour and nutritional quality but who cannot start the process until late in the evening. A possible schedule could work like this:

Day 1

2100   Mix dough at around 27°C, to give the yeast a bit of a start
2200   Put in fridge at 5°C

Day 2

0730   Divide and mould and place in tins or on trays in a warm place
0930   Into the oven
1010   Loaves are baked

The proof time of around two hours is an approximation. The dough will be cold as it comes out of the fridge so it will take quite a while to get going, but provided it is in a reasonably warm place, two hours is quite possible.

The advantage of this system is that you have fresh bread, not first thing in the morning but certainly a good deal sooner than you would from a standing start.

Overnight proof

The same idea can be used to get bread ready for baking even earlier in the morning. In this example, there is still a reasonable bulk fermentation of four hours at ambient temperature. But there is a greater risk. If your dough is too lively, or your fridge not powerful enough, the loaves may over-prove before morning. If this happens, try reducing the yeast quantity a bit and make the initial dough cooler.

Day 1

1800	Mix dough at around 27°C
2200	Divide, mould and put in fridge at 5°C

Day 2

0730	Switch on oven
0730	Remove loaves from fridge; if fully proved, cut or dress with topping as required; if not fully proved, transfer to a warm place to complete proof
0800–0900	Into the oven
0840–0940	Loaves are baked

Overnight sponge and dough

As mentioned above, an overnight sponge is a way of starting a dough with a small amount of yeast and allowing time for it to reproduce, and for lactic acid bacteria to develop flavour and nutritionally beneficial qualities in the dough.

Day 1

2000   Mix sponge at around 27°C and leave at ambient temperature

Day 2

0730   Make the dough with the fermented sponge and the rest of the
        ingredients
0800   Short fermentation in bulk because the sponge will contribute flavour
0900   Divide, mould and set to prove
1000   Into the oven
1040   Loaves are baked

Daytime sponge and dough

This timetable enables the working person to get the benefits of the sponge-
and-dough system and produce a loaf within a day.

Day 1

0700   Mix sponge at around 27°C and leave at ambient temperature
1900   Make the dough with the fermented sponge and the rest of the
        ingredients
1930   Short fermentation in bulk because the sponge will contribute flavour
2030   Divide, mould and set to prove
2130   Into the oven
2210   Loaves are baked

There are, of course, many possible variations on the timetables outlined here.
The point is, however, that all it takes is a little advance planning to be able to
make good bread slowly and in complete harmony with a busy life.

I will deal with the timing of sourdoughs and leavens in Chapter 7. But
now it is time to turn theory into practice with some recipes for typical breads.
Just as I hope that you will experiment with timing in order to fit baking into
your everyday life, I urge you to approach the recipes as exemplars of baking

methods and styles, to be adapted to your own special purposes once you have grasped the principles involved.

What to do when things go wrong

Although baking bread is, in essence, a fairly simple process, there are enough variables to make it likely that things will not always turn out the same.

A loaf that looks a bit odd is not necessarily a failure. It may not look quite like a shop loaf (how could it, without all those additives?) but it is very probably still edible. And the best thing about mistakes is that they are better teachers than instant success.

So, if things go wrong, don't worry. Remember what you did and check the symptoms of your distress against the following list of common faults. Then have another go.

Fault	Possible causes
The bread doesn't rise very much.	The dough is too tight. Make it softer by adding more water at the mixing stage. The yeast may be exhausted or may not have a sufficient supply of fermentable sugars in the dough at the time of the final rise or proof. This may be due to using a flour with a naturally low level of amylase or flour that is a bit old. If the problem persists, try using a small amount of diastatic malt (available from home brewing suppliers) in the dough or add some flour from a different source. The dough may have skinned over during its final rise, making it hard for the yeast to expand it fully. Cover the dough (loosely) with a polythene bag and keep it away from draughts. If the dough shows signs of skinning, brush or spray the surface with warm water or put a cup of steamy water next to the loaf under the bag in which it is proving.

Fault	Possible causes
	Check that you haven't overdone the salt. Salt can inhibit the yeast's working, leading to too little gas being generated to expand the dough. Consider the temperature of your final rise: although it is quite possible to prove bread at a low temperature over a long period, there is a danger that the yeast will run out of steam as the dough gradually becomes more acid. By contrast, a very warm, fast final rise often leads to excessive dough expansion and crumbly bread which doesn't keep well.
The crust splits randomly and the top of a loaf baked in a tin seems to be trying to part company with the rest.	This is caused by under-proof, not letting the dough expand enough before putting it in the oven. It may also happen if you do not allow the dough sufficient time for its first rise. While random splits in the crust can give a pleasingly rustic appearance, they can be constrained by 'slashing' the crust with a series of regular cuts before baking.
The loaf collapses during or after baking and has a sad-looking rumpled crust.	Usually a result of over-proof, i.e. too long a final rise. The yeast expands the dough beyond its ability to retain gas and the structure deflates when subjected to the stresses of heat in the oven. This can also be a symptom of weak flour, i.e. one with low protein and low-strength gluten. If you are stuck with this sort of flour, try baking it in shapes that do not require as much vertical lift as a tin, e.g. as a flat bread like a ciabatta.
The loaf has a pale crust despite having been in the oven for ages.	This may be due to insufficient oven heat. Try to start with your oven as hot as it will go (except for breads enriched with sugar, egg, fruit etc.) and turn it down by 10–20° C after about 10 minutes of baking. It may also be due to a lack of natural sugars in the dough at the time of baking, either because they were not there in

Fault	Possible causes
	the first place (see 'The bread doesn't rise much' above) or because they have been used up as the bread rises. Try reducing the first and final rise times a bit. Failing that, try mixing in some flour from a different source.
	You can disguise this effect by glazing the top of the loaf with an eggy or sugary solution before baking. Such glazes take on a golden or brown colour in even moderate oven temperatures.
The bread (especially if baked in a tin) has a hole or a very weak and crumbly area just under the crust.	There are several possible causes:
	Weak, low protein flour whose gluten is not strong enough to retain the gas produced by yeast fermentation.
	Too wet a dough for the type of flour being used.
	Over-proof, or allowing the dough to rise too much before baking the bread.
	Using excessive amounts of yeast in a fast-made bread with strong flour.
	In the case of flat breads or baps, rolling them out too thinly or without letting the dough relax first. Of course, this is precisely what to do if you want to get a pitta bread to burst in the oven and produce its characteristic cavity.
Crackly crazy-paving effect develops on the crust as the bread cools.	Not a fault, in my opinion. It seems to happen only with certain kinds of flour, usually strong ones. If you really don't like the effect, brush the dough with oil before baking; this produces a softer, more pliable crust.
Blisters or spots on the crust.	Blisters can be caused by uneven shaping of the dough, during which pockets of gas are trapped rather than evenly expelled. In wet, extensible doughs like ciabatta, blisters are part of the character of the loaf and not a fault.
	Blisters can also be caused by too much humidity during the final rise, which can cause patches of the dough surface to

Fault	Possible causes

become more extensible than the rest, thus erupting as thin blisters which may well burn to a darker colour than the main crust.

Small spots are usually caused by a long final rise at low temperature and high humidity, e.g. an overnight proof in the fridge. If you don't like this effect, sprinkle the dough surface with seeds like sesame or poppy just before baking, or brush it with oil, milk or a weak egg mixture.

CHAPTER SIX

FIRST BREAD AND ROLLS

'Bread recipes are almost valueless,
because they are so dependent on yeast
speeds and the variable nature of flours.'
WALTER BANFIELD,
Manna: *A Comprehensive Treatise on Bread Manufacture*
(Maclaren, 1937)

There are not many different ways of making bread. It could be argued that all you need to make bread are flour, water and some form of yeast. Other bits and pieces may be interesting but they don't change anything fundamental. So I promise not to confuse you with a load of superficially different recipes. I would rather introduce you to a few basic doughs, suggest some variations and take you with me on an open-ended journey into bread. Simple bread and rolls are a good place to start.

In the recipe for Basic Bread I describe the method in some detail. Treat this as a template for many of the other breads, where repetition of the same instructions might become boring.

A note on ingredients

To avoid endless repetition I do not preface every ingredient line with the word 'organic'. However, all the recipes have been developed with organic ingredients and I recommend their use throughout, for reasons explained in Chapter 2. If you cannot get hold of everything you need from a certified organic source, the recipes will work just as well with non-organic ingredients.

You can substitute wholemeal flour for white or vice versa in all the recipes. Loaves made with a substantial amount of wholemeal flour will need a bit more water and will expand less than those made entirely with white flour.

Basic Bread

This is the simplest possible yeasted dough. It can be worked into all kinds of shapes or augmented with other ingredients to produce different flavours and textures.

To complete this bread in about 4 hours, aim to make the dough at about 27°C. If you want to do this accurately in order to get a feel for what dough at this temperature feels like, follow the formula on page 68.

The yeast quantity shown in the recipe is fairly small. In winter you may wish to increase it a bit to allow for the difficulty of keeping a relatively small piece of dough warm in normal kitchen conditions.

Makes 1 large or 2 small loaves

600g	Stoneground strong wholemeal flour
5g	Sea salt
400g	Water
8g	Fresh yeast
1013g	**Total**

Flour or seeds for the top

Weigh the flour and salt into a bowl. Measure the total amount of water and pour about a quarter of it into a small jug or bowl. Dissolve the yeast in this water by stirring it gently with your fingers. (If you are using traditional active dried yeast, stir the granules around for a moment or two and then leave them to soften; they will probably float to the surface. In a few minutes they should be beginning to dissolve and foam a little.) Pour the yeasty water into the bowl with the flour and salt and add the rest of the water. Use one hand to hold the bowl and the other to begin mixing the dough (you could use a wooden spoon but it's just another thing to wash up, and hands are more effective anyway). As soon as all the dry flour has become wet and the dough has begun to form, scrape it out of the bowl on to the worktop and begin kneading.

Do not add any flour at this stage, even if the dough seems to you to be rather wet. If it seems too dry, add some more water. As you knead, the flour will absorb the water and the gluten structure should begin to develop. Knead for 10–15 minutes. If you are using a mixer, rather less time will be needed. At the end of the mixing/kneading process, the dough should be soft, slightly silky to the touch and with a definite elasticity that was not there at the beginning.

Make sure the bowl is reasonably clean and put the dough back in it. Don't worry about oiling the bowl: it's a waste of oil and makes washing up more difficult. Cover the bowl with a polythene bag that is big enough not to come into contact with the rising dough. Leave the bowl in a warm place (around 25°C, if possible).

After 2 hours, the dough should have risen appreciably. If it has grown significantly in less than 2 hours, you can either 'knock it back' by gently folding it over on itself a couple of times and leaving it to rise again, or you can simply progress to the next stage.

Grease one large loaf tin or 2 small ones with some fat or vegetable oil; a hard fat such as butter is better than liquid oil because the latter tends to run down the sides of the tin and form a pool in which the base of the loaf partially fries. Tip the dough on to the worktop again. If you plan to make 2 small loaves, divide it in half. Using the barest flick of flour to prevent the dough sticking to your hands or the worktop, roll the dough into a sausage about twice as long as the longest side of the tin. Flatten this sausage with your knuckles and then fold it in three. Again, knuckle the dough down until it is a flattish rectangle about two-thirds the length of your tin.

Starting at the edge furthest from you, fold it over and roll it up, trying to keep the dough under some tension but not folding it so tightly that it tears. Finish your roll with the seam underneath and then pick the whole thing up and place it in the tin. If you intend to cover the surface with seeds or flour, it is better to do this before the dough goes into the tin. Have a shallow bowl of flour or seeds available and roll the freshly moulded dough piece in it, ensuring that what will be the top of the loaf, i.e. the side opposite the seam, gets well covered. If the stuff doesn't stick very well, your dough surface is too dry. Get some water and rub it over the dough or spritz it using a household sprayer with warm water in it. Then dip the dough. Place it seam-side down in the tin. The dough should roughly half fill the tin (a little less if the dough is made from white flour).

Set your bread to prove in a warm place, covered with a stiff plastic bag or large bowl to stop it drying out too much. It is important not to let the dough touch the cover as it rises otherwise it may stick and damage the loaf structure when the cover is removed.

Preheat the oven to 230°C or its hottest setting. When the dough has risen appreciably but still gives some resistance when gently pressed with the pad of one finger, put the loaf or loaves carefully into the oven. Bake for 30–40 minutes, turning the heat down to 200°C after 10 minutes.

Turn the bread out of the tin and check that it is done (see page 122). Don't be afraid to put it back in the oven for a few minutes if you are not sure that it is fully baked. If the bottom seems rather pale by comparison with the top, turn the loaf out of its tin and put it on one of the oven's wire shelves to finish baking.

When you are happy that it is done, cool it on a rack to stop the bottom sweating and going soggy.

Bread with Old Dough

This is identical to the Basic Bread recipe except for the old dough, a piece of basic bread dough that has been kept for at least 24 hours, preferably in the fridge. The difference in flavour and texture contributed by the old dough is considerable. If the tangy flavour from the acids in the old dough is too strong for your liking, reduce the proportion of old dough in the recipe. You will still enjoy improved texture and keeping quality. The salt level is reduced because some salt comes into the mix via the old dough.

Makes 1 large or 2 small loaves

500g	Stoneground strong wholemeal flour
4g	Sea salt
330g	Water
8g	Fresh yeast
160g	Old dough
1002g	**Total**

Make a dough with all the ingredients except the old dough, as for Basic Bread. Knead for about 5 minutes, then add the old dough. If the latter has become very soft and sticky, you may need to add a little more flour to achieve a dough that is just manageable. As you continue to knead, you may notice the acids in the old dough beginning to condition the gluten, i.e. making it softer and more extensible.

Let the dough rise for about 2 hours, then divide it as required, mould it and place in greased tins. Prove and bake in a hot oven as for Basic Bread.

Milk Bread

The addition of milk to a bread dough has a pronounced softening effect on the crumb. This, and the nutritional benefit of the extra calcium, is probably why it was a nursery favourite. For those striving for softness in dough, milk is a much better way to achieve it than the hidden enzymes added by the baking industry. Whole milk gives the fullest effect, but semi-skimmed will still make some difference.

Putting 4 round pieces of dough together in a tin creates a slightly corrugated top, reminiscent of the fluted, tubular tins traditionally used for milk bread.

Makes 1 small loaf and a mini plait

260g	Whole milk
5g	Fresh yeast
200g	Stoneground strong wholemeal flour
200g	Strong white flour
4g	Sea salt
669g	**Total**

Egg, beaten with a little milk, to glaze

Warm the milk to the required temperature (see page 68) and dissolve the yeast in a little of it. Combine all the ingredients, then turn the dough out on to the worktop and knead for about 10 minutes. You should notice that it has a softer feel than one made with water. If it feels rather sticky on the surface, persevere with kneading and adjust the flour only towards the end. This should remain a fairly soft dough.

Let it rise for up to 2 hours. Then divide the dough into 2 pieces, one weighing 500g and the other about 150g (you always seem to lose a little along the way). Divide the larger piece into 4, mould into rolls and place them side by side in a greased small loaf tin. To enhance the crust colour, brush the top with egg beaten with a little milk. Roll the smaller piece of dough into a sausage about 30cm long and make it into a one-strand plait or knot it as if you are tying the first part of a bow. Put it on a baking tray lined with baking parchment and brush with egg glaze, being careful not to leave a 'tide mark' round the edges.

Prove under cover as usual. The freestanding plait will probably be ready to go in the oven first, partly because, not being constrained by a tin, it will have expanded in all directions and partly because it will look more attractive if it jumps and splits just a little in the oven – if it is over-proved, the dough strands are more likely to merge into one another, reducing the definition of the shape.

Start baking at 210°C and reduce the temperature to 190°C after 10 minutes. A slightly lower temperature is required because the milk sugars in the dough make it more likely to take colour as it bakes and the egg glaze accentuates this effect. If you get it right, the result will be a glossy, dark brown crust and a crumb that is soft without being pappy. The plait, being smaller and unprotected by a tin, will bake in as little as 15 minutes, the loaf in 30–40, as before.

Rolls

Rolls are essentially very small loaves of bread, but size does affect them in various ways. They have a greater proportion of crust than loaves, so they have to be baked in such a way as to avoid becoming all crust with not much crumb. One very common strategy is to place them so close to each other that, as they expand, they touch their neighbours and 'batch' together: where two rolls touch there is no crust, only crumb. Another way of limiting the formation of a hard crust is to dip the rolls in flour before proof: the flour coating interferes with the development of a firm crust and produces a softer surface, which teeth can tear more easily. Rolls often have some fat in the dough to help keep the crumb soft.

Heat can penetrate to the centre of a small volume of dough quite quickly, so baking time is reduced, as is the danger of the dough not being cooked in the middle. Rolls can therefore be baked at a high temperature, quickly forming a crust and retaining maximum moisture in the centre.

Hot rolls

I fired my first 'Scotch' brick oven in 1977, using hardwood offcuts from local saw-mills, and it built up a prodigious heat as I piled on the logs in the afternoon and evening ready for the next morning's baking. We never knew its precise temperature because it didn't have a thermometer, but we knew it was right when a certain crack in the front of the oven started to widen. As the bakery got busier, we needed to get the oven ever hotter so that it would bake more bread on a single firing: there wasn't time during the baking day to heat it up again. The first things into the fiercely hot oven were baps – ten trays with 54 baps on each. The whole oven full baked in three minutes. A few seconds' delay in getting them out could have been disastrous, but quick work with one person on the peel (the flat shovel on the end of a long handle) and another shooting the baps off into wire trays resulted in wonderfully moist rolls with a thin crust flecked with a hint of toasted flour.

Baps

This recipe is for a straight bap dough. You could use white flour instead of wholemeal but if it is made with white flour in 3 or 4 hours from start to finish, there will be insufficient time for much flavour to develop by comparison with the sponge-and-dough method given for Scottish Morning Rolls (see page 149). One way of improving an all-white dough is to use a fat with definite flavour. Lard was the traditional favourite. Vegetarians might prefer butter or a well-flavoured olive oil. Remember, however, that fats that are liquid at room temperature tend to depress dough volume a little.

Made with wholemeal flour, these rolls have plenty of flavour even after a relatively short fermentation. But even wholemeal gains a roundedness and pleasing tang from an overnight sponge and, more importantly, the long fermentation helps break down phytic acid from the bran (phytic acid can make certain important minerals in the flour inaccessible to the human body).

The recipe uses a higher percentage of yeast in order to create a lively dough that will give the baps good lift in the oven. If you use salted butter, you could reduce the amount of added salt in the dough a bit, although some people may find the amount recommended quite low already.

Have a bowl of flour (wholemeal or white, as you prefer) ready to dip the rolls in.

Makes a dozen good-sized baps

10g	Fresh yeast
390g	Water
600g	Stoneground strong wholemeal flour
5g	Sea salt
30g	Butter, lard or olive oil
1035g	**Total**

Aim to finish the dough at about 27°C. Dissolve the yeast in the water and then combine all the ingredients and knead until the dough is pliable and the gluten properly developed. Cover and leave to rise for 1–2 hours, but in any case take the dough to the next stage before it collapses.

Without completely de-gassing the dough, divide it into 12 equal pieces, then mould each one tightly and evenly by rolling it on the work surface under cupped hands. As soon as each piece is moulded, dip it into a bowl of flour, making sure that the whole piece is covered. Place the floured rolls about 2cm apart on a baking tray lined with baking parchment. Line them up neatly so each has an equal space in which to rise. If you want to make a flatter sandwich roll or burger bun, let the freshly moulded and floured dough pieces stand for about 5 minutes to relax the gluten and then press or roll them out with a rolling pin until they are about 50 per cent wider than they were. Line them up on the tray, still 2cm apart.

Cover the whole tray with a loose polythene bag to create a warm, moist atmosphere in which the dough can rise easily. The baps are ready for the oven when they have risen appreciably and are just touching their neighbours.

Bake in a very hot oven (230°C), turning down the heat after 5 minutes or so to 210°C. They may take as little as 12–15 minutes, depending on your oven. Checking is not easy if the baps have batched together as they should. Gently tear one away from the rest and check its top and bottom crusts. If the torn side where it was attached to its neighbour still looks a bit raw, it probably needs a minute or two more in the oven, but the baps will firm up a little as they cool.

Scottish Morning Rolls

Although this recipe is for rolls, it can be applied to all kinds of breads. It uses the classic sponge-and-dough method – the way most bread was made until the second half of the last century. A very small amount of yeast is used in the sponge. This reproduces itself by feeding on the sugars available in the sponge flour, so that by the time the final dough is made there are enough active yeast cells to give a good rise to the rolls.

If, after fermenting your sponge for 18 hours, you discover that you haven't time to make bread after all, don't worry. Just leave the sponge in a coolish place or the fridge for another day. It will get a little more acid and the yeast will be rather more starved of food, but nothing drastic will happen to render it incapable of reviving when mixed with fresh flour.

For some thoughts on how a sponge can be turned into a 'natural' leaven, see pages 213–214.

Makes a dozen rolls

1. The overnight sponge

5g	Fresh yeast
130g	Water (at 20°C)
50g	Stoneground strong wholemeal flour
100g	Strong white flour
285g	**Total**

The water for the sponge does not have to be particularly warm, since the yeast has a long time to get to work and the sponge will gradually reach room temperature.

Dissolve the yeast in some of the water and add it to the flours with the rest of the water. Mix until the dough has 'cleared', i.e. all the ingredients are thoroughly combined. There is no need to knead the sponge, since time will develop the gluten sufficiently. In fact, after 18 hours the gluten will be so softened that, if then kneaded hard, it would turn quite quickly into a sticky mess.

Put the sponge in a bowl large enough to allow it to expand to at least 3 times its original size. Cover with a lid or polythene bag and leave it at ambient temperature for 12–18 hours. If ambient happens to be more than 25°C, find somewhere a bit cooler, so that the yeast does not start fermenting too quickly.

2. The final dough

285g	Overnight sponge (above)
350g	Strong white flour
100g	Stoneground strong wholemeal flour
5g	Salt
270g	Water
15g	Butter, lard or olive oil
1025g	**Total**

Before you do anything else, take the lid or cover off your sponge and enjoy a first whiff of the fruity, beery, slightly vinegary aroma. Notice how the mixture has obviously bubbled up and collapsed. The yeast is still working a bit, but it is running out of available food and the gluten structure has collapsed because enzymes have softened it and it has been stretched beyond endurance by vigorous pressure from the fermentation gases.

Aim to make the final dough at about 27°C for a reasonably quick rise. If you are calculating the water temperature accurately according to the formula given on page 68, measure the temperature of both the sponge and the flours, take an average and use that as the value for the 'flour' component.

Mix all the ingredients together into a soft dough. Knead until it is silky and slightly stretchy. Leave to rise for 1 hour, during which time the yeast will begin to use the fermentable sugars in the fresh source of flour. A long period of rising is not needed because both flavour and gluten-conditioning elements have already entered the dough with the overnight sponge.

Divide, mould, prove and bake as for Baps, above. Proof may take a little longer but, in my experience, a sponge-and-dough started with half as much yeast as a straight dough, if set to prove at the same time, will be ready for the oven only a few minutes later, if that.

No-time dough, straight yeasted dough, sponge and dough ... each uses progressively less industrial yeast and time assumes ever greater significance. Not time for the sake of it, but time as the essential condition if the benign potential of grain is to be fulfilled in bread of incomparable flavour and nourishing ability.

The best way of harnessing time to make good bread is to dispense with industrial concentrated yeast altogether and to rely exclusively on natural fermentations.

CHAPTER SEVEN
SIMPLE SOURDOUGH

'... on establishing a well-grounded
theory on this subject [fermentation]
depends the whole art of baking bread.'
ABRAHAM EDLIN,
A Treatise on the Art of Bread-Making
(Vernor & Hood, 1805; reprinted by
Prospect Books, 2004)

'Sourdough' means a dough fermented with naturally occurring yeasts and lactobacilli and without industrially manufactured yeast of the kind used by bakers and sold for home baking. Making sourdough bread is easy. People have made bread this way for thousands of years. This simple folk knowledge has been rediscovered by a new community of enthusiasts and some terrific naturally fermented breads can now be had from artisan bakers and even some supermarkets. But if you look for guidance on making this sort of bread at home, it seems strangely complicated.

Even if you are not flummoxed by words like *desem* and *levain* (both of which refer to types of natural fermentation), you may be expected to wade through pages of instructions, assemble a clutch of special ingredients and spend up to a fortnight fussing just to create a starter which, if it survives, becomes as demanding as a pet. Over the whole enterprise hangs an aura of mysticism, a sense that the processes involved may be accessible only to a chosen few. The sourdough grail is guarded by zealots, who expatiate interminably on the size of the holes in their *miches*.

It doesn't have to be like this. All that is needed is a clear understanding of what happens when flour and water are mixed and left in a warm place. The rest is detail. Forget the milk, the yoghurt, the orange peel, the grape skins, the apple juice, the raisins and all the other things that are suggested as aids to developing a starter. There is nothing wrong with them in themselves. They are just not necessary.

Naturally occurring ('wild') yeasts and lactic acid bacteria (lactobacilli) are present in any sample of wheat or rye flour (and many other flours). Water and warmth provide the conditions for their growth. They feed on sugars converted from flour carbohydrate by the action of enzymes (also naturally occurring). What's more, sourdough is an object lesson in cooperation, with its various constituents depending on, and not competing with, each other. Yeasts do not compete for food directly with lactobacilli and lactobacilli actually generate antibiotic compounds that neutralise potentially harmful bacteria.

Flour contains everything necessary to sustain a sourdough, including its own yeasts, just as grape skins harbour the yeasts that help turn grape juice into wine. Some overlap is likely, given the enormous number of species of yeast. But grape yeasts work best with grapes, not bread. In the same way, using milk or yoghurt confuses the bacteria commonly found in dairy cultures (*acidophilus*, *bifidus* etc) with the lactobacilli (*brevis*, *plantarum*, *sanfranciscensis* and many more) that predominate in sourdoughs.

Of course, flour is not the only source of yeasts and lactobacilli. Moulds, bacteria and yeasts of innumerable species permeate our environment. So it is by no means impossible that some organisms can enter a sourdough from the air, or indeed (as some evidence suggests in the case of *Lactobacillus sanfranciscensis*) from the hands of bakers. But the shortest, simplest route to a sustainable sourdough is flour and water.

Instructions for starting and using a sourdough follow shortly, but a few definitions may be helpful first:

Sourdough

Sometimes called simply a 'sour'. A self-sustaining fermentation of flour, water, lactobacilli and naturally occurring (or intentionally introduced) yeasts of acid-tolerant strains other than *Saccharomyces cerevisiae*. I usually confine the word sourdough to fermentations of rye and rice, and use leaven for wheat and other flours, but essentially the words are interchangeable.

'Wild' yeast

A genus, species or strain of yeast not normally used in the industrial production of baker's yeast. In baking, wild yeast generally refers to naturally occurring species that ferment symbiotically with lactobacilli in a mixture that is more acidic than a normal bread dough.

Lactobacilli/lactic acid bacteria

Bacteria of several different species, strains and varieties naturally found in flour and the baking environment and capable of symbiotic fermentation with certain kinds of naturally occurring yeasts. Lactic acid bacteria multiply in any dough left to ferment for long enough. They produce mainly lactic and acetic acids, which give sourdoughs and leavens their characteristic aroma and flavour.

Liquid assets

In an age before industrial yeasts had been selected and purified to deliver very rapid fermentation, bakers were naturally on the look-out for anything that would make their barms, or leavens, more reliable and vigorous. Writing in 1805, Abraham Edlin reported that 'most excellent bread is frequently baked on board of our ships of war that are on the West India station, with the water that has become sour in the casks and that the fermentation is as speedily excited as when made with yeast.' In the East Indies, bread was 'raised and baked by a liquor called toddy', which was the sap of palm or wild date trees. Apparently within two hours of being tapped, the sap fermented spontaneously into an intoxicating liquor, which was 'fit to bake with, in the same manner as yeast in this country'. And in the West Indies, there was another liquor 'peculiarly serviceable in exciting a speedy fermentation'. It was the dregs left in the bottom of a rum still and it was known as 'dunder' (presumably only 'dunderheads' overindulged). The cask water, toddy and dunder may have contributed both actively fermenting yeasts (some of which would work in dough) and a source of yeast food in the form of partially fermentable sugars.

Leaven

The same as a sourdough, but usually used to refer to wheat-based naturally fermented doughs. The French for leaven is *levain*.

Starter

Can refer to a bought-in preparation of selected yeasts and lactobacilli, as in 'starter culture'. This usually needs to be activated by mixing with flour and water and being allowed to ferment for several hours or days. Bought-in starters can be a shortcut to a viable sourdough and they can, in theory, contain yeasts and bacteria specific to a particular country or baking tradition.

However, they cost a lot more than simple flour, and some purveyors of these preparations imply, for understandable commercial reasons, that a fresh culture should be used for each batch of bread. That rather goes against the principle of a self-sustaining natural fermentation and is completely unnecessary.

I use the term starter in two ways: first, to denote the initial preparation stage of a leaven or sourdough; secondly, to describe a piece of fermented sourdough or leaven that is not baked into bread but is kept back to initiate a later cycle of dough development. In French/American artisan baking, this starter dough is sometimes called the chef, or mother.

Backferment

A German name for a proprietary sourdough culture based on honey, wheat and maize that is available in dried form. Honey, provided it has not been heated or pasteurised, is a good source of natural yeasts. *Backferment* has the ability to produce a vigorous natural yeast fermentation with less acidity than is usually associated with sourdoughs.

Refreshment

When you add fresh flour and water to a leaven or sourdough, the yeasts and lactobacilli can 'feed' on the new source of fermentable sugars. But the term 'feeding' is misleading because it suggests that a discrete body of organisms in the starter dough is being nourished with the new flour. In fact the new flour also brings into the dough fresh quantities of yeasts and bacteria; so the flora of the 'refreshed' sourdough comprise some of the original cells, some of their 'offspring' and some completely new ones that will bring their own fermentative power to the whole mixture.

I use the term 'cycle of refreshment' to describe the time it takes for a refreshed sourdough starter to reach an optimum balance of fermenting yeasts and lactobacilli. In the early stages of a refreshment, it is likely that yeast reproduction and fermentation will predominate, with the development of lactic acid bacteria coming along more slowly. You should normally use a refreshed sourdough to make a final dough when it has developed sufficient flavour and is likely to achieve the most effective aeration of the dough. I sometimes recommend a 'mini-refreshment', which is an interim addition of flour to a sourdough, designed to prompt a short-term upsurge in yeast activity. This can be useful if the sourdough is too acidic for your liking and seems to take ages to raise your bread under normal conditions.

Production sourdough/production leaven

This is the middle stage in the process of using a sourdough to make bread, as in:

starter > production sourdough > final dough > baked bread

In most sourdough systems, the majority of refreshed sourdough is incorporated into the final dough (to act as its yeast, as it were) but a residue is held back to become the starter for the next day's bread. Then all the starter is incorporated into the production sourdough and is thereby completely 'refreshed'. There is no need to maintain a separate starter with its own 'feeding' requirements, because a piece of the refreshed production sourdough does that job automatically. This is the simplest and most economical way of managing sourdough baking.

Of course, adjustments are required if you are increasing or decreasing the amount you bake and you may well end up with odd amounts of old starter. For more information on how to look after sourdoughs between baking sessions, see page 204.

Culture shock

It is safest to make sourdough in a plastic tub with a press-on lid. If the fermentation gets a bit lively, the worst that can happen is a loud pop from the kitchen in the middle of the night.

I was a little alarmed to see in a couple of recent recipe books pictures of glass preserving jars containing sourdough starters, with no warning not to seal the lids down with the steel clips. The gas produced by a rye fermentation (indeed any fermentation) can be considerable and, even if the jar remains intact, it could easily produce a messy eruption when the pressure is released.

I once made kvas, a Russian 'small beer' fermented from rye bread crusts, in some old cider flagons. One exploded with such force that it sent shards of glass right through a roll of aluminium foil.

Starting a rye sourdough

The ideal temperature for fermenting a rye sour is around 30°C. This can be difficult to maintain unless you have a hot water tank or airing cupboard. Lower temperatures will make the process take longer. Try to create a space on a shelf above a range cooker or a radiator that holds the required temperature, but be careful not to overdo it. There is a pronounced 'window' of reproductive activity in natural yeasts around 28–30°C; a few degrees lower *or higher* and the process slows down.

A cheap electric plant propagator is a simple way to provide a constant temperature for both developing a sourdough and proving bread. Use a thermometer to check the actual temperature being delivered.

Day 1

25g Wholemeal (dark) rye flour

50g Water (at 40°C)

75g Total

Mix the flour and water into a sloppy paste, preferably in a plastic tub with a lid. Press the lid down, or cover the bowl with a polythene bag, in order to stop the mixture skinning over or drying out. Keep this mixture as near to a constant 30°C as you can manage.

Day 2

25g Wholemeal (dark) rye flour

50g Water (at 40°C)

75g Starter from Day 1

150g Total

Stir the fresh flour and water into the mixture, cover and return it to a warm place.

Day 3

25g Wholemeal (dark) rye flour

50g Water (at 40°C)

150g Starter from Day 2

225g Total

Stir the fresh flour and water into the old starter, which may already show signs of frothing. If there is a layer of greyish liquid on top, don't worry: just stir it in with the other ingredients.

Day 4

25g Wholemeal (dark) rye flour

50g Water (at 40°C)

225g Starter from Day 3

300g Total

Add the fresh flour and water. After a further day, you should have a sourdough that has bubbled up and subsided and smells fruity. If you dip a finger in and lick it, the sour should taste mildly acidic.

That completes the preparation stage and you should now have a viable rye sourdough starter. (If you are worried that your starter doesn't seem to be doing much, there are some suggestions on page 181 that apply equally to wheat leavens and rye sours.)

From this point, you need to attend to your starter only when you want to make bread. As you will see, 300g is rather more than you need to make a large rye loaf. At this stage, because the starter is young, I would recommend keeping the whole amount, even though you probably do not need it all. This will give your starter time to gain in acidity. However, if you find that you have accumulated much more starter than you are likely to use according to the recipes that follow, you may want to consider reducing your stock. You can, of course, throw some away but there are more constructive alternatives:

- Give some away.
- Use some (a maximum of 10 per cent) in a wheat bread dough and enjoy the effect on gluten structure and flavour.
- Freeze some in case anything happens to your main sourdough. Yeasts do lose some viability in the freezer, but using a frozen sourdough is still much quicker than having to start from scratch.

Wholemeal rye flour (sometimes called 'dark' rye flour) has a rich population of yeasts and lactobacilli and a sourdough made with it can ferment with great vigour. For that reason, only a small amount of original starter is needed to seed a production sourdough. The ratio is 1:10, i.e. one part starter makes ten parts production sourdough. In wheat leavens, this ratio is normally 1:3.

When it comes to using a sourdough to make bread, you should think of it as an alternative to bought-in yeast. You need much more of it, of course, because the natural yeasts are far less concentrated than the industrial ones. But the principle is similar and it follows that the less sourdough you put into your dough, the slower it will rise, and vice versa.

Interest in rye bread is growing in the UK, even as it declines in traditional rye-eating areas such as Germany and Poland. The main reason appears to be the desire to avoid eating wheat. But 100 per cent rye breads are well worth trying in their own right. For flavour, texture, digestibility and nutritional quality, they are hard to beat.

Rye and sourdough are an ideal combination. Not only is rye flour probably the best medium for starting a spontaneous sourdough but rye bread baking actually needs sourdough. If you simply substitute rye flour for wheat flour in a conventional recipe, expect a brick. Rye needs an acid dough in order to inhibit the excessive amounts of alpha-amylase enzyme typically found in rye flour; too much of this enzyme means sticky and unworkable dough. More importantly, sourdough enables the pentosans in rye flour to absorb more water, producing a softer dough that keeps better after baking.

Here is what you need to know to make superb rye bread:

General notes about all-rye breads

Kneading and dough consistency

The key to all breads with more than 50 per cent rye flour is that the dough must be very soft. If you try to make a rye dough into a kneadable consistency, the end result will be close to concrete. Make it as soft as loose mashed potato and the bread will rise well and keep for many days. Prolonged kneading is unnecessary, since rye gluten does not develop the same elasticity as wheat.

Rising

No period of first rising is needed because the gluten in rye does not need the same ripening treatment as wheat gluten and there is plenty of flavour from the high proportion of sourdough. The relatively long proof time provides a further opportunity for flavour to develop.

Shaping

Rye gluten has none of the elasticity of wheat, so the most that can be expected of an all-rye dough is that it takes on the shape of its container, whether this be a baking tin or the basket in which it is proved before being baked on a tray or pizza stone. There is no point shaping rye other than to give it a smooth surface and to fit it into the tin or basket. Once there, it tends to find its own level.

Proof

All-rye doughs do not expand as much as wheat doughs because rye gluten does not form a coherent and elastic network. Breads made with wholemeal (dark) rye flour will expand by about 50–75 per cent during proof. Those made with light rye flour (which has had some of the bran removed) will expand by 75–100 per cent.

Baking time

All-rye doughs are soft and wet because rye flour has the ability to absorb more water than wheat. This, and the relative absence of available sugars in a rye dough (to support the Maillard reactions that create crust colour), make it desirable to bake all-rye breads in a very hot oven, at least for the first ten to 15 minutes. You will need to bake rye bread for longer than wheat bread because more water has to be evaporated from the wet rye dough.

Storage and eating

Because rye breads retain significantly more moisture than wheat breads, they keep well. Their crumb can be very gummy immediately after baking, so it is advisable to leave them for at least a day before attempting to cut them. After two or three days, the flavour of sourdough rye bread becomes noticeably more pronounced, the crumb darkens a little and the bread becomes more easily digestible.

Russian Rye Bread

This is one of the easiest breads to make, once you have created a viable sourdough. Although in Russia, the standard 'black' bread (which is actually a grey colour) usually contains 10–30 per cent wheat flour, using all rye flour is quite legitimate. It has the advantage of making this a bread suitable for people who wish to avoid both baker's yeast and wheat.

By the way, be wary of any truly black bread that you see. Unless it is a pumpernickel-type bread that has gained an authentic dark colour by very slow baking over many hours, the blackness may well come from an artificial colouring such as caramel. Ignore, too, recipes that call for coffee or cocoa powder in rye bread: again, these are alien ingredients, presumably included for reasons of appearance, not authenticity.

Makes 1 large or 2 small loaves

Stage 1: production sourdough

50g	Rye Sourdough Starter (page 160)
150g	Wholemeal (dark) rye flour
300g	Water (at 40°C)
500g	**Total**

Mix everything together into a very sloppy dough at about 30°C. Cover and leave in a warm place for 12–24 hours. Then use this production sourdough to make your final dough. If you are going to make only one sourdough, make this one. It can be the basis of many simple, delicious and nutritious breads.

Stage 2: final dough

440g	Production Sourdough (above)
330g	Rye flour (light or wholemeal)
5g	Sea salt
200g	Water (at 40°C)
975g	**Total**

By using 440g of production sourdough in the final dough, there is about 50g left to retain as a future starter (a few grams usually get lost on the side of bowls etc).

Mix all the ingredients together thoroughly. The dough should be soft and far too wet to handle on the worktop. Using wet hands, scoop the dough up and drop it into a well-greased large bread tin (or 2 smaller ones). Cover loosely with a polythene bag, inflating and tying its neck to prevent contact with the dough. Final proof will take anything from 2–8 hours, depending on the vigour of the sourdough and the temperature in your kitchen. The dough will be ready to bake when it has risen appreciably and feels quite fragile and unresistant to the (very gentle) touch of a finger. If the dough slightly more than half filled the tin before proof, it is ready for the oven when it has risen to the top of the tin.

Bake in as hot an oven as you can muster (230–240°C ideally), reducing the temperature by 20°C after 10–15 minutes. Typical baking time will be 50–60 minutes for a large loaf, 35–45 minutes for small ones. Rye bread holds a great deal of water, so if you are in any doubt, give it a bit longer in the oven.

Leave to cool completely before wrapping in cellophane or a polythene bag. Rest the loaf for a day before eating. The flavour develops significantly with keeping, though the crumb will begin to harden after 5–7 days. The acidity of the sourdough should keep this bread free of mould for many days.

Seeded Rye Bread

This is a simple variation on Russian Rye Bread, which uses a lower percentage of production sourdough in the final dough. There is still enough to raise the dough but the loaf has a milder flavour. The buttery texture of sunflower seeds and the crunch of pumpkin seeds make this loaf not just nutritious but a very satisfying eat. It's a bit like a rather indulgent pumpernickel.

For an original canapé or nibble, slice the bread very thinly and roll the slices up with a filling of pickled or smoked fish or hummus.

If it suits you, you can use the production sourdough for this bread only 4–6 hours after refreshment. This maximises the yeast activity and reduces the acidity of the dough.

Makes 1 small loaf

160g Production Sourdough (page 165)

240g Rye flour (light or wholemeal)

  5g Sea salt

 50g Pumpkin seeds

 50g Sunflower seeds

140g Water

645g Total

Bowl of sunflower seeds for dipping

Mix all the ingredients together into a very soft dough at about 30°C. Using wet hands, form the dough into a smooth rectangle the right size for your tin, then dip it into the bowl of sunflower seeds, rolling it gently so that seeds stick all over the surface of the dough. Pick it up and drop it carefully into a well-greased tin. The recipe should make enough to fill a generous 'small' tin, with a capacity of around 500ml, just over half full.

Cover and put in a warm place (28–30°C if possible) to prove. This can take anything from 2–6 hours, depending on the vigour of the sourdough and the warmth of the conditions. Bake in a fairly hot oven (200–210°C), reducing the heat a little after 10–15 minutes. This bread is baked at a slightly lower temperature than plain Russian Rye Bread because the seeds on the outside, with their high natural oil content, can turn bitter if too highly fired.

Borodinsky Bread

Borodinsky was the doyen of Russian breads when I lived in Moscow in the late 1960s. As with all good things, it wasn't always available. News would spread on the grapevine if a certain bread shop had a batch of Borodinsky and it would sell out in minutes.

Officials at the museum of bread in St Petersburg deny that there is any direct evidence of a connection between this bread and the Battle of Borodino, but I heard of a radio broadcast in which a well-known food historian insisted that there was a link, if only in folklore. It doesn't really matter, because the story is a good one.

The village of Borodino was the site of a decisive battle when Russian forces confronted Napoleon just outside Moscow in 1812. Although Napoleon subsequently entered a

semi-deserted Moscow, he was harassed by Russian partisans and eventually lost most of his army in the winter retreat. So for Russians, the battle has a powerful patriotic significance. The story goes that, on the eve of the fight, the wife of a Russian general wanted to bake some special bread to encourage the troops. She found coriander ripening in the early September sun and crushed some seeds to flavour her loaves. And so it was that Borodinsky acquired a heroic status among breads, through association with a crucial event. If Britons took their bread as seriously as Russians, it might be Waterloo or Trafalgar Bread that adorned our shelves instead of ... 'Mother's Pride'.

In Russia the sweetness of Borodinsky is provided by a rye malt called *suslo*, which has the appearance and viscosity of old engine oil. I have substituted a mixture of molasses and barley malt, which comes fairly near to the real thing. If these are hard to find, ordinary black treacle will do, though it is not quite malty enough.

Eat Borodinsky in open sandwiches with smoked salmon or salted herring, savoury or sweet spreads, soups or salads. It keeps for a good week. Then try it toasted with bitter marmalade. Victory shall be yours.

Makes 1 small loaf

270g	Production Sourdough (see page 165)
230g	Rye flour (light or wholemeal)
5g	Sea salt
5g	Coarsely ground coriander seeds
20g	Molasses
15g	Barley malt extract
90g	Water (at 35°C)
635g	**Total**

Whole coriander seeds, to sprinkle in the tin

Coarsely ground coriander seeds, for the top of the loaf

Grease a small bread tin with butter or a hard vegetable fat. Sprinkle a few whole coriander seeds over the base of the tin. The grease should stop them rolling around and all gathering in one place, so it is a good idea to grease even non-stick tins for this bread.

Use the production sourdough 12–18 hours after it has been refreshed. Mix all the ingredients thoroughly into a smooth, soft dough. The mixture will be too sloppy to mould on the table so, wetting your hands and a plastic scraper, scoop it into a ball and smooth it into a loaf-shaped rectangle. Enjoy the slippery, mud-pie feeling and the fragrance of this wonderful dough. Drop the glistening pillow of dough very carefully into the greased tin, trying to avoid scraping any grease from the sides. The tin should be just over half full of dough at the beginning of proof. Do not be tempted to fiddle with the dough once it is in the tin, even if it has gone in a little lop-sided; it will find its own level. The most you should do is to smooth the surface of the dough if it looks very stippled or uneven. Wet your hand and use the back of your fingers for this. Never, incidentally, follow the fatuous advice to 'press the dough into the corners of the tin'. At best, this will destroy the shape you have carefully created by moulding. At worst, it will key the dough into the seams of the tin, making it much more likely to stick.

Leave the bread until it has risen up the tin appreciably. If it was just over halfway up when you put it in, it should reach the top of the tin when fully proved. This may take 2–6 hours, depending on the warmth of your kitchen and the vigour of your sourdough.

The lack of a tenacious gluten structure in all-rye breads means that the dough tends to split into a crazed pattern as it reaches full proof. This is nothing to worry about. If the dough surface has dried out (if you can touch it without any dough sticking to your finger), you will need to moisten it a little so that the coarsely ground coriander sticks. Do not be

tempted to spray the top with water because some will inevitably run down the sides of the tin, making it less likely that the loaf will come out after baking. Use a soft brush with some warm water and carefully moisten just the top of the loaf. Then sprinkle it generously with coarsely ground coriander.

Immediately put the loaf into a hot oven preheated to around 220°C, turning the heat down to 200°C after 10 minutes. Bake for about 40 minutes. Borodinsky takes more colour than plain rye breads because of the extra sugars in the shape of the molasses and malt. If your loaf is getting too dark, shield its top crust with a sheet or two of baking parchment towards the end of baking. The loaf may begin to shrink away from the sides of the tin when it is done. If it doesn't come out of its tin immediately, leave it to sweat for a few minutes, then try again. If it is still reluctant to move, slide a plastic scraper down between the loaf sides and the tin to break any sticking points.

Leave Borodinsky to cool completely before wrapping it in cellophane or a polythene bag. Rest it for a day before eating. You may notice that the crumb goes darker as the days pass. I don't know why this happens.

Troubleshooting 100 per cent rye breads

Breads made entirely with rye flour can produce their own distinctive challenges. Here are a few typical problems and ways of dealing with them:

Problem	Reason	Remedy
Sunken crust.	Dough too wet.	Add a little flour.
Big split down side of crust with the top crust beginning to lift; poor overall volume.	Dough too tight and dry.	Use more water.
	Insufficient proof.	Have patience; try to create warm, moist conditions for proof.

Problem	Reason	Remedy
Compressed core of dough at bottom or sides of loaf.	Excessive enzyme activity has softened gluten to the point where the pressure of fermentation gases is too great and the structure compacts.	Use production sourdough after shorter refreshment (6–8 hours); make dough a little stiffer and cooler; consider changing flour source or mix with a new source.

Caraway Rye Bread

Caraway is a popular flavour found in rye breads from Scandinavia to the Ukraine. In Moscow, Rizhsky (Riga) bread used to be second only to Borodinsky in bread lovers' estimation. This recipe is based on breads from Latvia and Estonia and is similar to the German *Schwarzbrot*, although that is not literally a black bread. It is a sourdough rye and wheat bread in which the two grains are present in equal quantities. The wheat flour gives the dough sufficient structure to make a freestanding loaf possible, though it can equally well be baked in a tin. Some traditions call for the use of a little baker's yeast in addition to the sourdough. I find that the extra yeast hurries the dough along too much and produces a drier, more crumbly texture, but if time is short this may be your only option.

A first rise is suggested for this bread in order to allow some ripening of the gluten from the wheat flours in the dough. There should be adequate flavour from the sourdough and the caraway.

Makes 1 large or 2 small loaves

350g Production Sourdough (see page 165)

150g Rye flour (light)

100g Stoneground strong wholemeal wheat flour

200g Strong white flour

10g	Caraway seeds
5g	Sea salt
200g	Water
1015g	**Total**

Use the production sourdough 8–18 hours after refreshment; the longer the time, the more pronounced the acidic flavour. Mix everything together into a soft dough, aiming to finish it at around 28°C.

Some kneading is required to develop the gluten in the wheat flour, but you will notice that the presence of the rye flour makes for a softer, stickier dough. If you intend to mould this as a freestanding loaf, you will need to tighten the dough up just a little so that it is possible to knead it on the worktop without too much sticking. However, if you prove it in a basket or cloth-lined bowl you can contain a very soft dough's tendency to flow. The softer the dough, the more open the internal structure and the more attractive the eating quality.

After initial kneading, cover the dough and allow it 1–2 hours to rise. If you are pushed for time, you can shorten or omit this stage. You will not notice much expansion even after 2 hours, but the wheat gluten will have relaxed and softened, making it easier to mould the dough. Divide the dough in half if you want small loaves. Gently press the dough into a rectangle and then roll it up towards you, finishing with a fat sausage.

For a freestanding loaf, deftly roll the sausage backwards and forwards a few times, with your hands moving gradually from the middle to the edges to form slightly tapered ends. Put the loaf or loaves on a baking tray and brush with a little water to ensure that the dough surface remains moist during proof.

To prove in a cloth-lined wicker basket or *panneton*, dust the lining of your basket well with rye flour or wholemeal wheat flour, dip the moulded dough piece into the same flour and lay it gently in the basket. What will eventually be the bottom of the loaf, which is the side with the seam created by rolling up the dough as it was moulded, should be facing upwards at this stage. Do not prod or poke the dough, even if it is lying a little unevenly: it will find its own level as it proves.

Enclose the basket or baking tray loosely in a polythene bag and put it in a warm place to prove, preferably with a little moisture, perhaps from a cup of boiled water placed next to the basket, to stop the dough surface drying out. Proof will take 2–4 hours, depending on the conditions and the vigour of your sourdough. When you judge the dough to have expanded to somewhere near its maximum extent without collapsing, tip the loaf gently out of the basket on to a baking tray. Depending on the type of basket used, the loaf may come out with attractive striations or the imprint of the lining material. If you want to keep these features, by all means do so. If, however, you want to create the slightly glossy, leathery crust typical of this kind of loaf, clear any loose flour from the surface of the dough and then gently brush it with warm water, taking care not to leave a 'tide mark' round the sides, but also avoiding a puddle on the tray.

Carefully cut the loaf with 5 or 6 slashes at an angle across the top. Try not to press down very much as you cut, otherwise the knife or blade may drag into the dough and cause some deflation of the structure.

Bake in a hot oven (230°C), reducing the heat to 210°C after 10 minutes or so. Large loaves will take about 45 minutes, small ones about 35 minutes. After baking, an immediate wash or spritz with hot water will soften and shine the crust a little. For a varnish-like finish, brush on the cornflour glaze on page 249.

Whole Grain Rye Bread

This style of bread is often described as pumpernickel. Although pumpernickel is usually made with rye, there are similar wholegrain breads in Denmark using coarsely kibbled wheat. A tasty and healthy variation is to include a proportion of sunflower seeds with the kibbled grain.

Try to use a tin that, when exactly full of dough, produces a brick-like shape with an almost square profile. Though by no means essential, this will produce nice-looking slices of bread. Incidentally, you should not be discouraged from making this bread by bad experiences with the foil-wrapped slices of cardboard bearing the name pumpernickel that languish on the shelves of healthfood shops and supermarkets. Pumpernickel-type breads have, to their great detriment, been categorised as 'long shelf-life' products. It is true that they keep well, even without preservatives, because of the lactic and acetic acids generated by the sourdough fermentation. But acidity prevents mould formation; it does not prevent the gradual hardening of starches that begins the moment bread is baked (unless it has been spiked with artificial enzymes). So by the time these thinly sliced breads reach the end of their six-month shelf life, they are practically mummified. If you bake your own, however, you will be able to enjoy wholegrain bread at its best – succulent, chewy-textured and nutritious.

Makes 1 large loaf

Preparing the grains

300g Boiling water

300g Coarse kibbled rye or wheat grain

600g Total

Pour the boiling water over the kibbled grain, stir, then cover and leave at warm room temperature for as long as possible so that the grain can absorb all the water. This procedure is best done at the same time as the sourdough is refreshed, i.e. at least 8 hours before assembling the bread.

Wholegrain dough

300 g	Rye Production Sourdough (page 165)
600 g	Soaked grains (above)
7 g	Sea salt
907 g	**Total**

Let the rye sourdough ferment for at least 8 hours, preferably 16–24 hours. Then mix it with the soaked grains and salt. The mixture will resemble wet concrete. Using wet hands, gather it into a lump, squish it roughly into a brick shape and drop it into a greased large loaf tin. Ideally, if smoothed out evenly, the mixture should come about two-thirds up the side of the tin. It will not rise very much, since there is not much flour to hold the gas generated by the fermentation.

Cover the top of the tin with a lid (e.g. an inverted baking tray, either greased or lined with baking parchment. Weight this lid down with a heavy, heatproof object such as an ovenproof dish. The idea is to get the bread to rise up to the top of the tin and press against the lid, forming a flat top. Baking under a lid also retains moisture, which would otherwise escape.

Rising time will depend on the vigour of your sourdough but is likely to take 2–3 hours. Take a quick look every hour or so to see how the dough is rising. It is ready to go in the oven when it is just about up to the top of the tin.

Slow baking is critical to this type of bread. The longer the bake and the lower the temperature, the darker the bread will be. In a range-type oven, bake overnight in the bottom oven. In conventional ovens, bake for at least 4 hours at 130°C or less. A dish of hot water in the oven will help maintain a slightly steamy atmosphere. It is possible to bake this bread without a lid and in a hotter oven but the kibbled grains on the surface of the bread tend to become as hard as flint and a danger to teeth – at least for a day or so until they soften up.

After baking, turn the loaf out of its tin and wrap it in a tea towel, which will recycle some of the escaping moisture into the loaf, ensuring that the outer crust is soft. The loaf will be grey rather than black and will look pretty much like what it is – a brick-shaped coagulation of coarse grains. But wait! After a day to stabilise the moisture and mature the flavour, slice the bread very thinly and serve with smoked fish, cream cheese or an olive tapenade – quite a different experience from the commercial alternatives.

Pumpernickel

Legend has it that this supposedly German word is a corruption of the French *pain pour Nicole*, the female in question being Napoleon's dog, who was evidently partial to a bit of rough. Whether there is any connection between the imperial canine's preference for wholegrain bread and French scientist Magendie's experiment showing that dogs fed white bread did not survive beyond 50 days, history does not record. Despite such exalted associations, this bread is probably of humbler origin. It is easy to see how, using whole grains and very little flour, it might have been a do-it-yourself expedient for farmers who had no access to a proper mill.

Most sourdough baking systems involve an intermediate step between the original starter and the final dough. This is what I refer to as a 'production' sourdough or leaven. The purpose of this stage is to allow the yeast population to multiply so that there are enough active cells to aerate the final dough.

However, it is possible to cut out this intermediate stage and to put your sourdough starter straight into the final dough. This is probably the simplest way of making sourdough bread.

Really Simple Sourdough Bread

This recipe shows that you can use a rye sourdough to raise a predominantly wheat bread (which could be useful if you have only a rye sour on the go), although it will work perfectly well with a piece of wheat leaven instead of the rye sour. It really doesn't get much simpler than this. Just take a bit of old rye sour, mix it with wholemeal flour, water and salt, put it in a tin and let it rise.

Compared to most of the breads in this chapter, this one uses a relatively small amount of initial sour or leaven, so the rise is slow because it takes some time for the yeast population to increase sufficiently to raise the dough.

Some experimentation will be required to establish the right combination of sourdough starter, temperature and time in your conditions. The process can be speeded up by using more starter, though this may result in a slightly stronger-flavoured (more acidic) bread. The quantity given in the recipe is designed to make it possible to start the dough in the evening and have it ready to bake first thing in the morning.

Makes 1 small loaf

40g	Rye Sourdough Starter (page 160)
175g	Water (at 35°C)
250g	Stoneground wholemeal flour
4g	Sea salt
469g	**Total**

To be on the safe side, use a rye sourdough starter that has been refreshed within the last fortnight or so. It is quite possible to get good results with stuff that has been hanging around in the fridge for ages, but its acidity may have reduced the population of viable yeast cells and it could take quite a while to perk up. If you don't have time to do a full refreshment, which really amounts to the same as making a 'production' sourdough (as described on page 165), do a mini-refreshment, by dispersing some of your very old sour in at least double its weight of wholemeal rye flour and water. It should be about 30°C and as sloppy as runny porridge. Give it 4 hours in a warm place if you can. If absolutely nothing has happened in that time, it will need longer, but you can expect to see some bubbling after a few hours as the yeasts start to ferment.

To make the bread, disperse your old (or refreshed) rye sourdough in the water and then mix in the flour and salt. Knead to develop the gluten and adjust the moisture so that the dough is very soft. Any structure that you create by tight moulding will largely subside during a long proof, so do not expect a fine-domed top to a loaf such as this. Place the dough in a greased small loaf tin, cover it and leave to rise. Do not put the tin in an especially warm place unless you want to hurry the process along. At an average kitchen temperature of about 20°C, this dough should rise in 10–12 hours.

Bake as for any normal tin bread, i.e. in a hot oven (about 230°C), reducing the temperature by about 30°C after 10 minutes or so. Since all the flour in this loaf has been fermented for a long period, the crumb will be markedly stickier immediately after baking than in a conventional leaven system such as French Country Bread (page 182), so it is better to leave it for a day before cutting it. Its keeping quality, however, is remarkable.

Even better, the science suggests that a long rise with lactic acid bacteria from the rye sour will neutralise almost all the phytic acid present in the wholemeal flour bran, making important minerals such as iron, magnesium, calcium and zinc more available to your body than they would be in an ordinary yeasted wholemeal bread.

Starting a wheat leaven

The procedure for starting a wheat leaven is almost exactly the same as for a rye sourdough. Again, all that is needed is flour and water.

I find that a firm leaven is easier to control than a wet one: it does not ferment quite so quickly, so there is less risk of it going too far too quickly, i.e. becoming too acidic and exhausting its yeast food, both of which conditions can affect the quality of the final dough. There is no compelling reason why you should not make a wheat leaven fairly sloppy like a rye sour. But if you do use more water in your leaven than suggested below, you may need to use slightly less water in the final doughs.

The procedures for handling a wheat leaven are much the same as for a rye sourdough (see page 160), so only the differences are described below:

Day 1

40g Stoneground wholemeal wheat flour

40g Water

80g Total

Keep this mixture as near to a constant 28°C as you can manage.

Day 2

40g Stoneground wholemeal wheat flour

40g Water

80g Starter from Day 1

160g Total

Day 3

40g Stoneground wholemeal wheat flour

20g Water

160g Starter from Day 2

220g Total

The water proportion is slightly reduced to tighten the dough up a bit.

Day 4

120g Strong white flour

100g Water

220g Starter from Day 3

440g Total

White flour is added on the fourth day to lighten the leaven a little. If you prefer to stick with wholemeal only, that is fine. After fermenting the Day 4 leaven for another 24 hours, you should have a leaven that smells slightly acidic and has risen appreciably (and probably collapsed).

What if nothing has happened?

If there are really no signs of life in your leaven, even after you have kept it in a warm place as suggested, it probably just needs more time to get going. Give it another refreshment by repeating Day 4 (discard 220g of your starter or put it in a separate tub and observe what happens to it). If it did show signs of life and then appears to have 'died', it may be that it has become too acidic at a stage when the number of yeast cells is still rather limited. In this case, it needs to be diluted with fresh flour, which will bring in some more yeast resources. So discard all but 130g of your starter and do a refreshment as follows:

 60g Stoneground wholemeal flour

120g Strong white flour

130g Water

130g Old Starter

440g Total

If that doesn't work, give it another go and if you still notice no life in the leaven at all, start again from the beginning with a fresh source of flour.

It is unusual for a starter to fail completely. One possible explanation, if low temperature can really be excluded, is over-cleanliness. From the chlorine in the water supply to the sanitisers and bacteriocides in household cleaning products, modern life is on a mission to exterminate all suspicious organisms. If you have been over-zealous in your domestic duties, traces of some fragrant biocide may have done for your leaven. Be sensibly clean, by all means, but lay off the chemicals. A doctor who came on one of my courses described how he routinely sterilised his utensils in a medical autoclave before making a leaven. I persuaded him to abandon this overkill and his leavens never looked back. In harnessing the power of wild yeasts and beneficial bacteria, we are only repeating what generations of our forebears practised long before sterile conditions were understood, let alone possible. We are lucky that in natural fermentations of flour and water, the bacteria that predominate are almost always those that do us good, not harm. Leave them to it, I say.

Assuming that you have got a viable leaven, it can now be put to work making bread. With a wheat leaven, the cycle of refreshment is different from a rye sour. The stages are the same – starter, production leaven, final dough – but the quantities and timing are different. A wheat starter seeds a production leaven only three times its size (not ten) and the production leaven is fermented for only four hours, even less in hot weather.

French Country Bread

This is a straightforward way of making the classic *pain de campagne*, or just a simple, naturally fermented wheat bread. It can be made with all white flour or combinations of white and wholemeal, according to taste. While the basic dough makes a terrific everyday bread in its own right, it can also form the basis of a host of interesting variations, some of which are suggested below.

Although this bread is usually baked as a flattish round loaf on the bottom of the oven, there is no reason why it should not be baked in a tin. If you make the dough as soft as the recipe suggests, you may find a tin loaf coming out fairly flat topped, but this can be corrected by tightening the dough up just a little with extra flour. Don't expect the crumb to be close-textured and even, like a British sliced loaf. It will be more open and uneven – and infinitely more tasty.

The instructions here assume that you make this bread in one sequence with the doughs at ambient temperature, in which case the whole process, from beginning the leaven refreshment to taking the baked loaf out of the oven, will take 9–11 hours. However, it is possible to adjust the timing in various ways; see page 200 for some suggestions.

Makes 1 large loaf

Stage 1: Refreshing the leaven

160g*	Wheat Leaven Starter (from above)
50g	Stoneground wholemeal flour
150g	Strong white flour
120g	Water
480g	**Total production leaven**

Mix everything together into a fairly firm dough at about 27°C. If your starter was very wet, you may need to add a little more flour at this stage. Cover and leave in a warm place for 4 hours. In very warm weather, this period of refreshment may need to be reduced to 3 hours or even less. The production leaven is ready when it has expanded appreciably but not collapsed on itself.

---

* You may well have more starter than this. As with excess rye sour, you can either freeze the excess wheat starter, give some away, put it in the compost bin or use it to flavour another dough (at up to 10 per cent of the dough weight).

Stage 2: Making the final dough

100g	Stoneground wholemeal flour
300g	Strong white flour
7g	Sea salt
300g	Water
300g*	Production Leaven (from above)
1007g	**Total**

Mix a dough with all the ingredients except the refreshed production leaven. Make the dough pretty soft and aim for a temperature of about 28°C. Knead until the gluten is making itself felt and the dough is becoming smooth and elastic. About 8–10 minutes of vigorous action should see some changes. Then add the production leaven and work it into the dough until it is smooth. At this stage, the softness of the dough can be adjusted by additions of water or flour. If you are going to prove this dough in a basket, do try to keep it very soft. Even at the end of kneading (after another few minutes), the dough should not be so dry that it does not stick to your hands or the bench.

Smear some water over a clean area of worktop and lay your dough down on it, covering the whole thing with a clean upturned bowl whose inside rim has also been moistened with water. Wait an hour, during which time the gluten will relax and soften and the yeasts will begin to aerate the bubble structure inside the dough. Then, with wet hands and a couple of plastic scrapers, stretch and fold the dough. With one scraper in each hand, slip them under the middle of the dough, gently prising it from the table if it has stuck. Lifting the dough very slightly, stretch it away from you as far as it will go without forcing it and then fold it back on itself and let it rest on

---

* The remaining 180g or so of refreshed production leaven goes back into the pot and becomes the 'old starter', to be kept for another cycle of refreshment and breadmaking. For advice on looking after your starter, see 'What do I do with my sourdough between baking sessions?' on page 204.

the main body of dough. Do this again, this time getting hold of the 'front' part of the dough piece and pulling it towards you before folding it back on top of the main body of dough. Repeat the action, stretching the dough to your right and then finally to your left. You should end up with a tighter, more vertical pile of dough. The object of this folding action is to thin the gluten membrane by stretching it, allowing a greater subsequent expansion of the dough, at the same time squeezing as little gas out of it as possible.

Have a bowl of wholemeal flour ready. Pick the dough up and dip it gently in the flour, turning it over to ensure that it gets completely covered. Then transfer it to a floured proving basket with the seam (or more ragged) side of the dough facing upwards. Cover the whole basket with a large polythene bag, inflated so that it cannot touch the dough, and put it in a warm place to prove for 3–5 hours.

When it looks as though it has expanded a fair amount, test the dough with gentle finger pressure. This dough is going to be subjected to some indignity when you turn it out of its basket on to a baking tray, so it is best not to let it prove until it is fully aerated and quivering like a jelly. It is ready to be baked when an indentation made by your finger disappears fairly slowly, indicating that the pressure of gas in the dough may be passing its peak.

Line a baking tray with baking parchment. Invert the basket with a fairly quick action but be careful not to clatter the dough on to the baking tray – or you may hear a reproachful sigh as gas escapes from the ruptured loaf. Make 2 or 3 cuts in the top of the loaf and then put it into an oven preheated to about 220°C. Reduce the heat to around 200°C after about 10 minutes. Bake for about 40 minutes to ensure a good, deeply coloured, firm crust.

Variations

- Instead of strong white flour, try using some plain flour (perhaps from English wheat) to change the quality of the gluten in the dough. If you can get hold of a French T65 or T110, or an Italian-style ciabatta flour, these may also provide the kind of very extensible but not very strong gluten that is ideal for French Country Bread. The effect of using weaker flour may be to make the crumb structure more random. The wetter the dough, the chewier the crumb will be.

• Try substituting 50g wholemeal rye flour for the same weight of white flour in the production leaven. Even a small amount of rye can assist the production of gluten-ripening substances and contribute to extra moistness in the crumb.

Hop Bread

'The flowers make bread light and the lumpe to be sooner and easilier leavened, if the meale be tempered with liquor wherein they have been boiled.'

JOHN GERARDE, *The Herball or Generall Historie of Plants* (1597)

Brewing and baking are kindred crafts, united in their dependence on yeast fermentation. Bakers often used residues of brewer's yeast to start their sponges. So it is not surprising that people have periodically tried to revive an ancient fellowship by enriching bread with some of the flavours of the brewery. Typically, they substitute beer for some or all of the dough water.

Coming across Gerarde's observation about hops, I wondered whether it would be possible to put all the essential flavours of beer into bread without actually using the liquid itself. The recipe that follows is based on the basic wheat leaven given above. Incidentally, I take issue with Gerarde. In my experience, hops *slow down* the yeast fermentation. They contain strong essential oils and aromatic acids called humulones. These have a preservative (antifungal) effect in beer, which makes it likely that they would inhibit the action of yeast to some extent. But, apart from its delicious malty, hoppy flavour, this bread does keep mould-free for a remarkably long time.

You can buy hops from home-brewing shops. The amount of hops in the recipe is very small, but their flavour is pronounced and can easily be overdone. The malty flavour of beer is provided by malt extract.

Makes 1 small loaf

Ye hop water

1g	Hops
120g	Boiling water
121g	**Total**

Add the hops to the boiling water in a saucepan. Cover and simmer for 10 minutes. Cool and strain off the hops; you should have about 115g liquid.

Ye hop bread dough

50g	Stoneground wholemeal flour
130g	Strong white flour
3g	Sea salt
115g	Hop water (from above)
30g	Barley malt syrup
180g	Production Leaven (page 183)
508g	**Total**

Cracked wheat (or wholemeal flour or jumbo oats) for dipping

Make a dough with all the ingredients except the refreshed leaven. Knead until smooth and stretchy. Then add the leaven and work it into the dough until smooth. Mould into a round cob and dip in cracked wheat to cover the entire loaf. If you have made the dough too tight and dry and the cracked wheat does not stick, moisten the surface and try again.

This dough may take a good bit longer than ordinary French Country Bread to rise – up to 7 hours – so it is best to prove it in a basket.

When it is ready, turn it out of its basket (as described for French Country Bread above) and bake it in a fairly hot oven at around 200°C for 30–40 minutes, reducing the heat a little after 10 minutes. The malt content of the dough will make it take more colour than a plain loaf, so a really hot oven may burn it.

Broon Geordie

In the mid-1990s some bakers in northeast England made a bread called something like Broon Geordie, using Newcastle Brown Ale. They brought it over the Pennines each morning and put it on the lorry taking our bread to Waitrose. The problem with most beer breads is that an awful lot of liquor is needed to carry any flavour through the baking process and this gets pretty expensive. In my view, it's also a waste of good ale to evaporate all the alcohol in a loaf of bread.

Fruit and Nut Leaven Bread

Based on the French Country Bread dough, this recipe makes a loaf that is a meal in itself and, with the help of the succulent fruits, keeps for ages. If you cannot get hold of all the fruits and nuts specified, use what you have to hand. It is always a good idea to soak dried fruit before using it in bread to prevent it 'robbing' moisture from the dough itself. I recommend soaking the nuts, too, which gives them an almost buttery eating quality.

Makes 1 large cob

The fruit and nut mix

50g Dried figs

35g Dates

35g Prunes

35g Hazelnuts

35g Brazil nuts

35g Walnuts or cashew nuts

50g Water (any temperature)

275g Total

Chop the figs, dates and prunes into halves or quarters. Mix all the fruits and nuts together and put them into a strong polythene bag. Add the water, seal the bag and swirl it around to get everything wet. Try to do this a couple of times at intervals. Leave the bag at ambient temperature overnight, or for at least 4 hours. If you are in a hurry, use hot water.

Fruit and nut leaven bread dough

70g Stoneground wholemeal flour

200g Strong white flour

5g Sea salt

190g Water

200g Production Leaven (page 183)

275g Fruit and Nut Mix (from above)

940g Total

Make a dough with the flours, salt and water. Knead until smooth and elastic. Add the refreshed leaven and knead a little more until you have a fairly soft, springy dough. Put this back in the bowl, cover it and leave for about an hour. This allows the gluten (and you) to relax and the yeast to begin inflating the dough. Not a great deal of effect will be visible in an hour, but it will be much easier to add the fruit and nut mix at this stage than it would have been immediately after kneading.

Strain off any free liquid from the fruit and nuts and then tip them into the dough bowl. Gently fold the dough over, trying to envelop the fruits and nuts rather than force them into the dough. Go for a reasonable dispersion rather than complete evenness of distribution, which tends to come at the cost of breaking the dough up into a sticky mess.

Using a little flour on your hands and perhaps a tiny bit on the worktop, mould the dough into a round cob, pulling it quite tight so that it sits upright. During proof it will inevitably flow out fairly flat, but a bolder shape can be retained if the initial moulding process succeeds in creating some tension around the circumference of the loaf which will, as it were, 'hold in' the bulging insides. In your moulding, try to finish up with not too many bits of fruit or nut sticking out of the top of the loaf because these will tend to get overbaked. You can pick out the worst offenders and push them into the bottom of the loaf before putting it on to a baking tray lined with baking parchment.

Prove for 3–5 hours and bake at about 200°C, reducing the heat a little after 10 minutes. The whole loaf is so streaked with fruits and nuts that it will take colour quicker than a plain dough. If the top shows signs of getting too dark, shield it with a couple of sheets of baking parchment for the last few minutes of baking. This is a fairly big loaf, so it will take about 40 minutes to bake.

Arkatena Bread

If you like bread with a hefty crust, chewy crumb and intense flavour, this one is for you. It is like French Country Bread gone rustic. It is amazing what a difference the addition of a small amount of chickpea flour can make to a bread.

On a working trip to Cyprus, I visited a village bakery near Limassol. The area is known for bread and rolls called *arkatena* and made with a natural fermentation of chickpeas. In the bakery I was so amazed at the enormous tub of heaving, billowing leaven that I completely forgot to ask how it was made. In any case, it isn't really the done thing to waltz into a small bakery and ask for its trade secrets. I remembered reading in the Slow Food journal the memoir of a woman who described her Cypriot grandmother soaking chickpeas and somehow generating the yeast for a distinctive local bread. I suspect that this baking tradition is largely domestic, so I had to devise a recipe of my own.

Chickpea or gram flour seems to be teeming with yeasts because it ferments in no time at all. Within a day of mixing it with warm water it will be active. For the first day or two it smells, frankly, rather uninviting, but with the addition of some wheat flour on the third day it settles down to a pleasant acidity, with a hint of beany aroma from the chickpeas.

I am not sure if the addition of fennel seeds to the final dough is authentic – probably not. But they work well with the wonderfully chewy texture produced by this leaven. There is only about 5 per cent chickpea flour in the final dough, enough for a modest nutritional gain (chickpeas are a good source of folate and copper). This could be increased a little, but beyond a certain point a beany flavour begins to intrude.

Starting an arkatena leaven

The procedure is the same as for rye sourdough on page 160.

Day 1

30g Chickpea (gram) flour

40g Water

70g Total

Keep this mixture as near to a constant 28°C as you can manage.

Day 2

70g Starter from Day 1

30g Chickpea (gram) flour

40g Water

140g Total

Day 3

140g	Starter from Day 2
80g	Stoneground wholemeal flour
60g	Water
280g	**Total**

After a further few hours' fermentation, you should have a lively arkatena starter. You will need only 160g of this to make the recipe that follows. Throw away the remainder, or freeze it, or use it in small amounts in other breads.

Making arkatena bread

Makes 1 large cob

Stage 1: the production leaven

160g	Arkatena Starter (from above)
50g	Stoneground wholemeal flour
50g	Chickpea (gram) flour
150g	Strong white flour
120g	Water
530g	**Total**

Mix everything together into a softish dough at about 27°C. Cover and leave in a warm place for 4 hours. In very warm weather, or if your leaven is very lively, this period of refreshment may need to be reduced to 3 hours or even less. The production leaven is ready when it has expanded appreciably but not collapsed on itself.

Stage 2: arkatena dough

100g	Stoneground wholemeal flour
300g	Strong white flour
7g	Sea salt
300g	Water
20g	Fennel seeds
300g	Production Leaven (from above)
1027g	**Total**

Make a dough with all the ingredients except the fennel seeds and the production leaven. Keep it soft and work it until the gluten develops and feels elastic. Add the fennel seeds and the refreshed leaven and give the dough another few minutes' kneading. It should be very soft.

Treat it from here in all respects like a French Country Bread (see pages 182–185). Final proof may be shorter than for French Country Bread because the arkatena leaven is a bit livelier.

After baking, let the bread cool completely before you cut it. You will struggle not to wolf several slices of this delicious bread one after another, so they should at least be cool.

Starting a spelt leaven

One of the easiest flours with which to start a natural fermentation is spelt. In its wholemeal version, it seems to carry a generous population of yeasts and bacteria and should reach a usable state in only a few days. As you will have gathered, the start-up sequence is pretty much the same for any sourdough or leaven: mix the flour with some water, keep it warm, add some more from time to time until the organisms are reproducing and fermenting vigorously. For more details, see Starting a rye sourdough on page 160.

Here is how to start a spelt leaven.

Days 1 and 2

50g	Wholemeal spelt flour
100g	Water
150g	**Total**

Keep this mixture as near to a constant 28°C as you can manage. Ferment for 2 days.

Day 3

150g	Starter from Days 1–2
50g	Wholemeal spelt flour
50g	Water
250g	**Total**

At the end of another day, this leaven should be fermenting nicely. If it is not, give it another Day 3 treatment, tuck it up in a warm place and await developments.

Spelt Bread

I live about 30 miles from Hadrian's Wall, as the screaming jet flies. At various points along the wall, excavations have revealed evidence of granaries, drying kilns, mills and bakeries. When I became aware of spelt and its significance in the food economy of Ancient Rome, I realised that I could probably make a bread similar to that which was eaten by the legions stationed not far from my bakery 1,800 years earlier. The drying kilns were a clue to the kind of flour used: they would have been needed to roast spelt grain because it is a 'covered' wheat, whose husks do not fall off at threshing time. Roman ovens would have been fired with wood, as was mine. Their bread was fermented without the use of baker's yeast, as was mine. The mechanical dough mixer was the only aspect of our breadmaking that a Roman would not recognise. Then my Classicist brother dug out a recipe from Pliny, which described a bread made with spelt and the juice of raisins.

I am sure that demand for the resulting product had less to do with my fanciful historical musings than the still largely unexplained fact that people who found commercial yeasted wheat bread made them unwell were able to enjoy spelt bread with impunity.

The raisin juice is an optional addition, which provides a little sweetness to counter spelt's sometimes bitter flavour. It may also provide some fermentable sugars to aid the leavening process. The result is a hearty wholemeal loaf with a markedly stronger flavour than bread made with modern wheat.

Makes 1 large cob

Spelt production leaven

150g Spelt Starter (from above)

200g Wholemeal spelt flour

120g Water

470g Total

Mix everything together into a softish dough at about 27°C. Cover and leave in a warm place for 4 hours. In very warm weather, or if your leaven is very lively, this period of refreshment may need to be reduced to 3 hours or even less. The production leaven is ready when it has expanded appreciably but not collapsed on itself. At the same time as you refresh the leaven, prepare the raisin mush:

Raisin mush

50g	Boiling water
50g	Raisins
100g	**Total**

Pour the boiling water on to the raisins and let them steep for half an hour or longer. Then whiz them into a fine mush in a blender.

Spelt bread dough

400g	Wholemeal spelt flour
7g	Sea salt
100g	Raisin Mush (from above)
200g	Water
300g	Production Leaven (from above)
1007g	**Total**

Make a dough with all the ingredients except the production leaven. It will feel quite coarse and stodgy at first, but a few minutes' kneading will bring a change to the gluten and the dough will hold together better. Add the refreshed spelt leaven and give the dough another few minutes' kneading. It should finish fairly soft – a bit less so if you intend to prove it freestanding on a baking tray.

Treat it from here like French Country Bread (see pages 182–185) but the final proof will be a bit shorter. Do not expect enormous expansion of the dough. Spelt gluten is not all that strong and the bran in the flour does interfere with the formation of big gas bubbles.

Too many sourdoughs?

This chapter has, so far, described how to produce four different types of sourdough or leaven: rye, wheat, chickpea and spelt. Despite their obvious similarities, there is a danger that my initial claim – that sourdoughs are easy – will be belied by such a proliferation. Pausing only to defend myself with the observation that all these sours are simply flour and water left around for a while, I offer a solution for the home baker who would rather limit the number of tubs festering in the kitchen.

The one and only

The answer is to keep only a rye sourdough going permanently. In my experience, a rye sourdough is the easiest to get going, the quickest to regenerate and the most resilient. Any of the other leavens can be quick-started with a small amount of rye sourdough. For instance, instead of starting a spelt leaven from scratch, which would take at least 4 days according to the schedule given above, you can get one going overnight. The sequence and quantities would look like this:

Rye-seeded spelt leaven

20g Old Rye Sourdough Starter (page 160)

70g Wholemeal spelt flour

60g Water

150g Total rye-spelt starter

Keep this mixture as near to a constant 28°C as you can manage. Ferment for 12–24 hours. This then becomes the Spelt Starter in Stage 1 of the Spelt Production Leaven on page 195. The rye sour content of the refreshed Spelt Production Leaven is only 4.2 per cent and it is only 1.27 per cent of the final spelt dough, so the rye flour will not have any negative effect on the texture of the loaf. Indeed, small amounts of rye flour actually benefit the handling and eating quality of wheat and spelt doughs.

The same principle can be applied to any sourdough or leaven. Purists might argue that the yeasts and lactobacilli in rye are subtly different from those in other grains and flours and they may be right. But starting a wheat leaven with an initial population of organisms from a rye sour clearly works and does not preclude the probability that other yeasts and bacteria would emerge if that leaven were henceforth to be refreshed only with wheat flour.

The next loaf shows how easy it is to use a basic rye sourdough to make wheat bread – and how good it can be.

Cromarty Cob

This recipe may have come about because of my forgetfulness, but it has become one of my favourite ways of making bread. It is just so easy and the result is a loaf of wonderful flavour with a terrific crust.

In Cromarty, on the Black Isle just north of Inverness, Sutor Creek community restaurant serves wonderful pizzas from a wood-fired oven built by my Cumbrian colleague, Alf Armstrong. I was invited to run a breadmaking course for local people in the restaurant. I arrived the evening before and realised that I had forgotten to bring my wheat leaven starter. There was no time to create another one from scratch but a naturally leavened French Country Bread was one of my key course recipes. What to do? As I was stirring fresh flour into the rye sourdough that would be used for Borodinsky the next day, I realised that the solution was literally in my hands. Why not use some rye sour to refresh a wheat leaven? It worked perfectly. It is true that relief at not having my forgetfulness exposed may have coloured my judgement, but the Cromarty loaf seemed to have a particularly delicious chewy crumb and tangy crust.

So this recipe shows how an old rye sourdough starter can be used to refresh a wheat leaven and make a light wheat loaf. The rye flour content of the final dough is less than 5 per cent, but the lactic acid bacteria brought in with the original rye sourdough have a significant effect on the flavour of the bread. I have suggested using a mixture of strong white and plain white flour in the final dough in order to produce a weaker, more extensible gluten structure. This could equally well be done by using a white flour stoneground (and sifted) from English wheat, or indeed a French T110 flour. If you prefer a more intensely flavoured and more nutritious bread, use more wholemeal in the leaven and some or all in the final dough.

The production leaven

150g	Rye Sourdough Starter (page 160)
100g	Stoneground wholemeal flour
100g	Strong white flour
100g	Water
450g	**Total**

The rye sourdough starter does not have to have been recently refreshed. Provided that you are confident that it has at some time been a reasonably vigorous sour, it should revive quickly once it has access to fresh flour and warmth.

Mix everything together into a fairly firm dough at about 27°C. Cover and leave in a warm place for 3–4 hours. This rye-started leaven may ferment a bit quicker than an all-wheat one. It is ready when it has expanded appreciably, but try to use it before it has collapsed back on itself.

Cromarty cob dough

200g	Strong white flour
200g	Plain white flour
7g	Sea salt
300g	Water
300g	Production Leaven (from above)
1007g	**Total**

Make a dough with all the ingredients except the refreshed production leaven. Knead until the gluten is showing good signs of development. Then add the refreshed leaven and continue kneading for a few more minutes. At the end of kneading the dough should be soft and stretchy and coming away from your hands, but it should not be so firm that it doesn't stick to the worktop if left for a few seconds.

Moisten an area of worktop with water, put the dough down on it and cover it with a bowl. From this point, fold, mould and prove as for French Country Bread (page 184–185). When you tip the proved dough out of its basket on to a baking tray or peel (a baker's flat shovel for sliding loaves into the oven), cut it with a single large 'C', for Cromarty. Curved cuts are a bit tricky, but this one will make a nice break in the top crust – and it will be a kind of homage to the good people of Sutor Creek and their wood-fired oven.

Making sourdoughs work in real life

Sourdoughs and leavens may be fundamentally simple to make, as I hope I have demonstrated, but fitting this kind of breadmaking into domestic life takes a bit of figuring out. Once you get your head round the basic sequence of events, you can decide when to start (or aim to finish) the process of making a naturally fermented bread.

Even now, if I have a dough to prepare for a course or a new product experiment, I write down on a scrap of paper the sequence of starter refreshment, production sourdough and final dough with approximate timings. I find it helps to keep me straight. Below are some typical timings as examples that you may wish to follow, and also to show how you can control the process by adjusting the dough temperature.

The basic sequences for making bread with a rye sourdough or a wheat leaven at normal kitchen temperatures go like this:

RYE SOURDOUGH SYSTEM

Sourdough refreshment	20 hours
Mix and shape	15 minutes
Prove	3 hours
Bake	45 minutes
Total	**24 hours**

WHEAT LEAVEN SYSTEM

Leaven refreshment	4 hours
Mix, rest, fold and shape	1 hour 15 minutes
Prove	5 hours
Bake	45 minutes
Total	**11 hours**

The timelines below show how this works in real life. These are, of course, only guideline timings. A rye sourdough can be used to make a final dough at any time after about four hours, depending on the temperature and the liveliness of its yeast population. The yeasts tend to reproduce and ferment quicker than the lactic acid bacteria, so a young sourdough will be noticeably less acidic. Similarly a wheat leaven may be ready to use in as little as two and a half hours in very warm weather. Proof times, too, will vary with the ambient temperature and the general vigour of the sour or leaven being used.

I use the 24-hour clock because it makes it easier to keep track of day and night. Obviously the start times are just suggestions and can be changed at will.

CLASSIC RYE SOURDOUGH SYSTEM

Day 1	2200	Refresh sourdough
Day 2	1800	Mix dough and shape
	1815	Begin proof at 27–30°C
	2115	Into oven
	2200	Loaf baked

CLASSIC WHEAT LEAVEN SYSTEM

0800	Refresh leaven
1200	Mix dough and rest
1315	Shape and begin proof at 25–28°C
1815	Into oven
1900	Loaf baked

The rye system would work quite well for someone who is out all day. You refresh your sour one evening and then make bread the next evening. The only risk is that if the bread is slow to prove, you may have a late night. What happens, however, if you refresh your sourdough at ten o'clock one night, intending to make rye bread the following evening, but you are unexpectedly delayed and do not get home until ten? If you leave the sourdough for another day, it could get too acidic and the yeasts might lose vigour. If you do another refreshment you will have ten times as much refreshed sour as you want, or you will have to throw some away. The alternative is to make the dough at ten o'clock at night (it takes only a few minutes if it's a rye bread), and prove the bread slowly in a cool room or in the fridge. With a bit of luck, it will have risen by morning and you can put it straight in the oven and have it baked before going out. The timeline would look like this:

RYE SOURDOUGH SYSTEM – CHILLED PROOF

Day 1	2200	Refresh sourdough
Day 2	2200	Mix dough
	2230	Begin proof at 5–8°C
Day 3	0730	Into oven
	0815	Loaf baked

The rye sourdough refreshment, which was arbitrarily fixed at 20 hours in the ambient example above, can in fact last from four to 24 hours, providing considerable extra flexibility. The beauty of the rye sour is that it does not have to be slowed down by chilling at the refreshment stage because some extra acidity in the final dough will not affect the dough structure, merely its flavour.

The wheat leaven is different. If a wheat production leaven is over-fermented, it will bring too many acids into the final dough and the gluten will be quickly over-ripened. This causes a breakdown of the dough structure, which results in a ragged, sticky, poorly risen loaf. So, if the leaven refreshment period of four hours at ambient temperature does not fit in with your plans, you can extend this to 12 to 24 hours in the fridge. A cold leaven and ambient final dough system might look like this:

WHEAT LEAVEN SYSTEM – CHILLED LEAVEN, AMBIENT PROOF

Day 1	2300	Refresh leaven at 5°C
Day 2	1600	Mix dough at 27°C and rest
	1715	Shape and begin proof at 25–28°C
	2215	Into oven
	2300	Loaf baked

This lengthens the leaven refreshment stage to 17 hours, but it still requires the main dough to be made early in the evening if the bread is going to be out of the oven at a reasonable time. If the proof time, too, is extended by using a lower temperature, it becomes possible to have both the long processes (leaven refreshment and proof) occurring at times when you are either asleep or out.

The following timing has a 12-hour overnight leaven refreshment and a 12-hour daytime proof. If the bread has not fully proved by the time you get in at night, you can always finish it off with a little warmth.

WHEAT LEAVEN SYSTEM – CHILLED LEAVEN, CHILLED PROOF

Day 1	1900	Refresh leaven at 5°C
Day 2	0700	Mix dough at 5–10°C and rest
	0815	Shape and begin proof at 5–8°C
	2015	Into oven
	2100	Loaf baked

These are, I stress, indicative timings only. The one thing that can be said for certain about natural fermentations is that they are not completely predictable. But they do have the great advantage that they are generally slow, and can be made even slower with judicious temperature adjustments.

What the above timings do show is that slow baking is not incompatible with a busy life. And if the gratification seems rather delayed, remember that slow bread is more nutritious, more digestible, better flavoured and longer keeping than its fast-fermented counterparts.

What do I do with my sourdough between baking sessions?

I encounter many able and enthusiastic bakers, both domestic and professional, on the courses that I run. Quite a few of these are intimidated by sourdoughs, not least because looking after them seems to be such a hassle. This widespread perception is not dispelled by baking books that treat leavens and sourdoughs as if they need constant and fiddly attention. The notion of 'feeding' a sourdough may be the source of the problem. If empathy spills over into anthropomorphism, it is easy to see how people might worry that they are doing something wrong as their precious sourdough declines into a dormant sludge. It is only human to associate health with some signs of active life. So they fuss and poke, sprinkle and stir, or suffer pangs of remorse as 'feeds' are missed. People have recounted to me the demise of their sourdough in terms that could hardly be more guilt-ridden if they were confessing to starving the family cat. There's probably a psychotherapist somewhere doing a roaring trade in sourdough bereavement counselling.

All this angst is unnecessary. You need only think about your sourdough when you want to make a batch of bread. No hassle and no stress.

Once a sourdough or leaven is established, it is generally in one of two phases – maintenance or production. In the maintenance phase, a quantity of sourdough is held (in or outside a refrigerator) as a reservoir of yeasts and bacteria. In the production phase, it is refreshed with the addition of new flour and water. The greater part of this refreshed sourdough is used to produce bread, with the unused part returning to the maintenance phase until it is next needed for production.

Instead of 'feeding' the sourdough, we are incorporating it all into a bigger entity, the production sourdough. The piece that we keep back as a future starter is therefore a mixture of the old sour and the fresh flour and water. This is important because it guarantees that when an old sour is refreshed, a correct balance of old and new material is maintained. By contrast, the problem with 'feeding' is that if you simply make small regular additions of flour and water to a permanent stock sourdough, you are likely to cause a build-up of acidity, which will make it progressively more difficult for the yeasts to thrive.

One solution to the latter problem that I have come across is periodically to 'wash' your starter, which is a way of diluting its acidity and giving the yeasts a better chance. But this is yet another job waiting to be overlooked, another breeding ground for guilt and a great big waste of time.

Constructive neglect

So, the question that everyone baking with sourdough wants answered is: what do I do with it between bakes?

To which I respond: as little as possible, provided that it will still work when you next want to use it. That may be tomorrow, next week or in a month's time and the gap between outings will dictate your intervening treatment. First, a few principles, and then a simple look-up table as a guide to future action.

When a sourdough is left unrefreshed, first the yeasts, then the lactobacilli run out of nutrients; some of the yeast cells will die if the acidity goes beyond a certain point, others will go into a dormant state, as will the bacteria. The speed at which this occurs is dependent on temperature. If a sour is left in warm conditions it will grow more acid more quickly and it may also fall prey to extraneous moulds. So, if more than two or three days are likely to pass before the sourdough is used again, it is best to store it in the fridge. In this, as in other ways, rye sours are more tolerant than wheat leavens, but the basic idea is the same for both.

If your sour was viable when you last used it, it should keep for many weeks and revive easily. I keep (in the fridge) a bucket of old rye sourdough that is many months old; all I ever do to it is stir in the grey-brown liquid that settles on the surface and scoop out about 50g of sour to demonstrate how easy it is to maintain a sourdough. I never add fresh flour to this old sour. I take this icy-cold, not very fragrant 50g and mix it with 150g wholemeal rye flour and 300g very warm water. I cover it and leave it in the bakery, which is usually at about 25°C. Without fail, 16 hours later, I have a bubbling, pleasant-smelling, utterly normal refreshed rye sourdough. It is as simple as that.

Broadly the same holds for a wheat leaven. However, the usual four-hour period for a wheat refreshment may be insufficient for a really dormant old leaven to come to life again, in which case it may be worth leaving it to ferment for a bit longer.

Intermediate refreshment

If you have doubts about the viability of your old sour, you may want some prior assurance that it really will work before you commit to a full baking session. This is easily achieved by doing an extra refreshment the day before you would otherwise have begun the baking cycle. There is one problem: by doing two refreshments instead of one, you may end up with more sourdough than you want. So, you either make a bigger batch of bread, or you give or throw away some of your sourdough. Alternatively, you could freeze the unwanted portion, making a note of what stage it had reached. This could be used at a later date if a sudden increase in production were called for, or if some disaster had befallen your day-to-day sour.

If you think you are unlikely to use a wheat leaven for more than a fortnight or a rye sourdough for more than a month, it is probably best to freeze them. Freezing tends to reduce the power of the natural yeasts, if not the bacteria, so it is wise to refresh a sour immediately before putting it in the freezer and to give it an intermediate refreshment after it comes out, just to make sure that it has regained full vigour. You will need to work out what to do with the extra sourdough thus generated.

Storing leavens and sourdoughs

Type of fermentation	How long until next use?	Where to keep it	Special treatment
Wheat leaven	0–2 days	Store at ambient temperature	
	2–14 days	Store in fridge at 5°C	Optional intermediate refreshment before use

Type of fermentation	How long until next use?	Where to keep it	Special treatment
Wheat leaven *Cont.*	Over 14 days	Store in freezer	Intermediate refreshment before and after freezing
Rye sourdough	0–3 days	Store at ambient temperature	
	3–30 days	Store in fridge at 5°C	
	Over 30 days	Store in freezer	Intermediate refreshment before and after freezing

CHAPTER EIGHT
BREAD –
A MEAL
IN ITSELF

'"And they were filled", the Bible says.
No simpler words can be written to describe
happiness, satisfaction, gratitude.'
H. E. JACOB,
Six Thousand Years of Bread
(Lyons Press, 1944)

Once you have mastered a basic loaf, it won't be long before you feel like branching out. How about a light savoury bread, flavoured with olives, tomatoes, cheese or nuts? Suddenly, bread is liberated from the servile role of carrier to take its time-honoured place as the heart of a meal.

When you make flavoured breads you can be creative, you can indulge your favourite tastes, you can adapt breads to fit with specific dishes and you can take care of your nutritional concerns while making breads that are guaranteed to win over the most sceptical of families or friends.

How things have changed. Until the early 1990s, a flavoured bread usually meant, in the UK at least, a dough with added sugar, egg, fruit or spice. We liked teacakes, spicy buns and fruity malt loaf, but we preferred our savoury flavours *with* bread, not *in* it.

Then came the Mediterranean diet. We knew about pizza, of course, but travellers and food writers told of flat slabs of porous bread with an oily topping of herbs or local summer vegetables. Focaccia and *schiacciata* tied our tongues and tickled our taste buds.

Some bakers saw 'speciality bread' as a licence to put ever weirder combinations of bits into some pretty indifferent doughs. But the flavoured breads that have stood the test of time have been those in which the savoury element complements the texture and taste of the dough.

In this chapter I describe a basic dough that works well with a wide variety of savoury additions and I suggest ways of incorporating vegetable mixtures into the dough. This may seem obvious, but simply chucking in a load of Med Veg can produce a loaf with a strong resemblance to roadkill. However, with a sound basic dough and some idea about textures and flavours, there is no limit to the tasty and nutritious combinations that are possible in savoury breads. Perhaps they will inspire your creativity, or at least prove a most satisfactory way of using up vegetable leftovers. And to conclude, the Altamura recipe shows how to use the overnight sponge method to make a semolina bread, with a variation for a simple fruited bannock.

Basic Savoury Bread Dough

This recipe is similar to Scottish Morning Rolls (page 149), but whereas the sponge comprised about a quarter of the dough for the rolls, in this bread it is nearer half. The effect is to make this savoury bread dough slightly more acidic and therefore a better foil to the various ingredients that will be used to flavour and texture the bread.

The sponge

3g	Fresh yeast
150g	Water (at 20°C)
75g	Strong white flour or Italian Type 0 flour
75g	Stoneground wholemeal flour
303g	**Total**

Dissolve the yeast in the water. Add the flours and mix to a soft sponge. There is no need to mix this vigorously: gluten development by physical means is irrelevant in a dough that is allowed such a long time to ferment because naturally occurring enzymes and acids transform it anyway.

Put the sponge in a bowl with plenty of room for expansion (up to 3 times its volume) and cover with a lid or plastic bag to conserve moisture. Leave it at room temperature to ferment for 16–48 hours. During this time, the sponge will rise up and collapse. The yeast cells will multiply and lactic and acetic acids will begin to develop.

The final dough

225g*	Sponge (from above)
150g	Strong white flour
75g	Stoneground wholemeal flour
4g	Sea salt
15g	Olive oil
105g	Water
574g	**Total**

If the sponge has been in a cool place, you will need to use fairly warm water to bring the final dough to a reasonable temperature of around 27°C. To work out how hot the water should be, follow the formula on page 68. For the purposes of this calculation, treat the sponge as part of the flour. Since they are equal weights, you can add their temperatures together and divide by 2 to arrive at an average.

Mix all the ingredients together and knead until the dough is stretchy and 'silky' (not so easy to detect if you are using a high proportion of wholemeal flour). Cover and allow to rise for an hour or so.

This dough may be moulded into loaves or rolls and baked as it is or used as a base for flavoured breads.

Refreshing the sponge

While a sponge is usually created from scratch and then used up, it is perfectly possible to refresh what you don't use with flour and water (and no more baker's yeast). In this case, after 2 refreshments, most of the original baker's yeast will have disappeared (due to its dislike of acid conditions) and been

---

* Using this amount, there will be a little sponge left over. If you want to turn your sponge into a leaven, follow the instructions under Refreshing the sponge. Otherwise, include all the sponge in the dough.

replaced by 'wild' yeasts from the flour. Gradually, the sponge becomes a leaven – more acid, slower acting, with a fuller flavour.

From sponge to leaven

75g	Leftover sponge (from Final Dough above)
75g	Strong white flour
50g	Stoneground wholemeal flour
100g	Water
300g	**Total**

Treat this from now on as if it were a wheat leaven starter (see pages 179–181). If you use it to make the Basic Savoury Bread Dough, you can expect it to rise more slowly than if you were using a fresh sponge. But the flavour and keeping quality will be superior.

Sun-dried Tomato and Red Onion Bread with Tamari-roasted Sunflower Seeds

This bread is a feast for the eyes and the taste buds. With a hint of sweetness from the onions and the tomato purée and a savoury crunch from the sun-flower seeds, it really needs no accompaniment – except, perhaps, for a drizzle of olive oil. You can tear off hunks to mop up sauces or salad dressings, or cut slices to make the kind of sandwich in which the bread has as much flavour as the filling. Or you can toast a thick slab and top it with roasted vegetables for a brilliant bruschetta.

Tomato bread needs a bit of care. To get any tomato flavour into a bread, you need to use a purée or concentrate, but this can colour the dough a shocking and rather surgical pink. Sun-dried tomatoes have bags of flavour (and salt, by the way) but the flavour is almost too concentrated and they are very expensive. So if you simply add an affordable quantity of bits of sun-dried tomato to the dough, the flavour may not permeate the whole loaf.

My solution is to make a paste using a mixture of sun-dried tomato and tomato purée. This is swirled through the loaf so that every bite should find some. But there is another trick. A small amount of tomato purée tints the dough attractively and the spices augment its flavour in a way that deceives the palate into thinking that the tomato flavour is stronger than it really is.

Assembling the various elements of this dough is a bit of a fiddle, but the end product is worth it.

Makes 2 small loaves
Sun-dried tomato mixture

30g	Sun-dried tomatoes
50g	Boiling water
50g	Tomato purée
130g	**Total**

Prepare this in advance if possible. Chop the sun-dried tomatoes roughly and pour the boiling water over them. When the water has cooled, add the tomato purée and then whiz it all up in a blender, leaving a few small bits of sun-dried tomato evident in the mix. Set aside for use later. (This can be made in larger quantities and stored in the refrigerator.)

Red onions

50g	Red onions
15g	Olive oil
65g	**Total**

Finely slice rings off a peeled onion until you have 50g. Heat the olive oil in a small frying-pan or saucepan and drop the onion rings in without breaking them up at all. Sweat them on a low heat, stirring occasionally. When they are slightly softened but not mushy, turn off the heat and allow to cool.

Roasted sunflower seeds

30g Sunflower seeds

5g Tamari (or soy sauce)

35g Total

Put the sunflower seeds in a dry baking tray and into a fairly hot oven (200°C). Roast them, stirring every few minutes, until the seeds have begun to take a little colour but are not burned. Remove the tray from the oven and immediately throw the tamari on to the seeds and stir them around to distribute the liquid evenly. The heat should cause the seeds to soak up and become coated in the tamari. Allow the seeds to cool before adding them to the dough.

Tomato bread dough

1g Chilli powder

1g Turmeric

20g Tomato purée

65g Red Onions (from above)

35g Roasted Sunflower Seeds (from above)

570g Basic Savoury Bread Dough (page 212)

692g Total

130g Sun-dried Tomato Mixture (from above)

Stir the spices into the tomato purée and add the sweated onions with all the oil around them and the roasted sunflower seeds. Spread the prepared Basic Savoury Bread Dough (which should be nicely relaxed after an hour or so fermenting in bulk) out on the worktop, stretching it gently until it is about 1–1.5cm thick. Scrape the tomato, onion and seed mixture out on top of it. Fold the dough over the wet mixture, press it out and fold again, continuing until the mix is fairly evenly distributed through the dough. Do this gently, trying to avoid tearing the dough and mashing it up into a dog's dinner. A certain streakiness in the end result is fine.

If the wetness of the tomato, onion and seed mix has made the dough impossibly sticky, scrape the mess off your hands and dust with a little flour. Scrape the worktop free of any stickiness and flick a little flour over it. Then divide the dough into 2 pieces. Leave them for a couple of minutes to allow the gluten to relax.

Using either a rolling pin or your hands, stretch each piece into a rectangle about 20 × 15cm. Divide the sun-dried tomato mixture between them and spread it evenly over the surface, leaving a narrow line along one side without any mixture on. Fold this top edge over and then roll the whole thing up like a Swiss roll. Do this as tightly as you can. You will notice that, as you roll, the dough piece stretches out widthways until, when you have it all rolled up, it will be about twice as wide as it was at the beginning. Curl it into an 'S' shape so that it will fit into a greased small loaf tin. Don't worry if some tomato mix has oozed out and is smeared randomly on the surface of the dough. This adds to the generally uneven and multicoloured top crust that is a feature of this bread.

Cover the loaves loosely and prove until gentle pressure with your finger meets only feeble resistance from the dough, suggesting that the yeast is no longer gassing very vigorously. Proof may be slow but the loaves should increase to about twice their original size.

Bake in a moderate oven (190°C). The tomato in the dough will cause this bread to colour quite quickly. Care should be taken not to scorch it. The loaves are quite light and will bake in 20–25 minutes.

Olive and Pumpkin Seed Bread

There are many ways of combining olives and bread. This recipe uses a similar make-up method to that used in the tomato bread above: a swirl of black olive paste spreads flavour throughout the dough. The pumpkin seeds create a bit of crunch to contrast with the olives' soft oiliness and add significantly to the nutritional value. If you do not have any olive paste, it can easily be made by mashing a few pitted olives in a blender. If the olives have been stored in brine, drain that off and add a little olive oil to help form a succulent paste.

In the unlikely event of this bread not being wolfed down within hours of being baked, like the tomato bread, it makes a wonderful base for bruschetta.

Makes 2 small loaves

30g	Pumpkin seeds
20g	Olive oil
570g	Basic Savoury Bread Dough (page 212)
620g	**Total**
100g	Black olive paste
12	Black or green olives (pitted)
	Olive oil for brushing

Work the pumpkin seeds and olive oil into the prepared Basic Savoury Bread Dough. Divide the dough into 2 equal pieces. Scrape the worktop clean and dust with a little flour. Roll or stretch each piece of dough into a rectangle about 20 x 15cm.

Spread the black olive paste over almost all the surface of each dough piece. Roll up quite tightly like a Swiss roll. The dough piece will end up longer than it started, so tuck both ends under the middle of the loaf so that they meet underneath. This should reduce the length of the loaf by half and create a roughly rectangular shape. Now push six olives firmly into each loaf. Even spacing does not matter, but the olives should be pushed in hard enough to break the surface and disappear into the dough.

Place the loaves on a baking tray and brush them with olive oil. Cover and leave to prove. Bake in a moderate oven (about 190°C) for 20–25 minutes. Any olive paste that has been accidentally smeared on the exposed surface of the loaf will tend to burn more quickly than the plain crust, so be prepared to take action (for example by covering the loaves with a sheet or two of baking parchment) if your oven is a bit flashy.

Mushroom and Garlic Bread

A small quantity of dried porcini mushrooms can add great flavour to bread. In this recipe, fresh mushrooms are also used to give moisture to the crumb. Garlic, of course, goes with mushrooms like nothing else. The trick with this bread is to brush the loaf with garlic purée while it is hot, so that the crust soaks up and holds the flavour.

For the fresh mushrooms, use whatever you fancy, but note that the meatier varieties survive baking better; frilly, watery ones, like oyster mushrooms, tend to disintegrate and the extra expense will be wasted.

Makes 2 small loaves

Mushroom mix

100g Boiling water

10g Dried porcini mushrooms

50g Brown-cap mushrooms or your favourites

160g Total

Pour the boiling water on to the dried mushrooms. Cover and leave to soak for at least half an hour. Chop the fresh mushrooms coarsely and add to the soaked dried mushrooms. Swirl around together to coat the fresh mushrooms with the liquid.

Garlic purée

30g	Peeled garlic cloves
10g	Olive oil
40g	**Total**

Finely chop or crush the peeled garlic cloves and add to the olive oil.

Mushroom and garlic bread dough

570g	Basic Savoury Bread Dough (page 212)
160g	Mushroom Mix (from above)
730g	**Total**

Garlic purée (from above)

On a lightly floured worktop, gently press and stretch the prepared Basic Savoury Bread Dough until it is about 1–1.5cm thick. Spread the mushroom mix over it and then fold the dough over repeatedly in order to distribute the mix fairly evenly. Leave the dough a little streaky and then rest it for a couple of minutes.

Divide the dough into 2 equal pieces. Roll each out into a sausage about 30cm long and then fold into a knot as if you were tying the first part of a bow. Place the knots on a baking tray lined with baking parchment, cover and leave in a warm place to prove.

Bake in a moderate oven (about 190°C) for 20–25 minutes. As soon as the loaves are out of the oven, brush generously all over the visible crust with the garlic purée.

Cheese Bread

Bread and cheese go together in so many ways, all of them delicious in my opinion. One of my favourites is a large, flat roll with cheese baked inside and on top. Sliced horizontally and filled with salad leaves and perhaps a thin strip of ham, this is as good a lunch as I can think of.

The flavour of cheese can easily get lost in bread dough so it is important to use something strong, such as a mature Cheddar or a creamy Lancashire. The chilli and cumin in this recipe add a little something, which seems to boost the cheese flavour.

Makes 3 round cheese breads

1g	Chilli powder (a large pinch)
1g	Ground cumin (a large pinch)
120g	Grated cheese
570g	Basic Savoury Bread Dough (see page 212)
692g	**Total**
	Beaten egg, to glaze
100g	Grated cheese for topping

Stir the spices into the grated cheese and add this to the prepared Basic Savoury Bread Dough. Fold the cheese through the dough until it is fairly evenly distributed. You may need to add a little water if the dough shows signs of tightening up.

Divide the dough into 3 equal pieces and mould them up into round balls. Give them a minute or two to relax and then, with the palm of your hand, press them down so that they roughly double in diameter. Put these flat discs on a baking tray lined with baking parchment, far enough apart so that they will not touch.

With a plastic scraper or the back of a knife, mark the cheese breads with

2 cuts at right angles to make a cross. Simply press down on the dough, aiming to cut through almost to the tray but not quite. (If you do press too hard and the dough breaks in 2 (or 4), do not worry: it will probably join up again during proof or baking.)

Brush the visible surface of each bread with a little beaten egg. Divide the remaining grated cheese and place it as evenly as possible on top of each bread, but do not put it too near the edge. The cheese will partially obscure the cuts made by the scraper, but this does not matter. As the dough proves, it will spread the cheese out a bit.

Prove until nicely risen, then bake in a moderate oven (190°C) for 15–20 minutes. These breads are small and flat, so the heat will penetrate fairly quickly to the centre of the dough. Take care not to let the cheese on the top get overdone: it can go from softly melted to dried and 'foxy' in a few minutes.

The deep cross you pressed into the dough should be just visible after baking and the cheese breads should break easily into 4 wedges, which make good soup rolls. If you plan to fill a cheese bread, it is best to keep it as one, divide it horizontally, insert the filling and then cut the whole thing into halves or quarters.

Altamura (Semolina) Bread

Altamura is a small town in Puglia, not far from Bari in southeast Italy. It is now famous as one of the few places where a branch of McDonald's was forced to close through lack of trade, the locals preferring to get their takeaways from the artisan bakery. In July 2003 Altamura achieved DOP (Protected Designation of Origin) status for its bread, which is made with semolina milled from durum wheat grown exclusively in the immediate area. In deference to the Altamurans, I should make it clear that the recipe here is my own take on a semolina bread. Few of us will be lucky enough to get hold of genuine Altamura-region flour, but Italian-milled semolina is reasonably easily obtained from good Italian delicatessens.

Semolina has a slightly gritty feel when dry but can produce a surprisingly smooth and extensible dough. It has a creamy colour and considerably more flavour than white flour.

Makes 1 small loaf

135g	Sponge (see page 212)
270g	Semolina flour
4g	Sea salt
135g	Water
544g	**Total**

Ferment the sponge according to the instructions given above for 18–48 hours. Add the semolina, salt and water at a temperature that will finish the dough at about 27°C. Knead well, until the dough is silky and stretchy. If it is hard to stretch and seems to tear easily, add some more water. It takes the semolina a little while to absorb its full complement of water because the granules are bigger than flour. So be prepared to adjust the dough while you are kneading.

Cover and leave to rise in the bowl for 1–2 hours. This dough may be moulded up as a loaf or used as the base for other ingredients, as in the Semolina, Raisin and Fennel Bannock below.

Mould into an oval loaf that is slightly tapered at the ends, the shape of a rather fat rugby ball. As you finish moulding, dip the loaf into a bowl of semolina flour so that the whole thing is covered. If the dough is so dry that no semolina will stick, wet it and try again. The semolina coating gives a wonderful crunch and nutty flavour to the crust.

Dust a lined baking tray with plenty of semolina flour and place the moulded loaf on it.

This bread will expand a good deal, so allow plenty of time for a full proof. When the loaf is well risen, take a sharp blade and make 2 cuts, from point to point, about 8mm apart at their widest and following the 'contours' of the loaf. Place immediately in as hot an oven as you can muster – 230–240°C if possible – for about 30 minutes, dropping the oven temperature by 20°C after 10 minutes or so. The finished loaf should have a golden brown crust that is quite hard immediately after baking. The 2 cuts should have helped the inside of the dough to expand and push up a little through the crust and there will be a pleasing contrast between the cuts and the semolina-dusted crust.

If you have a baking stone or tile in the oven, prove Altamura Bread on a flat, lipless baking sheet that has been well dusted with semolina flour. Heat the baking stone up with the oven. When your loaf is fully risen, slide it gently off the baking tray on to the hot baking stone and close the oven door as quickly as possible.

Semolina, Raisin and Fennel Bannock

This extension of Altamura dough produces something like a tea bread, which is not so sweet it cannot be eaten with savoury accompaniments. I like it best with a very thin smear of unsalted butter. Wensleydale cheese is also a wonderful partner.

Soaking the raisins in advance brings a little extra moisture to the dough and pleasantly enhances its chewiness and keeping qualities. If you want to push the boat out, soak the raisins in something strong: grappa seems in the right spirit.

Makes 1 large bannock

Soaked raisin mix

220g Raisins

  10g Fennel seeds

  70g Water, fruit juice or spirit

300g Total

If you are using water to soak the raisins, make it hot. Put the raisins and fennel seeds in a strong polythene bag and add the liquid. Seal the bag and shake it about to wet the raisins thoroughly. Leave this overnight or longer. Swoosh it about from time to time if you are passing.

Semolina, raisin and fennel dough

540g Altamura Dough (from above)

300g Soaked Raisin Mix (from above)

840g Total

Prepare the Altamura dough as described above and leave it to rise for at least an hour. Drain any excess liquid from the soaked raisins and fennel seeds (and reward yourself with a tipple) and then gently fold them into the aerated dough. Try not to knock all the air out of the dough during this operation. Mould up gently and not very tightly into a round cob. If a lot of raisins are sticking out of the top surface of the loaf, pick them off and push them into the base – prominent fruits always get burnt and go bitter. Dip the moulded cob into semolina flour and place it on a baking tray that has been lightly dusted with semolina. Cover the tray loosely and put it in a warm place to prove.

The dough is soft and weighed down with raisins so this cob will flow out into a flattish bannock as it proves. When it is ready, bake it in a moderate oven (about 190°C) for 30–40 minutes. Leave it until it is completely cool before attempting to cut it.

CHAPTER NINE

OF CRUST AND CRUMB

'I didn't know that Life held
anything so ineffably delicious
as this bread ...'
KATHERINE MANSFIELD, 1908
(from *Selected Letters*, Clarendon Press, 1989)

Most bread is plain – just flour, water, yeast, salt and maybe some fat – and yet it comes in all shapes, colours and textures. Despite the best efforts of the industrial bakers, a considerable variety of breads can still be enjoyed around the world. How is this possible with so few basic ingredients?

There are two main reasons. First, the amount of water or fat in a dough makes a great difference to its texture and character; and second, how you treat the crust before, during and after baking greatly affects the appearance and eating quality of the loaf.

The following recipes explore the changing character of crust and crumb and demonstrate what is possible beyond the confines of tin loaf and toaster.

'The cheapest way to make water stand upright'

This was how some wag described standard white sliced bread after the 1977 Monopolies Commission Report[1] into the British plant baking industry revealed that the big bakers got an average of 4 per cent more bread from a given quantity of flour than the craft sector, due to the extra water incorporated into the dough. It was a clever way to allude to both the soggy texture of the bread and its producers' presumed greed. I admit to having used the phrase more than once.

That was before I had seen with my own eyes sloppy wet dough being transformed into great crusty, chewy *pain de campagne* at the Paris bakeries of Poilâne and Journot. When I learned how to make this bread, looked at the recipe and calculated the water percentage, I realised that extra water, far from being a trick that gave the public poor value, was essential to the life and character of some very tasty breads. So it is not the water content *per se* that is at fault in British sliced bread, as I now readily admit. What *is* remarkable is how the industrial loaf can use high water levels and still turn out so awful.

One of the commonest reactions from students on my breadmaking courses is, 'I now realise I have been making my dough too dry.' Once encouraged to add more water, they overcome the natural desire to avoid sticky hands and are amazed at how a wetter, softer dough is both easier to knead and more likely to expand as the fermentation gases inflate it. There may sometimes be reasons why a tighter dough is required – to make a freestanding loaf hold its shape, for instance. But in general, as one student put it, 'the wetter, the better'.

More water in the dough creates a chewier, more interesting texture in the crumb, and helps the keeping quality of the bread.

Ciabatta

After pizza, ciabatta must be the best-known Italian bread product, at least in the UK, where most people probably imagine it as part of a venerable national baking tradition. But Italy has a resolutely regional food culture and few genuinely national bread styles. Furthermore, ciabatta has not been around for very long; it is reputed to have been invented about 40 years ago by a baker who, in dreaming up the 'slipper' name, could not have imagined how popular it would become.

Ciabatta was popularised in the UK by a London bakery called La Fornaia, which still uses skilled handwork to shape this sloppiest of sloppy doughs. Sadly, popularity has turned ciabatta into a commodity and often it is no more than a plain white dough formed into the characteristic slipper shape. This is a shame, because the delight of ciabatta lies in its extraordinarily open texture, with vast and random gas bubbles and a flavour that mingles olive oil with a hint of acidity from a long-fermented sponge. The crust is thin and delicate – the result of the wet dough, its generous coating of flour and being baked quickly in a hot oven.

My version of ciabatta uses both a yeast-based sponge and a proportion of rye sourdough, which gives extra flavour and assists in the development of a very extensible gluten structure. If you do not have any rye sour on the go when you make this bread, it can be omitted, in which case some additional water will be required.

Makes 2 ciabatta loaves (double the quantity and you can bake crumpets as well – see below)

150 g	Sponge from Basic Savoury Bread Dough (page 212)
50 g	Refreshed Rye Production Sourdough (page 165)
180 g	Type 0 or plain white flour (not strong)
10 g	Olive oil
4 g	Sea salt
110 g	Water
504 g	**Total**

Ferment the sponge according to the instructions on page 212 for 18 hours. At the same time, refresh a small quantity of rye sourdough and ferment this, too, for 18 hours.

When both sponge and sourdough are ready, add the flour, oil, salt and water at a temperature that will finish the dough at about 27°C. To begin with, the dough will seem impossibly soft and sloppy. If you are kneading by hand, scrape it out of the mixing bowl on to the table. Using a plastic scraper, scoop the dough up into the other hand as best you can. Using both hands in an action that makes it look as if you are playing a concertina, 'air knead' the dough without letting it drop on to the table. Pinch the fingertips of each hand together and pull the dough away from the other hand, repeating the action in a rolling motion that should involve all the dough.

Stop once in a while, drop the dough on to the table, scrape the dough off your hands into the general lump and then pick the whole lot up again and continue air kneading. After a few minutes, you should notice the gluten beginning to 'fight back', making the kneading a little more difficult. Carry on for 10–15 minutes, by which time the dough should be showing signs of coming away from your hands as you knead.

Of course it is easier to do this in a mixer. But you won't experience the magical feeling as the gluten gradually develops. If you do use a conventional mixer, start with the cake beater, which will make contact with more of the dough than the hook. Keep an ear open for the motor: if it starts to strain as the gluten develops, change to the dough hook for the final few minutes of kneading.

Do not expect the dough to be very manageable even after a good knead. It will still be extremely sloppy and will want to stick to your hands and the table if given half a chance. So smear water on a convenient area, drop the dough on it and cover it with an upturned bowl to conserve moisture and keep it away from draughts.

After about an hour, the dough should have begun to aerate as the yeast gets to work on the fresh flour. Using wet hands and scrapers, gently fold the dough in the way described on page 114. Be careful not to deflate the dough as you do this. You are trying to thin the gluten so that it will stretch further as the yeast produces more gas; and you are also trying to preserve and elongate the gas bubbles that have already formed in the dough. When you have completed the folding, make a wet area on the worktop again and move the dough piece on to it. Cover the dough with the bowl and leave it for half an hour.

Remove the bowl and dust the worktop beside the dough piece with a good covering of flour. Holding a scraper in each hand, ease them under the dough and flip it over on to the floured surface. Using flour as the lubricant instead of water from now on, cut the dough in half by pressing down firmly with a plastic or metal scraper dipped in flour. As you cut, dust flour into the incision to prevent the surfaces rejoining.

Take one of the pieces of dough, very gently stretch it lengthways and put it on a floured baking tray. The end result should ideally be a slipper shape, but it is more important not to have handled the dough roughly than it is to produce a perfect shape. You can do a bit more gentle shaping once the gluten has relaxed again in a minute or two. Notice how what started as a semi-liquid pile of gloop has now acquired a definite structure, and how there is enough tension around the edges of the dough to stop it flowing into a random puddle.

Repeat this process with the other piece of dough, or divide it further into smaller pieces to make ciabatta rolls. Space them out on the baking tray because they will grow in size. Give all the finished pieces a final dusting of flour and then cover the baking tray(s) for the final rise.

Proof will take somewhere between 1 and 2 hours. Leave it until your fingers tell you that the dough is at its peak and there is not much more gas pressure coming from inside. Bake in a hot oven (about 220°C) for about 15 minutes. Ciabatta should be only slightly brown (because the floured surface prevents the crust from taking colour or going crispy). It will feel rigid as you take it from the oven but, as it cools, the moisture from the middle of the loaf will migrate to the edges and soften the crust.

Crumpets

It is odd that English baking has never seemed interested in the open, holey textures that are routinely found in the breads of mainland Europe. Perhaps the early industrialisation of our bakeries and the dominance of bread made from imported strong wheat and baked in tins put paid to the sprawling, unfettered doughs that may once have been more typical of cottage baking with home-grown grains. A possible memory of those textures survives in that baking oddity, the crumpet (or pikelet, as it is known in Yorkshire). In its standard English form, even the crumpet is a modern construction since it is baked in a metal ring. Indeed, Elizabeth David argues in her book *English Bread and Yeast Cookery* (Allen Lane, 1977) that 'crumpets are only yeast pancakes confined to rings and so made thick and of a uniform size.' But the characteristic very open, chewy texture of the crumpet is a result of baking a dough so wet that, if not confined by a ring, it would flow into a puddle – which is pretty much what a pancake is.

To make good crumpets you need a 'soft', low-to-medium-protein flour such as used to be milled from wheats grown in Britain and parts of the Continent. The strong, high-tensile, elastic gluten of North American wheat will produce a tight, bound result with the texture of carpet underlay. In the USA, the flour known as 'all-purpose' is about right. In the UK, a mixture of equal quantities of 'strong' breadmaking flour and plain flour should give the desired protein level of about 10–11 per cent. UK-grown wheat, ground at a small watermill or windmill, is often ideal for this kind of baking.

I don't like bicarbonate of soda as a chemical aid to crumpet making. It is used to provide a last-minute source of fizz to aerate the dough. I think it is unnecessary and can easily give a slightly soapy flavour to the product. My solution is to use a dough that already bears most of the hallmarks of a crumpet – soft, wet, very holey. I am referring, of course, to the ciabatta dough above. With a slight adjustment of the water content, it has everything needed to make the tastiest crumpets you have ever had.

Traditional steel crumpet rings are around 10cm in diameter and 2.5cm high, but nowadays kitchen shops tend to sell all-purpose rings designed for poaching eggs and forming mini cheesecakes; these are a bit deeper. However, a crumpet has to cook with bottom heat only and therefore should not be made too thick or the base will burn before the middle and top are cooked. Aim to pour the mixture out to an initial depth of about 1.5cm. It will rise a bit as the heat expands the dough.

Makes 5 crumpets

504g Ciabatta Dough (see above)

50g Water

554g Total

Prepare the dough exactly as specified for Ciabatta, but add the extra 50g of water at the mixing stage. It should be a gloopy texture, just pourable, but with clear evidence of a gluten network. Ferment the dough in a bowl for 1–2 hours, until it is bubbling up nicely.

Prepare a hotplate, cast-iron girdle or heavy frying-pan by heating gently. The crumpet rings should be oiled or buttered lightly. When the dough is ready, brush with a little oil the area on the hotplate where you are going to place the first ring. Put the ring down on this oiled area and immediately ladle or pour about 100g of mixture into the ring. It should run out and fill the ring and start bubbling quite soon. Cooking time will depend on the thickness of the mixture and the heat of the hotplate. Cook until the top of the crumpet has just solidified, then remove the ring, flip the crumpet over and bake it on the other side for a minute or two. Serve warm, with a good smear of butter.

Crumpets do not keep well, but can be revived from terminal toughness by gentle heating in a covered dish. Toasting, though frightfully pukka when done on the end of a long fork by languid youths over Oxbridge coals, does tend to harden the crust – but then perhaps that's all part of the experience.

'Let them eat cake ...'

Wet doughs make wonderfully chewy breads. But for sheer indulgence there's no substitute for fat. I don't mean the modest quantities that improve the size and keeping quality of plain breads. I mean serious amounts of oil or butter – the sort of dose that threatens to turn bread into cake and your waistline into a fading memory.

Breads enriched with fat (and eggs) were often called 'yeast cakes' and the definition survives in names like 'teacake', 'barm cake' (not particularly fatty) and 'lardy cake' (very). But adding a good amount of fat was traditionally a way of making everyday bread into something special – for a treat, a religious festival or a celebration. Fat used to be expensive, so for most people consumption of enriched breads was severely limited – a fact that clearly escaped Queen Marie Antoinette when she suggested that her starving subjects should eat 'cake' if there was no bread to be had. Linguists (and royalists) point out that she has been maligned: what she suggested the hungry Parisians eat was not cake but brioche or, according to Elisabeth Luard in *European Peasant*

Cookery (Bantam, 1986), *Kugelhupf* – both of which are really enriched yeast-raised breads. But little was lost in translation, because these breads have more fat in them than many cakes.

Brioche, of course, turned out to be bad for Marie Antoinette's health, but for political rather than nutritional reasons. And, on the principle that a little of what you fancy does you good, home-made brioche is a winner.

Brioche

Making brioche by hand is an experience: it's pleasantly energetic, and quite a challenge to incorporate so much butter into a seemingly unwilling dough. Eating it is the reward for trusting in a favourable result when all the evidence seems to suggest disaster. Doing it yourself means that you can avoid the strange compound fats that are used to eke out expensive dairy butter in bought brioche, not to mention the gratuitous additives that make it look good and 'keep' for an improbably long time. If you make it yourself, you can eat it genuinely fresh.

This is a two-stage dough. The ferment, made before the main dough, helps get the yeast bubbling vigorously before it encounters the egg and butter, which are not yeast foods.

Makes 1 large or 2 small brioche loaves

The ferment

15g	Sugar
5g	Fresh yeast
50g	Milk (or water)
50g	Strong white flour or a mixture of plain and strong
120g	**Total**

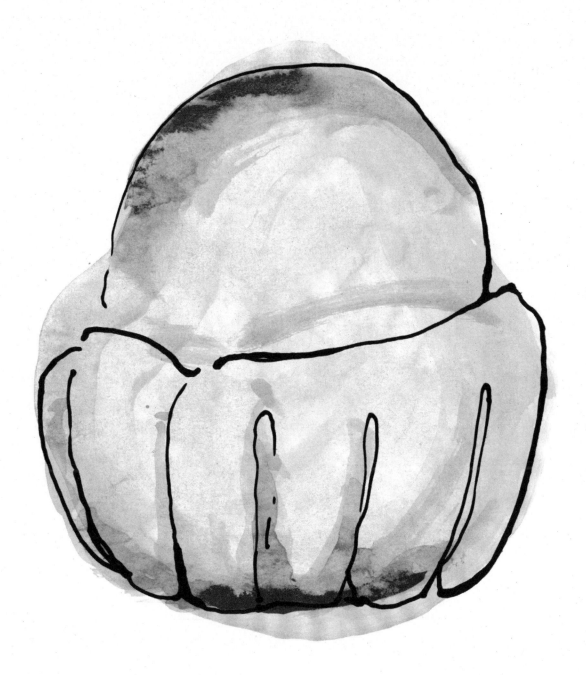

Dissolve the sugar and yeast in the milk, which should be warm enough to bring the ferment to a final temperature of about 27°C. Make a paste by mixing a small amount of the liquid with the flour, then gradually add the rest of the liquid. This prevents lumps forming. Mix until smooth, cover loosely and let it stand for about an hour in a warm place. The ferment should rise up in the bowl and should be used at just about its high point. If it 'falls', this is a sign that the yeast is producing more gas than the weak gluten structure can retain and it is time to make the main dough.

Brioche dough

120g	Ferment (from above)
200g	Strong white flour
100g	Egg (2 eggs)
5g	Sea salt
125g	Unsalted butter, lightly chilled
550g	**Total**
	Beaten egg for glazing

If you are using salted butter, reduce the added salt in the recipe by half. Mix the ferment with the flour, egg and salt to make a smooth dough. At this stage it should feel like a normal, fairly soft dough. Knead it for a few minutes until the gluten structure is beginning to develop.

Then add the butter. There is no elegant way to do this. Simply squidge the whole lot into the dough and enjoy the feeling of the cool, oily mass softening in your hands and disappearing into the dough. Work the dough between your hands, not on the worktop. As the butter softens and melts, the dough will turn into a greasy, sloppy mess. This is as it should be. Do not add more flour, even if it seems as though the dough is impossibly soft or even turning semi-liquid. Keep going, pulling the dough quickly and firmly with the fingers of both hands. As the gluten develops, you will be able to elongate the dough piece more and more until you have a 'concertina' of gloopy dough suspended perilously between your hands.

Keep going for about 10–15 minutes. Do not add any flour. Quite suddenly, the surface of the dough, which was rather ragged and dull, will take on an oily sheen. The dough will appear a bit lighter in colour because it will reflect more light and its surface will look a bit like chamois leather. The butter is now fully worked into the dough and you can stop kneading. Gratification will be all the greater for having been delayed.

If you ignore the above and add extra flour, you may appear to reach a satisfactory dough a bit sooner. But by altering the balance of flour and butter, you risk producing a rather cementy brick rather than the light and buttery texture of a true brioche.

If you have naturally warm hands, you may find that the butter turns to oil before the brioche structure is fully developed and the dough will appear to 'curdle'. This is a pity and, if chilling your hands in iced water does not do the trick, you may have to forego the pleasure of kneading and use a mixer.

Return the dough to the bowl and cover it with a polythene bag. At this point you can choose to ferment it at room temperature or in the fridge. It will need a good 2 hours at ambient temperature and up to 16 hours in the fridge. One advantage of chilling the dough is that it solidifies the butter and makes final moulding a bit easier, so it is a good plan to give it an hour at room temperature and then at least an hour in the fridge. Leaving it overnight in the fridge means that you can have a head start if you want to bake fresh brioche in the morning.

Prepare your tins by buttering them carefully. Despite being over 20 per cent fat, the dough will expand to more than double its original volume, so allow for this when choosing tins. The amount of dough in this recipe will fill a large fluted brioche tin or savarin mould or 1 large or 2 small loaf tins. I don't bother with individual small brioches because they do not keep at all well, having relatively little crumb in relation to their crust.

If you are using a decorative tin, you need do no more than mould the dough into a neat, round cob and drop it in. For extra effect, keep about

10 per cent of the dough back, mould this into a little ball and press it firmly into the top of the main piece. If you are using plain bread tins, something more interesting than a plain domed crust is required. Try rolling the dough out into a sausage about 30cm long and either forming it into an 'S' shape or folding it in half and then twisting it around on itself to form a corkscrew effect. Or divide the dough into 4 equal pieces, mould them up into rounds and drop them side by side into the tin.

Brush the top of the brioche with beaten egg, being careful not to let any run down the inside of the tin, where it may stick like glue. Give the brioche a good proof in a warm place until it has risen significantly. Test it with gentle finger pressure. If the dough is beginning to feel a bit fragile and reluctant to push back against your finger, it is time to put it in the oven. Bake in a moderate oven (about 175°C) until golden brown. Small loaves will bake in 15–20 minutes, larger ones in 30–35 minutes.

Crust

Almost everyone loves crusty bread. Perhaps it's because crunchiness is a sign that bread is not long out of the oven. Perhaps it's the combination of sound, texture and aroma that makes sinking one's teeth into a fresh crust so satisfying. There is more flavour in crust than in crumb because of the complex gelatinisation of starches and caramelisation of sugars that occur as they are baked. This crust flavour is arguably more significant in breads with a bland-tasting crumb. But 'crustiness' is not the only measure of a crust's quality. Thick or thin, crunchy or leathery, a crust performs multiple roles – as dust-guard, moisture retainer and handle, for example – in its mutual relationship with the crumb.

There was a traditional compromise that accentuated the differing qualities of crust and crumb. It was the Scottish batch bread which evolved to make efficient use of coke-fired brick ovens. In this system, dough pieces were half proved in boxes and then transferred with a long peel (a flat shovel on the end of a pole) to the sole of the brick oven. They were placed very close to each other so that they could expand only vertically. The whole oven was filled with dough, divided only by L-shaped beechwood frames, which made it easier to remove whole sections of bread once it was baked. No precious energy was wasted in heating up tins and trays, and no space in the oven was wasted as it is when round loaves are set apart from each other to gain an all-round crust. In a Scotch oven full of batch bread it took a long time for the heat to penetrate through the solid mass of dough, so baking took ages. The resulting bread had thick, dark crusts top and bottom and no crust at all on the sides.

There are other ways of tipping the balance of a bread in favour of crust. Flattening it is the most obvious. Before ovens were invented, all bread must have been baked on some kind of hot surface. The greater the contact between dough and heat, the quicker the bread would bake – an important consideration if fuel was scarce. Of course, a bread with little crumb would dry out quickly, but we are talking subsistence, not 'shelf life'. Indeed, in some traditions, dryness was a precondition of long-term storage. From the Finnish rye breads baked with a hole in the middle, to be strung on a pole above the stove away from damp and rodents, to the oatcakes and ship's biscuits that were dehydrated to last out long journeys, crust was often the necessary condition of bread.

Nowadays, it seems, crust is both a selling point and a dirty word. On the one hand, 'crusty' is a commonplace and always approving description of bread, and considerable effort, in the form of steam during baking and the use of special packaging films, goes into making bread with a particular kind of brittle, crunchy surface. On the other hand, many people cut off the crusts, thereby wasting prodigious amounts of bread – or so we are told by the marketing department of one of the country's leading bakeries. Believe it or not, this company has recently spent a small fortune developing that ultimate symbol of the infantilisation of our food culture: 'crustless' bread, baked in special tins and ovens, which presumably poses no challenge to delicate gums and teeth[2].

In the world of real food, most people want breads that balance the different attractions of crust and crumb. One of the nicest examples of this is the stottie. It is really just a large roll, but baking it on both sides gives it a subtly different character. Stotties are easy to make and are excellent for filling: with the same sort of crust top and bottom, they hold together well – even if stuffed, as any Geordie would expect, with prodigious amounts of filling.

Stotties

To 'stot', I learned from my Scots mother, is to bounce, perhaps slightly unpredictably. The connection with stottie cakes, to give them their full name, must be the fact that they are flipped over during baking. If they were light enough, perhaps they might bounce a bit.

Stotties are a rare example of a truly regional bread. It is almost impossible to find them outside the Northeast, but in their home territory they are enormously popular and have probably assured their future by being an ideal vehicle for sandwich fillings.

Like many flat breads and yeast cakes, they may well have originated among people who had no ovens to bake in. If you have only a girdle or hotplate, your loaves will not bake through unless they are fairly flat and/or baked on both sides. Muffins and stotties are essentially the same thing, though muffins are smaller. Nowadays, it is a rare bakery that flips its stotties halfway through baking. Most just roll them flat and dock (prick) them to stop the middles puffing up. But bottom crusts, especially if they have been in direct contact with the oven sole or a hotplate, have a distinctive texture and flavour, which is very different from the crust formed on the top of a loaf. So baking on both sides is essential if the true character of a stottie is to be discovered.

Makes 5 stotties (or 8 muffins)

1025g Scottish Morning Roll Dough (page 151)

Rice flour, semolina or coarse maize meal for dusting

Make a roll dough as described on page 151. If anything, add a little more water to the final dough. The end result should seem almost too soft to handle.

After the first rising, divide the dough into 5 pieces (or 8 for muffins) and mould these up into rounds. If the dough is sticky, lightly dust your hands with flour but do not put any flour on the worktop where you are moulding because this will simply make the dough pieces skid around rather than tighten up into neat rounds. When they are nicely rounded, put the pieces on a floured area of worktop to rest for about 5 minutes. This will let the gluten relax, which will make it easier to roll them out.

You will need to be able to transfer the stotties from their proving place to the hotplate (or a girdle or a large heavy frying-pan), so it is important that they should not stick. Rice flour (ground rice), semolina or coarse maize meal are all better than wheat flour for 'lubricating' dough in these circumstances (rice flour is known in the bakery trade as rice 'cones' because of the shape of the particles). Dust a tray or an area of worktop liberally with rice flour. Using a little rice flour to dust your hands, the worktop and the rolling pin, roll out each dough piece until it is about 12.5cm in diameter (7.5cm for muffins).

Stotties should not be given maximum proof or they may collapse as you move them to the hotplate (or oven). But they should have increased in volume enough to ensure that they do not split drastically during baking. Unless you have a big hotplate, you will have to bake the stotties in batches, so start the first one bearing in mind that the last one will continue proving for some time.

Using a wide fish slice, 2 plastic scrapers or something like a loose cake base, pick up a stottie and place it on the preheated hotplate. Do not overheat the hotplate or the crust will take too much colour before the inside is done.

Bake for 5–7 minutes on one side, until quite dark underneath, then flip over and finish baking on the other.

If you prefer to use the oven, heat it to about 220°C and try to arrange a surface, such as an unglazed quarry tile, which can be preheated. This will give a better crust than if the stotties go in on trays. Bake them for about 10 minutes, then turn them over and bake for another 5 minutes or so.

Crispbread

It is possible, of course, to bake bread that is almost pure crust. We tend to call it crispbread these days, though often that term refers to an extruded mixture rather than a dough. The recipe below shows how to use breadmaking techniques to make a dough that might easily be baked into a soft-crusted, porous flatbread, but which in this case is rolled out so thinly that it bakes all the way through.

These crispbreads are easy to make. There are no worries about getting the rising time just right and baking is simply a question of leaving them in the oven until they dry out. They look pretty authentic and go well with spreads and dips of all kinds. Broken up into small pieces, they make a tasty, grease-free alternative to potato crisps. They will keep in an airtight bag for several weeks.

The use of a sponge and the presence of oil in this dough give the crispbreads a crunchy, melt-in-the-mouth quality that they would not have if they were baked from flattened unleavened dough. You can vary the herbs and spices to your heart's content. Try substituting 15g fennel seeds for the chilli powder and poppy seeds.

PLATE SECTION II

Makes 5 crispbreads

150g Sponge from Basic Savoury Bread Dough (page 212)

100g Strong white flour

50g Stoneground wholemeal flour

25g Semolina flour

5g Sea salt

20g Olive oil

75g Water

5g Chilli powder

15g Poppy seeds

445g Total

Semolina flour for dusting

Prepare the sponge according to the instructions on page 212 and ferment it for 16 hours or so. Add all the other ingredients except the chilli powder and poppy seeds and knead until the dough is well developed. Cover and leave to rise for at least an hour.

Once the dough has puffed up a little, fold in the chilli and poppy seeds, leaving the dough slightly streaky but dispersing the seeds fairly evenly. Divide the dough into 5 pieces of approximately 85g. Mould them into loose rounds without knocking all the air out of the dough. Rest the dough for a couple of minutes, then, using semolina flour for dusting, roll each piece out until it is a very thin rectangle about 30 x 8cm. Place the pieces on baking trays lined with baking parchment and lightly dusted with semolina flour. Prick the dough well to prevent it ballooning up like pitta bread when it is baked. After about 45 minutes, when the gluten is fully relaxed and the dough pieces slightly aerated, pick each one up in turn and stretch it lengthways to put the gluten under tension. Put the stretched pieces back on their tray and immediately place in a gentle oven (160°C or less). Bake for about

20–30 minutes or until the dough is completely dried out and crisp. The crisp-breads should not take much colour while baking but they ought to ruck up into slightly contorted shapes. If they go a bit limp after baking, put them back in a very low oven to dry them out completely.

As soon as the crispbreads are cold, store them in airtight bags (cellophane is good) to prevent them absorbing moisture from the atmosphere and softening up. They can always be crisped up in the oven again if necessary.

Putting on the style

I make no apology for going on a bit about nutrition. After all, if bread is the staff of life, it does matter what we put in it and how we make it. But that doesn't mean that the way it looks isn't important. One of the joys of good food is surely in the variety of shapes, colours and textures that can be conjured by skilful preparation. Once the basic nutritional quality is right, good looks can only enhance the experience of eating.

It is easy to vary the appearance of bread and rolls by applying some sort of glaze or covering to the crust before, during or after baking. Whether it's a film of egg to create a shiny glaze or a sprinkling of seeds for a textured topping, simple treatments can transform the look and flavour of the plainest dough.

Here are a few principles and ideas for smartening up your act *before* baking, see pages 247–248, and *after* baking, page 249.

Before baking	Detail	Effect
BATCHING	Placing rolls or loaves close to each other so that they touch, or 'kiss', when they expand.	Reduction of hard crust; softer eating quality; in loaves, can produce more even slices.
DUSTING	Covering the exposed dough surface with flour.	Interferes with crust formation (depending on thickness of flour), resulting in a thinner, softer crust. Coarser flours like semolina or maize meal give a crunchier crust. Dough surface needs to be tacky or flour will stick only patchily – mist it or brush with water if necessary.
DIPPING	Covering dough piece (either all over or just the top) with seeds, flakes etc. The following work well: Sesame seeds Poppy seeds Sunflower seeds Linseeds Pumpkin seeds Oat flakes (whole, not porridge) Oatmeal Barley, wheat, rye flakes Grated cheese Herbs (only woody, oily types like rosemary, thyme etc).	Depending on coverage, can prevent hard crust formation, but will tend to caramelise in their own right. Often contribute flavour that permeates whole loaf (e.g. sesame seeds). Larger seeds like pumpkin tend to fall off easily. General danger of burning, especially with herbs. Cheese can overbake easily and is not very nice unless eaten fresh. Herbs are generally better inside the loaf than on top.

Before baking	Detail	Effect
SLASHING	Cutting the surface of the dough at various degrees of proof.	Allows controlled expansion of dough, especially the final expansion caused by dough moisture turning to steam. Cuts made early in proof will open widest. Deep cuts may collapse and 're-seal' themselves, especially in a sluggish or weak-structured loaf or one that is over proved.
GLAZES	**Whole egg wash** Beat an egg, perhaps with a dash of milk or water to make it flow better.	Simplest all-purpose glaze for milk bread, brioche, croissants etc; gives a glossy golden-brown finish.
	Egg yolk – often with a dash of cream.	Gives even deeper golden colour than whole egg.
	Egg white with a little water.	Gives a shiny glaze, especially to rye breads.
	Milk.	Gives a little shine and softens the crust.
	Butter (melted).	Gives a soft, silky crust.
	Hot rye 10g light rye flour boiled with 50g water.	Gives a 'fused-on' shine akin to a thin pottery glaze, especially on breads with a very smooth crust (such as light rye or rye/wheat breads).

After baking	Detail	Effect
GLAZES	Hot water brushed or misted on to rye bread immediately after baking.	Gives a slight shine and softens the crust; useful for dark, all-rye breads with a thick crust.
	Cornflour Boil 10g cornflour and 100g water together until clear.	Take the mixture off the boil and brush over loaves as soon as they are out of the oven; gives a very shiny, if slightly unreal, gloss.
	Honey and cream Warm 50g honey until it is clear, then stir in 25g whipping or double cream.	The ultimate sticky, glossy glaze; makes hot cross buns a nightmare to handle but a real treat, especially if you add a pinch of nutmeg or mixed spice to the glaze.
	Egg, sugar, water Dissolve 25g sugar in 25g water and add 50g beaten egg (1 egg).	Less sticky glaze for sweet breads, spicy buns etc; brush on while the bread is hot.

A final thought on crusts. Despite my dismissive remarks about baguette crusts and the rather daft advice (like putting ice in the oven) offered even in serious baking books to create this sort of effect, I don't deny that there are few sights more gratifying than a loaf of bread with a shiny crust crackling and splitting as it cools. Rather than messing about trying to trap enough steam in a domestic oven, you might like to try the cloche method.

. This involves covering your bread with an upturned ceramic bowl (earthenware, stoneware or ovenproof glass) as it bakes. The idea is that moisture escaping from the dough re-condenses on the surface of the dough and causes a partial gelatinisation of the starch, which eventually solidifies as a thin, crisp, shiny crust.

A further effect of baking under a bowl is that it takes longer for the oven heat to penetrate the dough, so the yeast survives longer in the oven and, in a dough with the gluten strength to take it, expands the whole structure more than it would under normal conditions.

Some trial and error is required if you attempt this with whatever large bowl you have to hand, rather than shelling out a large sum for a purpose-made earthenware cloche. I suggest preheating your bowl as you would a baking tile, in order to minimise the drop in oven heat when you insert your bowl-covered loaf. You may find that you can keep the bowl on all through baking but, if the top crust remains rather pale, remove the bowl for the last half of baking; all the good work as far as crust formation is concerned will have been done by that time.

CHAPTER TEN SWEET BREADS AND CELEBRATIONS

'All lovely things are also necessary.'
JOHN RUSKIN,
Unto This Last
(1860)

Bread is sustenance, comfort, celebration and sacrament. It can be each and all of these when at its plainest. But every bread-eating culture has demonstrated an urge to enhance the specialness of bread through some form of enrichment or embellishment. It could be the simple addition of fat and sweetness before a period of fasting or the intricate decoration of the centrepiece for some important occasion. In making something special out of the everyday, people link simple gratitude for having enough to eat with a more profound sense of connectedness with the community and the natural world that sustains it.

Making festive breads is easy and rewarding. A special dish or meal seems much more memorable if you have made it yourself rather than warmed up something from a shop. The hot cross buns that you make a day or two before Easter are a gift and a link with a tradition whose meaning is another casualty of the supermarkets' assault on the seasons.

You have probably got most of the ingredients for special breads in your kitchen already: eggs, sugar, fat, spice, fruit, nuts, maybe some alcohol. Using them to turn plain dough into something exceptional is pretty straight-forward. Here are a few principles and recipes.

Basic Sweet Bun Dough

This is a simple recipe, which can either be made into plain sweet buns or teacakes or used as the basis for more elaborate buns or loaves with the addition of nuts, spices and exotic fruits.

Yeast cannot feed on ingredients like fat, egg and spice, so it is a good idea to get it working vigorously before mixing it with these things. That is the purpose of the 'ferment' – a mixture of flour, yeast, liquid and a little sugar that is made before the main dough.

The ferment

20g	Sugar
10g	Fresh yeast
280g	Milk (at about 32°C)
140g	Stoneground wholemeal flour
450g	**Total**

This is a very liquid ferment, so dissolve the sugar and yeast in the milk, then make a paste by adding some of this mixture to the flour. Gradually add the rest of the milk, whisking the mix until it is smooth and creamy. If some lumps remain, don't worry. They will disappear when you knead the main dough. Leave the ferment covered in a warm place until it has risen to its full extent and then 'dropped'. This should take about an hour, depending on the temperature.

Bun dough

450g	Ferment (from above)
200g	Strong white flour
110g	Stoneground wholemeal flour
50g	Butter
35g	Sugar
50g	Egg (1 egg)
5g	Sea salt
900g	**Total**

To make a plain dough, mix all the ingredients together and knead until the gluten structure is well developed. This dough should be very soft. Indeed, at the end of kneading, it should still be difficult to stop it sticking to your hands.

If you add flour to tighten it up, it will make kneading easier, for sure. But the end result will be rather solid buns or loaves.

If you are going to make this into a spiced dough, stir the spices into the flour before adding the rest of the ingredients. If fruit or nuts are to be used, they should be folded in towards the end of the kneading process. Add them too soon and they interfere with the formation of a good gluten structure during kneading, and there is a risk that the fruits will become smeared through the dough in an unsightly manner.

Return the dough to the bowl, cover it and allow it at least an hour to rise. It should grow in size appreciably before you take it to the next stage. This might be simply to form buns or loaves, or you may wish to enrich it further with nuts, fruit etc.

Hot Cross Buns

In medieval days it was common for bakers to place a cross on their loaves, perhaps to repel any evil spirits that might infect the bread and prevent it rising. After the Reformation, such practices were frowned on as 'popish', but the cross remained as the symbol for the Easter bun.

Rich, spicy, fruited doughs were allowed at holidays or public burials and by the seventeenth century the hot cross bun was established fare for Maundy Thursday. Until quite recently, people ate hot cross buns on just this one day of the year. Needless to say, supermarket culture has diluted such seasonal pleasure and hot cross buns now appear on shelves almost before Christmas is over, if not all year round. However, perhaps the supermarkets have learned from baking history, for what is 'One a penny, two a penny' if not the original 'buy one, get one free'?

Makes 16 hot cross buns

Fruit mix

180g	Sultanas
80g	Raisins
40g	Water (hot) or other liquid (e.g. fruit juice or port)
300g	**Total**

Soaking the fruit is not essential; indeed some baking authorities insist that it should merely be washed and dried. However, dried fruit tends to absorb moisture from the dough, so plumping it up first with some liquid makes for a more succulent and longer-lasting bun.

Put the fruit in a strong polythene bag and pour on the water or other liquid. Seal the bag and shake it so that all the fruit is covered in liquid. Leave this for at least an hour, but preferably much longer, giving the bag an occasional shake if you remember. For even tastier buns, use fruit juice or a sweet alcoholic drink like port.

Hot cross bun dough

900g	Basic Sweet Bun Dough (from above)
10g	Ground mixed spice (to be included in the basic dough)
300g	Fruit Mix (from above)
1210g	**Total**

As mentioned above, add the spice to the dough ingredients before mixing. The best time to add the fruit is about 10 minutes after you have finished kneading. The dough's gluten will have relaxed a little, making it easier to work the fruit in. Drain any excess liquid off the fruit first, otherwise the dough may become unmanageably soft. Either in the bowl or on the table, add the fruit to the dough and gently fold and press until it is fairly evenly dispersed. If you are using a mixer, use the slowest possible speed and keep a watchful eye on the dough. The danger is that excessive force, of either hand or machine, will break the dough up into a sticky mess and smear the fragile fruit into brown streaks. It is better to stop folding sooner rather than later, even if the fruit seems rather unevenly spread. The act of moulding buns or loaves later will help to disperse it. The amount of fruit given in the recipe may seem rather large at this point, but it is surprising how it thins out once the buns have expanded and been baked. Cover the fruited dough and leave it to complete its first rise.

To make buns (crossed or not) weigh the dough out into 16 pieces of about 75g each, placing them on a lightly floured area of worktop. If some gas remains in the dough as you do this, so much the better: it will make shaping easier. Mould the pieces up into fairly tight rounds, dusting your hands, but not the worktop, with a little flour if the dough shows a tendency to stick. Place the rolls in straight lines about 5cm apart on a baking tray lined with baking parchment. Cover them loosely with a polythene bag and put them in a warm place to prove until they are almost touching.

If you want your buns plain, simply put them in an oven preheated to 180°C. They will go quite brown on account of the added sugar in the dough. Check them after 15 minutes and try to remove them from the oven when they are just done.

If you want to put crosses on your buns, don't do what I did for my first ever batch, i.e. roll out very thin strips of white pastry and laboriously lay them on. Piping a runny dough mix (see below) with a fairly fine nozzle is so much easier and a lot more fun. If you don't possess a piping bag, use a reasonably thick polythene bag. Gather the mixture into one corner, screwing up the rest of the bag behind it to avoid leaks. Then cut a very small piece off the corner of the bag to allow the crossing mix to flow. Test the rate of flow and the width of the trail and enlarge the hole if necessary. Ideally, the trail of crossing mix should be no more than 5mm wide as it comes out of the bag. It will spread a little as it settles on to the buns.

Crossing mix

50g	Plain white flour
1g	Baking powder
5g	Vegetable oil
50g	Water (cool)
106g	**Total**

Bake the buns as soon as you have finished crossing them. If you leave them for any length of time, the crossing mix will tend to flow out too wide and thin.

The ideal hot cross bun has a clear contrast between the dark brown bun surface and the white crosses. If you bake them in too hot an oven or for too long, the crosses will also go brown and will be less distinct. If the oven is too cool, you will have to leave the buns in for so long that the crosses will bake into the same biscuity colour as the rest of the dough. So some trial and error may be necessary to get the right oven temperature and baking time.

If you consistently have trouble getting a good contrast between the bun surface and the crosses, try egg-washing the buns immediately after they are moulded up. The egg will thin out as the buns expand and its effect will be to accentuate the brown colour of the parts of the dough surface not covered with crossing mix.

When the buns, crossed or not, come out of the oven, brush them generously with a sweet, spicy glaze. My favourite is the honey and cream glaze described on page 249.

Bun Loaf

The Hot Cross Bun Dough can also be baked as a loaf. Divide it between 2 greased small loaf tins. Mould up as for a normal loaf. Prove and bake in a moderate oven of around 180°C.

A nice addition to the bun loaf is provided by nibbed roasted hazelnuts or other small pieces of nut. Have the nuts in a shallow bowl or tray and dip each moulded loaf thoroughly in them before putting it in its tin. The dough surface must be moist and tacky in order to get a generous and even covering of nuts.

Glaze a plain loaf after baking but leave the nut-covered one as it is.

European festival breads

In the past, the enrichment of bread with sweetness, fat and egg was often associated with special times of year, notably the major religious festivals. People would also put relatively scarce and valuable extra ingredients into bread either before or after a period of fasting. When you compare various festive baking traditions, there is really very little difference in the basic recipes, which is not surprising – after all, there were not that many different ingredients available. It is shape and decoration that distinguish one national or religious tradition from another. Special loaves often illustrate or represent one or more significant aspect of a culture's history or pattern of observance. The Jewish plaited challah is a prime example; its many strands may represent the tribes of Israel and the braided structure allows the baked loaf to be broken easily by hand, thus obeying a prohibition against using a cutting knife on the Sabbath.

There is so little difference in the recipes for a bunch of European festive breads that I have arrived at a common dough which can be used as the basis for panettone, *colomba pasquale* (Italian Easter bread), stollen, kulich, *christopsomo* (Greek Christmas bread) and so on. I give the full recipes for stollen, the very popular German Christmas bread, and kulich, the Russian yeast cake eaten at Easter with its delicious cream cheese accompaniment, paskha.

Basic Festive Bread Dough

This dough is usually made with milk to give a slightly richer, softer texture. However, water will work just about as well: there is enough additional enrichment in the form of egg, butter and sugar to make the difference between milk and water fairly slight. Proportionally more butter, sugar and egg are used than in the bun dough given at the beginning of this chapter. For the same reasons as for the bun dough, an initial ferment is required to condition the yeast before the main dough is mixed.

The ferment

5g	Sugar
5g	Fresh yeast
60g	Milk or water (at 32°C)
50g	Stoneground wholemeal flour
120g	**Total**

Dissolve the sugar and yeast in the milk or water and then beat in the flour to make a soft paste. Leave the ferment covered in a warm place until it has risen to its full extent and dropped. This should take about an hour, depending on the temperature.

Festive bread dough

30g	Sugar
70g	Strong white flour
40g	Stoneground wholemeal flour
50g	Egg (1 egg)
120g	Ferment (from above)

50g **Salted butter**

360g Total

Stir the sugar into the flours, then add the egg and the ferment. Work into a dough, knead for a minute to begin developing the gluten, then add the butter. Knead energetically for about 10 minutes by hand (5 minutes in a mixer). Do not be tempted to add extra flour: the dough should be very soft and quite sticky. It will firm up a bit as it ferments. Cover loosely with a polythene bag and leave in a warm place to rise for about an hour. Then turn the dough out on to the worktop and add any spices, fruits or nuts that are called for.

Kulich

This delicious and impressive festive bread is very similar to the Italian panettone. It is ideal with a cup of tea or strong coffee.

Kulich is the traditional Russian Easter cake, made with an enriched yeasted dough, spices, fruit and nuts. This recipe comes from *A Gift to Young Housewives* by Elena Molokhovets (1904), widely regarded as the Russian Mrs Beeton. The recipes in *A Gift* are for quantities appropriate to a well-to-do pre-revolutionary family. The copy I saw belonged to a Leningrad family who had survived the siege of 1941–2, when hundreds of thousands of Russians starved. They told me that, when they had literally nothing to eat, they used to read Elena Molokhovets out loud to each other: the descriptions of mammoth feasts somehow assuaged their hunger by transporting them into a forgotten, fantastic world.

Kulich (pronounced 'cool-each') and its cousin krendel are made from the same dough. Whereas kulich is usually baked in a cylindrical cake mould and is often accompanied at Easter by paskha (a cream and curd cheese mixture with fruit and nuts), krendel is a freestanding loaf or plait.

Makes 1 kulich

Fruit and nut mix

80g	Raisins
30g	Candied mixed peel
30g	Flaked or nibbed almonds or other nuts
20g	Rum, brandy, vodka or fruit juice
160g	**Total**

Put the fruit and nuts in a small bowl or strong polythene bag and pour the liquid over them. It is best to do this the day before making the kulich. Stir the fruit through with your fingers or give the bag a shake from time to time to help the liquid soak in.

Kulich dough

160g	Fruit and Nut Mix (from above)
360g	Basic Festive Bread Dough (page 260)
520g	**Total**

Drain any excess liquid from the fruit and nuts and fold them gently into the prepared festive bread dough. Cover the dough and let it rise for another 30 minutes. Meanwhile, prepare a baking case. You can use a bought-in panettone case or improvise as follows. Line the sides of an ordinary 12.5cm round cake tin with stiff brown paper, extending it to a height of 15cm. Inside this, line the bottom and sides of the tin

with baking parchment. You can do the same sort of thing with a catering-size vegetable or fruit tin with both ends removed, placed on a baking tray.

Taking care to knock as little air out of the dough as possible, shape it so as to present a neat, unbroken surface on the top of the loaf and drop it into the prepared baking case. Pick off any pieces of fruit that are projecting through the top surface, otherwise they will burn.

When the dough has proved to a point where the finger test tells you that it is nearing its maximum expansion, place the tin in a moderate oven (about 180°C) and bake for 30–40 minutes. Check to make sure the inside is baked by inserting a thin skewer. If it comes out clean, the kulich is done.

Paskha

The word *paskha* means Easter in Russian. In culinary language, it refers to a mixture of cream and curd cheeses, sweetened with sugar and sometimes flavoured with various combinations of raisins, citrus zest, vanilla and nuts. Paskha was traditionally pressed into conical wooden moulds whose sides were indented with religious symbols, such as the Orthodox cross and the initial letters (XB) of the Russian Easter greeting 'Christ is Risen'. Weights were placed on the cheese to squeeze some of the moisture out. The firmed cheese was turned out and cut into slices, which were served with kulich.

The recipe below is known as Royal Pashka. It is delicious in its own right and would make a great accompaniment to fresh or stewed fruit. Served with kulich, it turns teatime into something special.

Some shops supplying the large Russian community in London now stock the curd cheese (*tvorog*) and soured cream (*smetana*) mentioned in the recipe. If you cannot get hold of the exact equivalents, don't worry. Use as natural a cream cheese as you can find (but not cottage cheese) and soured cream or crème fraîche.

For those of us who do not have a wooden paskha mould in the pantry, some alternative must be improvised. Home cheesemaking suppliers sell something called a coulommier mould – an aluminium dish with holes in it, designed for making soft or semi-soft cheeses. A square pyramid mould is available at modest cost. Otherwise, a polypropylene pudding basin with a few holes drilled in the lower half would do the trick.

Makes 1 paskha

225g	Curd (or cream) cheese
50g	Egg (1 egg)
50g	Unsalted butter
90g	Soured cream (or crème fraîche)
75g	Golden granulated or caster sugar
2g	Vanilla powder or natural vanilla extract
15g	Almonds
15g	Currants or raisins
522g	**Total**

Pass the curd cheese through a fine sieve into a saucepan and add the egg, butter and soured cream. Heat this gently, stirring all the time, until you see the first telltale bubble showing that the mixture is coming to the boil. Remove it from the heat and cool it completely (Elena Molokhovets suggests putting it on ice to speed the process). Add the sugar, vanilla, almonds and currants or raisins and mix the whole lot well. Line your mould with muslin, put the mixture in it and put some weights on top to compress it and squeeze out some moisture. Leave it on a tray in the fridge for a few hours.

To serve, turn the paskha out of its mould on to a plate and remove the muslin. Slice and serve alongside a piece of kulich.

Stollen

Rich Christmas tea breads of German origin are found in various parts of northern Europe and seem to have had Christian or even earlier connotations. In one version from Dresden, the marzipan running through the middle of the loaf is used to create a shape suggestive of the infant Jesus wrapped in swaddling clothes. Other versions omit the marzipan altogether. In the recipe below, I use marzipan because it gives a wonderful moistness to the loaf, but I like to disperse it more evenly than in the Dresden stollen by rolling a sheet of it up with the dough, so that every mouthful benefits.

Makes 1 large stollen

Stollen fruits

70g	Sultanas
60g	Raisins
50g	Candied mixed peel
20g	Rum, brandy or fruit juice
200g	**Total**

Place the fruit in a small bowl or strong polythene bag and pour the rum, brandy or juice over it (you can be more generous with the rum if you feel inclined). It is best to do this a few hours before making the stollen or even overnight. Stir the fruit through with your fingers or shake the bag periodically to help the liquid to soak in.

The marzipan

60g	Ground almonds
20g	Caster sugar
20g	Icing sugar
20g	Egg (whole, beaten)
120g	**Total**

Mix these ingredients together to make a firm paste suitable for rolling on the worktop. It is a good idea to make this the day before and store it in a polythene bag in the refrigerator. Using two types of sugar may seem a bore, but with just one or the other the marzipan becomes either too gritty or too smooth. If you don't have any icing sugar handy, whiz up the total quantity of ordinary sugar in a blender or coffee grinder to reduce its grittiness.

The stollen dough

200g	Stollen Fruits (from above)
360g	Basic Festive Bread Dough (page 260)
120g	Marzipan (from above)
680g	**Total**
	Beaten egg, to glaze
	Melted butter
	Icing sugar for dusting

If you have been generous with the rum to soak your fruit, your largesse is now rewarded. Drain any excess liquid from the fruit and enjoy a cup of anticipatory good cheer. Fold the drained fruit gently into the prepared festive bread dough after it has had its hour of bulk fermentation, trying not to break up its structure completely but aiming to distribute the fruit reasonably evenly. Relax – the dough (and you perhaps) – for 10 minutes.

Using a light dusting of flour on the worktop and your rolling pin, roll the marzipan into a rectangle about 20 × 15cm. Then roll or stretch the dough out to make a rectangle very slightly larger than the marzipan. Place the marzipan on the dough, press down gently and then roll the whole thing up like a Swiss roll, finishing with the seam underneath the resulting log. Transfer to a baking tray lined with baking parchment.

Brush the stollen thoroughly with beaten egg, being careful not to leave any tide marks around the edge. Cover loosely and put in a warm place to prove, making sure that the cover cannot come into contact with the dough. When the stollen is proved, bake in a moderate oven (180°C) for 30–40 minutes, until it is golden brown all over. As soon as it is out of the oven, brush it liberally with melted butter, then leave to cool. Sprinkle all over with icing sugar and, if you like, decorate your stollen with a red ribbon.

Simple icing sugar will soak quite quickly into the surface of the stollen (you can be sure that the everlasting dusting on commercial stollen with a long shelf life is fortified with strange additives). The traditional remedy is to dust your stollen afresh with icing sugar just before serving. Some traditional German products are sold with a little sachet of sugar for just this purpose.

Schiacciata di Uva (Tuscan Harvest Bread)

Schiacciata (roughly pronounced ski-a-charter) means 'squashed' in Italian. The savoury versions of schiacciata are the Tuscan variant of Genoese focaccia and Neapolitan pizza. This is a slightly sweetened dough made into a filled flat bread, which celebrates multiple harvests. The Vin Santo is a fortified sweet wine fermented from raisins, not fresh grapes, and so is at two removes from this year's harvest. The raisins are last year's product, and the fresh grapes on top are this year's. The best grapes to use for the topping are very ripe black ones (ideally seedless), which will bleed a little crimson juice into the dough as they are partially cooked during baking.

Warmed very slightly, this bread makes a great centrepiece on the table for pudding. It is equally good in slivers with fresh espresso.

Makes one fairly large (30cm) schiacciata

The fruit

30g	Vin Santo, sherry or port
200g	Raisins
230g	**Total**

Pour the alcohol over the raisins and soak thoroughly, overnight if possible. Drain before using. Reserve any liquor as a reward for later.

The ferment

20g	Sugar
5g	Fresh yeast
100g	Water (at 35°C)
75g	Type 0 or plain white flour
200g	**Total**

Dissolve the sugar and yeast in the water. Pour some of this on to the flour to make a paste. Mix until smooth, then gradually add the rest of the yeasty water. Whisk all together. Leave, covered, in a warm place until the ferment rises and then drops. This should take 40–60 minutes.

The dough

200g	Ferment (from above)
100g	Stoneground wholemeal flour
75g	Type 0 or strong white flour
2g	Sea salt
10g	Raw cane sugar
30g	Olive oil
50g	Water
467g	**Total**

Adjust the water temperature so that the final dough works out at about 27°C. Mix all the ingredients together and knead the dough until it is soft and supple. Cover it and put it to prove in a warm place for about an hour or at least until it has roughly doubled in bulk.

Divide the dough into 2 equal pieces and roll them into circles, each approximately 1cm thick and no more than 15cm in diameter. Line a baking tray with baking parchment and dust it with a little wholemeal flour or semolina. This will help the schiacciata to stretch as you complete its assembly.

Lay one disc of dough on the baking tray and spread the drained raisins over it evenly, almost to the edge. There will seem to be rather a lot, but don't worry. Lay the second circle of dough on top of the raisins and seal the edges well. This is best done by using a little of the moisture from the raisins to dampen the edge of the bottom piece of dough, then pulling this bottom piece over the top of the upper piece and pressing down with a finger end to make the seal, Cornish-pasty fashion. Work your way round the whole thing like this.

You may now have a rather domed centre to your loaf, so press down gently with the flat of your hand to squash it a little. You may also have trapped some air between the dough layers, so get a skewer (a digital probe thermometer works well) and make a few holes for the air to escape. You should end up with a reasonably flat disc about 20cm in diameter. The final stage is to decorate the top with grapes.

The topping

150 g	Black grapes
20 g	Raw cane sugar
170 g	**Total**

Wash and dry the grapes and pull them off the bunch. In a random, free-spirited, Italian sort of way, push them firmly into the dough. You need to break the surface of the dough to make them stay in position, otherwise they will not survive final proof and baking, which will simply eject them and leave you with a ring of grapes around a naked schiacciata.

By the time you have finished pushing the grapes in, the schiacciata will have expanded to about 30cm in diameter. Sprinkle the sugar evenly over the whole thing. Prove for about an hour, then bake for approximately 30 minutes in a moderate oven (180°C), which should not scorch the top.

Serve slightly warm, just as it is with a cup of coffee, or with cream or thick yoghurt as a dessert.

CHAPTER ELEVEN
EASY AS PIE

'Bread is the new chocolate.'
JOSEPHINE FAIRLEY, co-founder of Green & Black's,
(*Living Earth*, Spring 2006)

Like it or not, fat is a health issue: we eat more of it than is good for us. The obvious answer is to eat fewer fatty things. But even if we have the will-power to follow such advice, there is still a place for occasional treats, not to mention the sheer convenience of pies and pasties that can be eaten on the hoof and without plates or cutlery. So here is some good news: yeast can replace fat.

Not directly, of course, but if you use a yeasted dough to make pies and pasties, croissants and Danish pastries, you may be eating half as much fat as you find in some traditional types of pastry. How can this be? So-called 'shortcrust' pastry, in which fat is combined with a soft (low-protein) flour and a minimum of liquid, can contain upwards of 40 per cent fat. Puff pastry, in which the flaky structure is achieved by folding fat between layers of un-leavened dough, has about 30 per cent fat. By comparison, my croissants contain 20 per cent fat, pirozhki (Russian pasties) just over 18 per cent, and calzoni and trenchers less than 5 per cent (fillings are excluded from these calculations).

You are unlikely to find the forms of yeasted pastry described below in baker's shops. Nowadays most pies and pasties are bought in from large specialist manufacturers and baked off from frozen. Almost all British pies and pasties are made with either shortcrust or puff pastry. So if you want to discover the delights of savoury snacks that are not running with grease, you will need to make your own. In most cases, this is as easy as making bread.

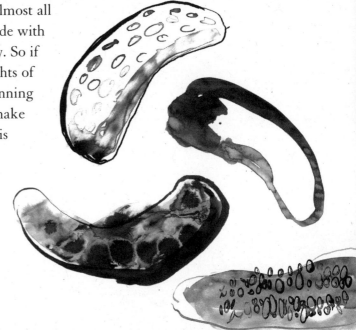

Here are some ideas for delicious pastries that build on your breadmaking expertise.

Pirozhki

This Russian word means 'little pies'. They vary in size and filling, though mushrooms and cabbage usually feature. Food memories are notoriously nostalgic, but few tastes can be more satisfying than warm pirozhki in a sliver of brown paper, bought for a few kopecks from a well-wrapped *baboushka* on a freezing Russian street. In those temperatures, the extra fat from deep-frying is a positive benefit. But pirozhki can equally well be baked in an oven. They can be reheated to good effect and make an excellent and traditional accompaniment to the soups for which Russian cuisine is famous.

The lightness of this pastry, which is quite a revelation, comes from the complementary effect of the yeast and the fats and egg. You need have no fear of overworking it and causing the gluten to toughen, which is one of the major concerns with conventional short pastry. Indeed, you must develop a satisfactory gluten network in the pastry so that it can aerate well; the fats lubricate the gluten network but they also expand with the heat of baking and contribute to lightness.

Makes 12 pirozhki

The pastry

10g	Fresh yeast
50g	Water
125g	Unsalted butter
200g	Plain white flour
200g	Stoneground wholemeal flour
5g	Sea salt
50g	Egg (1 egg)
50g	Soured cream (smetana) or low-fat yoghurt
690g	**Total**

Dissolve the yeast in the water. Rub the butter into the flours. Add the salt, egg (keeping back a little to glaze the pastries), soured cream or yoghurt and yeasty water and mix to a soft dough. Knead for a minute or two, until smooth, then cover and leave to ferment in bulk for about 1 hour.

The filling

50g	Onion, finely chopped
15g	Chives, chopped
15g	Butter
225g	Cabbage, finely shredded
100g	Hard-boiled eggs (2 eggs)
	Sea salt and pepper to taste
405g	**Total**

For the filling, fry the onion and chives gently in the butter until they are soft. Add the finely shredded cabbage and cover the pan with a lid. Steam the cabbage over a low heat, stirring every now and then to prevent sticking. The moisture released by the cabbage should be sufficient to lubricate the whole mixture. Remove from the heat when the cabbage has softened but not gone completely limp. Chop the hard-boiled eggs. Mix everything together and season to taste.

To make the pirozhki, divide the dough into 12 pieces and roll out each into a 10cm round. Fill with a generous heap of the cabbage mixture. Moisten the edges of the pastry with water, fold over to enclose the filling and crimp the edges together well. A Cornish pasty-style edge, in which the bottom layer is pulled up over the top and then crimped, helps prevent the filling leaking out. Brush the pirozhki evenly with beaten egg and arrange them, with plenty space to expand, on baking trays lined with baking parchment. Cover and prove until the pirozhki have grown appreciably. Bake in a moderate oven

(180°C) until golden brown; 15–20 minutes should do. Serve at just above room temperature.

Calzoni

Calzoni are, in effect, low-fat pasties – bread dough shaped into pockets and filled with the savoury ingredients of your choice. Easier to transport than pizza, they are, of course, best eaten slightly warm.

You can fill a calzone with almost any kind of pizza topping – vegetable, fish, meat and so on. One thing to bear in mind, however, is that a very wet filling will tend to generate a lot of steam as it bakes and will reduce in size, so there is a danger of ending up with a half-empty calzone. The filling below avoids the bane of Italian cooking – tasteless mozzarella – in favour of something with a bit of real flavour. But you can use whatever cheese you have to hand, as long as it melts reasonably well.

Makes 4 good-sized calzoni

The dough

160 g	Sponge from Basic Savoury Bread Dough (page 212)
120 g	Type 0 or plain white flour
40 g	Stoneground wholemeal flour
75 g	Water (30°C)
3 g	Sea salt
10 g	Olive oil
408 g	**Total**
	Beaten egg for sealing and glazing
	Olive oil for brushing

Ferment the sponge for at least 8 hours, preferably 16–24. When you are ready to make the calzoni, mix the flours, water, salt and olive oil into the fermented sponge. Knead until silky smooth, then cover and leave to rise for about an hour.

The filling

50g	Red onion, chopped
150g	Sweet peppers (any colour), finely sliced
10g	Olive oil
30g	Rocket
150g	Jutland Blue or Gorgonzola cheese
390g	**Total**

Gently fry the onion and peppers in the olive oil for about 10 minutes, then leave to cool. Chop the rocket fairly small and crumble the cheese into it. Add the cooled onion and peppers and mix everything together. If the cheese you are using is not very salty, you may wish to add a little salt at this stage.

To make the calzoni, divide the dough into 4 pieces each weighing about 100g. Roll these gently into rounds and leave them to relax for 2 minutes. Then flatten each one out with a rolling pin into a round about 15cm in diameter and 5mm thick.

Brush a little beaten egg round the edge of each dough piece. Place a good dollop of filling in the middle, fold over the dough and seal the edges together, pasty-style. Arrange the calzoni on a baking tray lined with baking parchment and brush them with beaten egg. Cover the tray loosely with a polythene bag (but don't let it touch the calzoni) and prove for about an hour, until the calzoni have grown appreciably in size.

Bake in a fairly hot oven (200°C) for 15–20 minutes. As soon as the calzoni are out of the oven, brush them with olive oil (which can be flavoured with garlic and/or herbs, if you like).

Trenchers

This recipe stretches the definition of pastry somewhat but I have included it here because you would eat this on the same occasions as pasties or calzoni. And after a foray to Russia and Italy, the inspiration for this delicious bread/pastry is decidedly home-grown.

Trenchers (perhaps from the French *tranche*, a slice) are mentioned in medieval times as thick slices of dark bread that were used as a kind of edible crockery: people would help themselves to meat and vegetables from large communal dishes, using their trencher to soak up the juices. In an early manifestation of conspicuous consumption (or maybe just waste), rich people would leave their soggy trencher to the servants, the poor or the dogs.

In the mid-1990s I found the trendy fascination with Mediterranean vegetables rather tiresome and wanted to create a baked snack based on English flavours. Thinking back to the tradition of the trencher and the 'trencherman' with his wholesome appetite, I came up with the idea of baking the vegetables into the bread. The problem was to find vegetable combinations that would compete with the intensity of Continental flavours. An experiment with beetroot and horseradish worked pretty well, but was rejected on the grounds that it was visually alarming. We eventually launched three varieties, with Chestnut & Ale among them. They were a commercial flop but I had fun trying out the fillings. Much to my surprise, my children loved the buttered parsnip one best.

The whole idea is essentially very similar to the flavoured breads described in Chapter 8. I offer a simple carrot filling below, but I suggest using your imagination and anything that is in season.

Makes 5 trenchers

570g Basic Savoury Bread Dough (page 212)

Spiced carrot filling

300g Carrots, finely grated

50g Butter

20g Honey

20g Cider vinegar

5g Fresh ginger root, finely grated

5g Ground cumin

400g Total

Put all the ingredients for the filling in a saucepan or frying-pan, cover and sweat over a low heat until just soft. Stir everything to ensure a good mixture.

Divide the prepared dough into 5 pieces. Roll these out into rectangles about 15 × 10cm. Spread the carrot filling over each piece of dough, almost to the edges. With the pieces of dough in 'portrait' orientation (i.e. with the shorter sides top and bottom), roll them from top to bottom towards you, like a Swiss roll, trying to avoid trapping too much air. If you roll too tightly, you risk elongating the tube that you are forming and thinning out the filling too much. If you roll too loosely, you may not spread the mixture sufficiently, with a risk of creating pockets of filling that may bake into a rather wet, doughy mess.

Place each piece of rolled-up dough seam-side down on a lightly floured baking tray and press down gently to form a reasonably neat rectangle. Dock (prick) the dough several times with a skewer to minimise the chance of it puffing up like pitta bread. Cover and prove for about an hour at room temperature.

Bake in a fairly hot oven (200°C) for about 15 minutes. If you want to keep the crust soft, brush it with a little oil or butter as soon as the trenchers are out of the oven.

Laminated dough

The family of pastries of which croissants are the best known exemplifies the combined effect of fat and yeast in a dough, which is deliberately manipulated to create a laminated (i.e. layered) structure. This basic principle can be deployed in a variety of pastries, both savoury and sweet. I offer below examples of three types of laminated dough: unsweetened croissant dough, sweetened Danish pastry dough, and lardy cake, which is both sweetened and fruited and assembled in a distinctive way.

In a laminated yeasted dough, the action of the yeast expands each thin layer of dough and the layers of fat melt and expand when subjected to heat, which vaporises the 20 per cent or so of the fat that is water. When the dough cools down, the fat solidifies again but a new open (and therefore light) structure has been created.

I cannot pretend that croissants, Danish pastries and the like are essential food or particularly healthy. A case might be made that anything as pleasurable as eating a pure butter croissant with a cup of fresh coffee must be good for mental health, but only the seriously addicted would resort to special pleading of this kind. I should know. For years I justified my habit on the grounds that my croissants were different and somewhat healthier than the rest. In the early days at the Village Bakery, we never used white flour because our one supplier, the local watermill, did not produce any. So anything lighter than wholemeal was made with the mill's '85 per cent flour', which had had about 15 per cent of the coarsest bran sifted out. Croissants made with this flour were browner than usual but they had a wonderful nutty taste and reasonable flakiness. Purists thought them rather earnest, but I clung on to the verdict of a French couple, who said they were as good as anything they had eaten at home.

The obvious problem with using anything other than the most refined white flour was that the bran particles tended to cut through the laminations and disrupt the uniformity of the fat/dough structure, making a slightly denser croissant. No problem, I used to say, with a mixture of defensiveness and self-righteousness, I am willing to trade a little flakiness for flavour and health.

I now take a different view. The *point* of a croissant is precisely that it is a deliciously unnecessary confection. The deliciousness comes from two elements: flaky texture and buttery flavour. Using a slightly branny flour reduces the flakiness and does nothing for the buttery flavour. Any supposed health gain from the bran is marginal. It would be healthier to eat more wholemeal bread and fewer croissants.

So why go on about them and suggest making them at home? Well, turning out your own hand-made croissants is a satisfying challenge for the home baker who wants to push the limits of yeast fermentation. But, just as important, if I am going to have an occasional indulgence I want it to be as good as it can be, and in this case that means made with proper butter and no additives.

The croissants and pains au chocolat that tempt us at every coffee shop and forecourt may well be made with combinations of fractionated butter, hydrogenated vegetable oils and various synthetic colours and flavours. Fractionated fats concentrate the highly saturated element from oils such as butter or palm; hydrogenation of oil creates trans-fatty acids, which are widely accepted as harmful to human health. Worse still, undeclared enzymes may be used to make the gluten in the dough more pliable and stretchy, in order to create thinner layers and a flakier structure.

One enzyme in particular is increasingly used in laminated doughs for croissants and Danish pastries. It is called transglutaminase. You won't see this name on any ingredient list because enzymes are called 'processing aids' in food labelling law and do not have to be declared. Why might you like to know that your croissants were made with transglutaminase? Because a recent study has shown that this enzyme acts on the gliadin proteins in dough to generate the peptides responsible for triggering the coeliac response in susceptible people[1]. The scientists who brought this disturbing possibility to public attention in late 2005 took the unusual step of making a recommendation to the food industry – that transglutaminase should not be used in baked products until further urgent research has been done to ascertain the extent of the risk to health. Whether this advice will be acted on by the food industry remains to be seen. If you are concerned, ask the supplier of your croissants whether they are made with transglutaminase. Don't hold your breath while you wait for an answer.

In the meantime, as you can see, there is every reason to make your own croissants. All that's needed is flour, milk, yeast, salt, ordinary dairy butter and absolutely no additives.

Croissants

Without the specially engineered fat and dough-modifying enzymes, you can't expect to achieve the same exaggerated flakiness that is sometimes found in commercial croissants. But if you follow the method given below, you should be able to turn out light and delicious croissants.

A fairly high-protein strong flour is needed, although the ability to stretch without shrinking back is more important than absolute strength. In practice this means using a 'strong breadmaking' flour, but you might experiment by mixing in a small percentage of a lower-protein flour – perhaps French or Italian if you can get hold of it. In theory this should make the dough a bit more extensible.

In all stages of making croissants (except final proof) it is important to keep the raw materials as cold as possible. A marble worktop is ideal. If you have naturally warm hands, try to chill them in icy water just before you handle the dough.

Makes 16 croissants or pains au chocolat

Croissant dough

10g	Fresh yeast
385g	Milk (cold)
600g	Strong white flour
5g	Sea salt
1000g	**Total**
250g	Butter (slightly salted or unsalted)
	Beaten egg for brushing

Dissolve the yeast in the cold milk. Make up a fairly stiff, stretchy dough with the flour, salt and yeast mixture. The texture of the dough must not be too soft or the butter will break through it during the folding and rolling process. Once the dough is developed to the right extent, put it in a polythene bag and into the refrigerator for a minimum of 30 minutes.

Dusting the worktop with light scatterings of flour as often as is necessary to stop things sticking, roll the dough out into a rectangle twice as long as it is wide and about 8mm thick. You now need to prepare a sheet of butter that will cover two-thirds of the dough. This can be done in two ways.

First, put the block of butter into a strong polythene bag and press down on it with a rolling pin, gradually changing to a rolling action as the butter gets thinner. The advantage of this method is that if the butter starts to melt, you can put the bag back in the fridge until it firms up again. The problem is getting the butter out of the bag on to the dough; this involves turning the bag inside out, preferably without touching the butter with your fingers.

Alternatively, cut slivers of butter about 2mm thick from the block and lay them over two-thirds of the dough. This is easier to control, but you may run out of slivers before you have covered the requisite area of dough and the end result will in any case not be quite as smooth a layer as with the bag method.

Once you have arranged the butter, fold the uncovered third of the dough over half the buttered part and the remaining buttered part back over the resulting sandwich. This will form a 'billet', or parcel, with alternating layers of dough-butter-dough-butter-dough. It is usual to keep a count of the number of fat layers: at this stage you have 2. Make sure that the edges are neatly aligned. Pinch the rims of the dough together to stop the butter slipping around when you roll the billet out.

Roll the dough out in the opposite direction to the first roll. You should aim to produce another rectangle about twice as long as it is wide. This time, instead of folding the dough in 3, do a 'book turn'. Pick up the short edges of the dough and fold them inwards until they meet in the middle. Then fold the 2 'pages' together as if you were closing a book. You have now got 8 fat layers. Put the dough back in its bag and into the fridge for at least half an hour and up to 2 hours. If you leave it for too long, there is a risk that the butter will go very hard and break up into flinty pieces when you next roll the dough. This can be remedied by allowing the dough to warm up a little before rolling. But the problem is usually to keep the dough cool enough to stop the butter melting. If it does, it will not form proper layers. The other reason for keeping the dough cold is to control the rate at which the yeast is fermenting: you don't want it to be too lively at this stage because it is hard to create good dough-butter laminations with a puffy dough.

Roll the dough out again (in the opposite direction to the previous roll) and do another book turn. You now have 32 fat layers, which is the maximum desirable number for a croissant dough, according to the experts. Return the dough to the fridge for another half an hour or so to keep the butter firm.

The dough is now ready for its final roll. Roll it out to a thickness of about 5mm. Cut into equilateral triangles with sides measuring 10–12.5cm. You can, of course, make your croissants smaller or larger, as you wish. Before you commit yourself to cutting the dough, mark out the triangles (or squares for pains au chocolat) to make sure that you are going to get about the right number. Rest the cut pieces for a few minutes to allow the gluten to become more extensible. To make a croissant, proceed as follows:

Grasp the apex of the triangle with one hand and the base with the other. As gently as you can – without tearing the dough – stretch the triangle until it is almost twice as long (from base to apex) as it was. Pick up the base in both hands and stretch it slightly outwards. You should now have something resembling the Eiffel Tower. Fold the edge of the base firmly over on itself and then, with the fingers of your left hand, grasp the top of the tower but keep it close to the worktop. Gently pulling with the left hand, roll up the croissant towards the tip with the right hand, keeping it under slight tension as you roll. This helps to create further layers of dough; more importantly, by putting the gluten under some tension, it creates a structure that will prove up into a bold, lively and flaky croissant. Place on greased or parchment-lined baking trays in such a way that the tip of the croissant is held down under the weight of the body; if you leave it showing, it may unravel during proof or baking. Turn the 'claws' inwards slightly to form the classic croissant (crescent) shape.

Brush carefully with beaten egg, ensuring that there are no unsightly tide marks round the edges. Cover and set to prove in a place that is not so warm that there is any danger of the butter melting. If it does, you will see disappointing puddles of butter oozing from your croissants as they bake; and if the butter is visible, it certainly won't be doing its job between the layers of dough.

After sufficient proof, the croissants should be appreciably bigger and the finger test will tell you that their structure has become puffy and decidedly fragile. Bake them in a fairly hot oven (200°C) for about 15 minutes, until they are golden brown.

Pains au chocolat

Only 30 years ago, Elizabeth David could write that *petit pain au chocolat* 'has never, so far as I know, crossed the Channel' (*English Bread and Yeast Cookery*, Allen Lane, 1977). Well it certainly has now. But the late, great Mrs David would be appalled at most of what passes for pain au chocolat in coffee shops and bake-off units the length and breadth of the UK. For one thing, she reckoned that they should not be made with a croissant dough at all; and she mourned the passing of the 'crude, rather gritty chocolate of those days'. Sadly, she did not live to see the arrival of the new breed of dark organic chocolate, satisfyingly bitter and high in cocoa solids. This is the only kind of chocolate worth using in a home-made pain au chocolat.

If you, like I, disagree with Elizabeth David about not using croissant dough for pains au chocolat, here is how to do it. You can, of course, put a stick of chocolate in any dough of your choosing – and why not?

To make pains au chocolat, cut the prepared croissant dough not into triangles but into rectangles about 10 × 5cm. Place a generous stick of choco-late along one short edge and roll the dough up around it. Pinch the ends together to stop the chocolate flowing out during baking. Egg wash, prove and bake as for croissants.

Marzipan wheels

This is another way of using a croissant dough that enjoyed some popularity at the Village Bakery when I could get around to doing it. Adding something as rich as marzipan to a croissant dough is rather gilding the lily. But the same principle and method can be used with a savoury filling, such as olive tapenade or a vegetable pâté.

Makes 10 marzipan wheels

300g Croissant Dough (see page 283)

120g Marzipan (see page 266)

420g Total

Beaten egg, to glaze

Take the croissant dough through all the stages until it is ready to be cut into triangles. Cut off a piece weighing about 300g, which will be about a quarter of the total, and use this to make the marzipan wheels (the rest can be made into croissants or pains au chocolat). Ideally the piece will measure about 15 × 10cm, but if you need to adjust the dimensions, make sure that you do not roll it any thinner than 5mm. Dusting the worktop with a little flour, roll out the marzipan until it is almost the same size as the dough. Place it on top of the dough with just a little uncovered at the top edge. Fold this edge of dough over on to the marzipan and then roll the whole piece up towards you like a Swiss roll. Do this quite tightly and use your fingers to keep the marzipan in close contact with the dough. Keep the final seam underneath the body of the roll and press down and rock back and forth gently a couple of times to help it to seal.

With a bread knife, cut slices off this roll, about 1.5cm thick. Lay them flat on a baking tray lined with baking parchment, allowing enough space for them to expand laterally. Brush the wheels with beaten egg. Cover, prove for about an hour and then bake in a moderate oven (180°C) until golden brown. If the oven is too hot or you bake for too long, the sugars in the marzipan will burn. For a really porky finish, brush the wheels with a honey and cream glaze (see page 249) as soon as they are out of the oven.

Storing croissants

There is no question that croissants and their ilk are best eaten warm (not hot) from the oven. So the question arises as to the best way to arrange this. It is possible to freeze croissants at various stages of production. If frozen immediately after being shaped, before proving and baking, they take up a minimum of room in the freezer and can be handled easily. However, they will take quite a while to defrost and prove. If you have sufficient space in the freezer to put the croissants in almost fully proved on flat trays, this has the advantage that they can be egg-washed and baked pretty much straight from the freezer. Any attempt to freeze croissants before baking needs to take account of the damaging effect of freezing on yeast: it definitely loses some vigour after being in a frozen state. So you may wish to increase the amount of yeast in the recipe accordingly. Be aware, however, that the more yeast there is in the dough, the more difficult it will be to build up good laminations.

My preferred option is to bake the croissants lightly and then freeze them. There are not many other baked products that are as good, if not better, from the freezer as fresh, but the effect of reheating a frozen baked croissant is to crisp up the 'horns' while leaving a moist bit in the middle.

To reheat frozen croissants, arrange them on a baking tray and put them straight into an oven preheated to 180°C. Bake for about 12 minutes, depending on their size. To check whether they are done, squeeze one in the middle: if there is no hard, frozen core, they are ready. Let them cool a little before eating; as with many foods, their full flavour is accessible when they are just a little above room temperature.

Home-made (and therefore additive-free) croissants do not keep well once baked. Never store them in the fridge but in a polythene bag at ambient temperature. To freshen them up immediately before eating, 'show them the oven', as bakers used to say, for as little as 3 minutes. The aim is to soften the hardening starches without drying the thing out.

Never microwave a croissant. I was once served one for breakfast on a plane; only the vague outline of its shape distinguished it from the hot towel that was dished out shortly afterwards.

Danish Pastries

This is another product that has been degraded from the special to the everyday by a food industry eager to advance the illusion that luxury can be a perpetual condition, forgetting that it is only in contrast to the plain that the fancy has any meaning. The road from treat to commodity is paved with cheap ingredients, manipulated to make less seem more.

Making Danish pastries at home with simple, real ingredients is a revelation – and anything as time consuming and fiddly as this is destined to remain the occasional indulgence that good sense suggests it should only ever have been.

The dough for Danish pastries is different from a croissant dough only in that it contains some sugar and egg and so is slightly richer and cakier. The rolling and folding method is the same as for croissants.

Makes 16 pastries

15g	Fresh yeast
180g	Milk (cold)
500g	Strong white flour
2g	Ground cardamom
15g	Raw cane sugar
2g	Sea salt
100g	Egg (2 eggs)
	Zest of 1 lemon
815g	**Total**
250g	Butter (slightly salted or unsalted)
	Fruit purée (such as apple, apricot, gooseberry or blackcurrant) for filling
	A few dried apricots
	Beaten egg, to glaze

Dissolve the yeast in the milk and add to the other ingredients. Knead into a smooth, elastic dough, as for croissants. Laminate with the butter and fold exactly as for croissants. After the final turn, roll the dough out into a large rectangle about 6mm thick.

There are many possible shapes for Danish pastries, ranging from wheels,

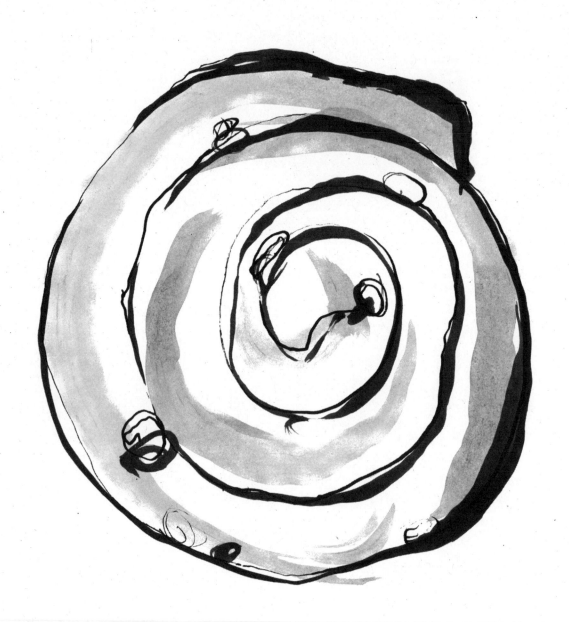

like the Marzipan Wheels described above, to strudel-shaped strips. The following is a classic shape, suitable for a soft filling.

Cut pieces of dough about 10cm square. Make a cut right through the dough from each of the corners halfway towards the centre point. Place a generous teaspoonful of fruit purée on the middle of the dough. Fold one half of each split corner over so that its end reaches the middle point on top of the filling. Gently press the 4 ends down on the filling and weight them down with a dried apricot or similar piece of fruit.

Carefully brush the exposed areas of dough with beaten egg. Cover and prove as for croissants. Bake in a moderate oven (180°C) and take care not to allow any rich, sugary filling to take too much colour.

After baking, glaze with a honey glaze (see page 249) or drizzle with the following lemon icing:

Lemon icing

30g	Butter
30g	Golden caster or granulated sugar
30g	Lemon juice
110g	Icing sugar
200g	**Total**

Melt the butter over a low heat and add the caster or granulated sugar and the lemon juice. Mix together until combined. Pour this mixture on to the icing sugar and whisk until smooth.

Lardy Cake

Lardy cake was a treat for the English rural poor. In its simplest manifestations it involved no more than a piece of ordinary bread dough with some sugar and lard rolled into it. It is associated with the pig-rearing areas of southern England, notably Wiltshire, but was probably more widespread in times gone by. Some versions used not lard but scratchings, the residue after pig fat had been melted and clarified.

While the very name is enough to make a centrally heated vegetarian queasy, lardy cake is packed with just the sort of tasty calories required to sustain hard manual work in winter. If you would rather not use lard, butter works just as well. The loaf is assembled using the rolling and folding method already seen in croissants and Danish pastries. The end result is not as fine, but it is unpretentiously English.

I haven't come across organic lard yet, though it ought to be a by-product of organic pork production. Until it appears in shops, you might prefer to use butter from happy organic cows than lard from intensively reared non-organic pigs.

Makes 2 small lardy cakes

605g Hot Cross Bun Dough (see page 256)

100g Lard or butter

100g Light muscovado sugar

805g Total

Prepare the Hot Cross Bun Dough as described on page 256, using some candied mixed peel in the fruit mix if desired.

Cream the lard or butter and sugar together. Roll the dough out into a rectangle, as for croissants. Spread two-thirds of this with the lard/sugar mixture. Fold up in 3 and then give 2 book turns, as for croissants. The rests between turns can be shorter, since their object is purely to relax the gluten rather than to keep the butter scrupulously cold.

After the final turn, pin the dough out into a rectangle and then roll it up tightly like a Swiss roll. Cut this in half and place each piece, cut edge down, into a greased small loaf tin or an 18cm round cake tin.

Cover, prove at ambient temperature and bake in a moderate to hot oven (190°C) for about 30 minutes. Tradition has it that the loaf should be tipped out of the tin and cooled upside down to allow the fat to run back into it.

CHAPTER TWELVE GLUTEN-FREE BAKING

'The industry has concentrated its economic and
technological effort into the production of a nutritionally
inferior loaf. More and more people are phasing bread out
of their diet, indicating that the bread industry has failed
both the consumer and itself ... The consumer has a right to
full information and thorough government protection on
matters affecting the nutritional value and safety of food.'
Bread: An Assessment of the British Bread Industry
(The Technology Assessment Consumerism Centre (TACC)
Report, Intermediate Publishing, 1974)

Coeliac disease is a serious digestive disorder. The only treatment is to avoid gluten. For life.

So how does the food industry cater for coeliacs – people who, by definition, must be eternally vigilant over what they eat? Why, by stuffing gluten-free products with substances such as methylcellulose (E461) and xanthan gum. These, like the plethora of additives, colours and flavours used to brighten up otherwise dull and tasteless products, are not, of course, 'foods'. Our ancestors did not cultivate or gather them, so we have no evolutionary experience of eating them. Maybe they are harmless. But maybe they are not. Perhaps people with a sensitivity to gluten deserve better than to be fobbed off with highly processed chemical additives. If coeliacs are already excluded, through an accident of genetics, from bread made with wheat, rye, barley or oats, perhaps they are entitled to the most nutritious alternative. Well, they might have to make it themselves.

What's wrong with additives?

In case you think I am being unfair to additives and 'processing aids', all of which are approved by learned committees before they can be used in food, just consider the alarming news about transglutaminase. In a recent study this enzyme, which is added to bread, pastry and croissants, was shown to act on the gliadin proteins in dough to generate the peptides responsible for triggering the coeliac response in susceptible people (see page 15). This is just one enzyme, of course, and I am not suggesting that all additives have such harmful potential. But it is surely common sense for people such as coeliacs and those known to be sensitive to wheat to avoid possible stress to their already compromised digestive systems by taking a cautious approach. After all, these additives are not food: they are only there to enable the manufacturers to present their product in an attractive form.

There are a few companies making gluten-free products without weird additives. But too often the food industry uses its ingenuity and functional additives to make overprocessed ingredients into superficially attractive but indifferent products, rather than saying to itself: 'How can we make the most nutritious food possible out of the ingredients which these people can eat?' When you can tolerate only a limited range of raw materials, it is especially important that every aspect of your diet is as wholesome as possible.

(Dis)comfort food

In the case of gluten-free bread, bakers use all the chemical contrivances in the book to create something that displays as many of the characteristics of standard white wheat bread as possible, such as:

- Soft, squishy texture.
- Enzyme-extended shelf life.
- Reduced dietary fibre and micronutrients (compared to whole wheat).
- Excessive baker's yeast.
- Minimal fermentation time, leading to suspect digestibility.
- Bland flavour.
- Significant dose of artificial additives.

If it is argued (as it often is) that this is exactly 'what the gluten-free market wants', I can only suggest that people with dietary sensitivities deserve something better than such self-serving infantilism. We sometimes give infants what they appear to like, irrespective of its quality, in order to avoid a tantrum. But if we are wise, we teach our children as they grow up that immediate gratification has to be balanced against future benefit and that with food, as with many other things in the real world, some effort may be required to gain a reward worth having.

Good reasons to bake gluten-free

So, if you or a family member has coeliac disease, or if you are avoiding or reducing gluten in your diet, you will naturally want to fill the gaps in your menu with wholesome, appetising food. Baking your own is the answer, for two reasons. First, you can control what goes into your food and avoid all the rubbish described above. Second, you can save money. Shop-bought gluten-free bakery products can be expensive, partly because there are fewer economies of scale than in the massive wheat-based market, and partly because there is less competition between suppliers. Registered coeliacs can, of course, get gluten-free food on prescription but the choice is limited, almost invariably, to products whose long shelf life is dependent on artificial preservatives.

After a bit of experimentation, you will probably decide that you need just a few gluten-free flours to make most of your breads, cakes and biscuits. You can then arrange to buy these in reasonable quantities to keep the cost down.

Why gluten-free baking is different

So you want to avoid the unpronounceable additives and you wouldn't mind saving a few quid. You're going to bake your own, gluten-free. Before you start, you need to learn a few principles – and *un*learn a few more.

Wheat gluten is unique. A grain of breadmaking wheat contains 12–15 per cent protein, whose main fractions are known as glutenin and gliadin. When these are made into a dough with water and subjected to physical mixing or kneading, an insoluble 'visco-elastic' web is formed. This is the gluten. It can be visualised as a series of tiny balloons, which expand when they are inflated by the gases from fermenting yeast. The result is a light, open dough structure that holds together well.

The gluten in rye, barley and oats does not have the ability to form the same stretchy network as wheat gluten. These flours make very different breads from wheat, though their gluten is still toxic to coeliacs.

Wheat gluten is amazing. It can form part of a dough that will expand to several times its original volume, that can be formed into an elaborate shape which is maintained throughout the baking process, and that produces bread with a variety of textures – soft, chewy, rubbery, firm, leathery, crunchy – to suit almost every occasion and taste.

Lower-protein wheats contain less gluten and are therefore used for making pastries, biscuits and cakes. These things need a 'short', crumbly, melt-in-the-mouth consistency and too much gluten (or a gluten network that is over-developed) will make them tough and chewy.

If you take the gluten out of wheat (yes, I'm afraid that there is such a thing as de-glutenised wheat flour), it will not make ordinary bread. Neither will other flours (such as rice, millet, soya etc) that do not contain gluten in the first place. This may seem obvious, but it needs to be emphasised. Making bread without gluten can be done, but it will not be the same as ordinary bread. It may be as nutritious and as delicious, but it is not the same. How could it be, when it lacks the very thing that defines bread?

I know how hard this can be for people who have to avoid gluten, especially for those forced to end a lifelong love affair with bread. What they really want is something that looks, tastes and behaves like 'proper' bread. It cannot be done. Unless, that is, you are prepared to let the food technologists loose with their chemistry sets. They are ingenious souls and can probably contrive something pretty plausible. But will it be food?

My approach is not to mourn the absence of gluten but to relish the qualities of flours that do not contain it. After all, despite wheat's global importance, many cultures feed themselves very nicely without it. By thinking creatively about ingredients and processes, we can turn out things that are good to eat.

Gluten-free baking is not just ordinary baking without certain ingredients. It requires a few adjustments, of mind and method.

Rules for gluten-free baking

Rule	Comment
Enjoy it!	Break the rules of wheat baking. No more kneading bread (no gluten to develop). No faffing about with pastry: work it, roll it and recycle it to your heart's content – there's no gluten to go all leathery on you. Enjoy the feel of sloppy, wet dough. It's child's play.
Don't expect it to be the same	Wheat gluten is unique. You can't mimic it except by using strange additives that aren't food. Enjoy the different tastes and textures of gluten-free ingredients as you learn how to put them together to make foods that fit your lifestyle.
Think laterally	If gluten-free flour doesn't produce a loaf suitable for sandwiches, why not make wraps instead? They are just pancakes by another name, easy to make and pretty darn fashionable these days.
Make it wet	Gluten-free flours need much more water than wheat ones. There's no point kneading a gluten-free dough because it won't become any more stretchy and if you make it firm enough to be kneadable it will bake into a brick. Gluten-free doughs and cake mixes must be sloppy – really sloppy.
Don't expect it to keep	The starches in gluten-free flours turn crystalline quite soon after baking. You won't be using dubious enzymes or preservatives (I hope), so your bread will age fairly quickly. To preserve that first-day freshness, slice the loaf and freeze it. Slices are quick to defrost and always in peak condition. Gluten-free cakes, especially if there are nuts in the mixture, keep fairly well.

The main ingredients

The following table lists the principal flours used in gluten-free baking, their nutritional profiles and functional properties[1]. If you find it difficult to get hold of some or all of these ingredients, there are some composite gluten-free flours available in most supermarkets. Check the ingredients list for unwanted additives.

For an excellent general guide to grains and cooking with them, see *A Cook's Guide to Grains*, by Jenni Muir (Conran Octopus, 2002).

Name	Amaranth flour	Buckwheat flour	Chestnut flour
Other names		Saracen corn (*farine de sarrasin* in France)	*Farina dolce* (in Italy)
Description	Made from the seeds of the amaranth (*Amaranthus paniculatus* or *caudatus*), an ancient South American plant used for both its leaves and its grain. Very nutritious.	Milled from the de-husked seeds of the buckwheat plant (*Fagopyrum esculentum*), an annual belonging to the rhubarb family (*Polygonaceae*). Popular in Eastern Europe and Japan (e.g. soba noodles). Flour usually comes as 'wholemeal', i.e. all the de-husked seed crushed into a grey meal with dark flecks.	Milled from dried and roasted sweet chestnuts (*Castanea sativa*). Main European source is Piedmont, in Italy.
Nutrition (analysis per 100g)	Protein 15.3g Carbohydrate 63.1g Fat 7.1g Fibre 2.9g	**Wholemeal buckwheat flour** Protein 12.6g Carbohydrate 70.6g Fat 3.1g Fibre 10g	Protein 5.2g Carbohydrate 57.4g Fat 1g Fibre 22g
Useful source of	Protein (good amino-acid balance), calcium, iron (better than spinach).	Rutin (helps prevent heart disease), B vitamins, lysine (important amino acid, deficient in many cereals),	Vitamins C, B_1, B_2, protein, fibre.

Name	Amaranth flour	Buckwheat flour	Chestnut flour
Useful source of *Cont.*		calcium, phosphorus and other minerals. Nutritionally among the best gluten-free ingredients.	
Good qualities	Very nutritious. Easily digestible when cooked. Cooks to a sticky paste and therefore has a certain binding power. Mild flavour, so suitable for plain breads and cakes. Often found as popped grains, which are even more like polystyrene than millet.	Traditionally used in Russia (in wholegrain form) to make *kasha* (porridge) and as flour to make blini (pancakes), usually in combination with wheat flour. In modern gluten-free baking, mainly used sparingly to provide some flavour and nutritional value in breads, cakes and savoury biscuits.	Nutritionally useful source of flavour and texture in gluten-free baking. Used in distinctive regional recipes (e.g. *castagnaccio*), sometimes on its own and sometimes with wheat flour. Has a natural sweetness.
Problems	Not as easy to find as flour. Quite expensive at present.	Disliked by some on account of its pungent flavour, which is an acquired taste.	If too much is used, flavour can be overwhelming. Some people dislike the 'pasty' mouthfeel of chestnut. May be hard to find in shops. Available by mail order on the internet. Expensive.

Name	Amaranth flour	Buckwheat flour	Chestnut flour
Cooking notes	Use at up to 20 per cent of flour weight in bread and cakes but beware of its tendency to produce a crumb that is too gluey.	Similar water absorbency to rice. As flour, has very little binding power but, despite its rough appearance, can confer a kind of lightness, e.g. in pancakes. In baking, limit to no more than 10 per cent of the mixture weight unless you are used to its flavour.	Can be used successfully, at around 10 per cent of flour weight, in breads, cakes, biscuits and even pastry. Not as absorbent as rice flour unless pre-cooked to form a purée.
General assessment	Currently underrated, especially in the UK, amaranth is a nutritious and versatile food, with some useful possibilities in gluten-free baking.	Can often add body, flavour and nutritional value to products that are mainly composed of lighter refined ingredients such as cornflour, tapioca or white rice. Go easy at first until you and/or your family get used to the flavour.	An underrated gluten-free ingredient, offering flavour and nutritional quality in a flour that has an impressive culinary history. A fine product of a theoretically 'sustainable' forest agriculture.

Name	Cornflour	Gram flour	Lupin flour
Other names	Corn starch, maize flour or meal (polenta)	Chickpea or garbanzo bean flour; known as *besan* in India and *ceci* in Italy	
Description	Cornflour is the purified starch of *Zea mays dentata*, a variety of maize. Corn meal or maize meal (also known as polenta) is the whole maize seed ground into flour. Maize flour is very finely ground maize meal from which all bran and germ have been removed. Maize meal is yellow; maize flour is almost white; cornflour is whiter than white.	Milled from chickpeas (*Cicer aretinum*), the base of hummus, felafel and channa dal. Black gram is a different kind of dried pea (*Phaseolus mungo*).	Made from the seeds of the sweet lupin (*Lupinus angustifolius*), which has been bred to remove most of the bitter alkaloids that made it unsuitable as an animal and human food. In some ways similar to soya, but grows in temperate climates.
Nutrition (analysis per 100g)	**Cornflour** Protein 0.6g Carbohydrate 92g Fat 0.7g Fibre 0g **Maize meal** Protein 8g Carbohydrate 77g Fat 3g Fibre 10g	Protein 20.2g Carbohydrate 50g Fat 5.7g Fibre 15g	Protein 43g Carbohydrate 57.4g Fat 12.5g Fibre 25.5g

Name	Cornflour	Gram flour	Lupin flour
Useful source of	**Maize meal** Vitamin A, protein, fibre.	Protein, magnesium, iron, folate (good), copper (rich).	Protein, fibre, antioxidants (especially alpha-tocopherol). Good balance of omega-6 to omega-3 essential fatty acids.
Good qualities	Cornflour is a useful base flour and thickener with considerable binding properties. The meal is much more nutritious but, being coarser, does not have the same functional properties as the refined starch.	Very nutritious and flavoursome. Its high protein content gives it a firming and binding effect in, for example, pastry and cake batters.	Exceptionally nutritious. Grows in Europe, so potential alternative to possibly GM-contaminated US soya. Even a small quantity adds significant protein and fibre to less nutritious gluten-free mixes.
Problems	Maize meal oxidises easily and often leaves a bitter taste in breads and plain cakes. Cornflour avoids this problem, but at great nutritional cost.	Has a pronounced beany flavour and slightly pasty mouthfeel, so best used in moderation.	Strong flavour limits dosage. 68 per cent of patients who are allergic to peanuts have shown positive reactions to lupin flour.
Cooking notes	For a light bread or cake, use cornflour for up to half the total flour, with additions of gram, millet or	Use at a maximum of 10 per cent of the dough or batter weight. More than this and you can taste	Use at around 5 per cent of flour weight in bread for an improved protein and fibre content. Smaller

Name	Cornflour	Gram flour	Lupin flour
Cooking notes *Cont.*	soya to improve nutrition. Cornflour absorbs about twice as much water as rice flour. Cornflour is good for pastry but needs balancing with tapioca and some protein source such as gram. It is, of course, an excellent general-purpose thickener for sauces etc.	the beans in a plain recipe. Make sure that the gram is finely ground – some samples have bits of bean left in. A little gram stops a light pastry based on corn or tapioca flour from falling to bits in a pile of dusty crumbs. If gram flour is unavailable, chickpeas can be cooked (in plenty water for about 3 hours) and mashed as a dough addition.	amounts can be added to cake and pastry flour mixes, where the lupin has a firming effect.
General assessment	As with other refined ingredients, the lightness we desire carries a big nutritional price. The best compromise is to mix cornflour with better (but possibly heavier) ingredients. If you can't tolerate maize, tapioca flour is a good substitute.	A nutritious and useful flour for the gluten-free baker, but it should be used judiciously for the right balance between functionality and flavour.	Apart from the issue of a peanut-like allergenicity, lupin is a nutritionally valuable gluten-free ingredient.

Name	Millet flour	Potato flour	Quinoa flour
Other names	Bajoa, jowar. Very similar to sorghum, which is sometimes known as Indian millet	Potato starch, *fécule*	(pronounced 'keen-wah')
Description	Flour milled from the hulled grains of a number of species of cereals of the grass family. White millet is usually *Panicum miliaceum* or *Setaria*. Red millet is *Eleusine coracana*, usually used for animal feed only.	Potato flour is dried and ground potato. Potato starch is a more refined derivative of potatoes.	Light creamy flour, ground from the seeds of the quinoa (*Chenopodium album*), a very nutritious member of the spinach family. Staple food of the Incas in South America for thousands of years, it is enjoying a revival.
Nutrition (analysis per 100g)	Protein 10g Carbohydrate 73g Fat 2.5g Fibre 3g	**Flour** Protein 8g Carbohydrate 80g Fat 0.05g Fibre 3.5g **Starch** Protein 0.05g Carbohydrate 77g Fat 0g Fibre 0g	Protein 13.8g Carbohydrate 55.7g Fat 5g Fibre 5.9g
Useful source of	Magnesium, protein.	**(Flour only)** Vitamin C, B_6, copper.	Protein (very good amino-acid balance), calcium, iron, B vitamins, phosphorus, vitamin E.

Name	Millet flour	Potato flour	Quinoa flour
Good qualities	Considered more nutritious than rice. Flavour is pretty bland but can be improved by lightly roasting the tiny grains before either milling to flour or using them whole in bread.	Both the flour and the starch, used in moderation, have the ability to bind liquid and create a certain amount of tenacity and lightness in the structure of breads and cakes. They can help hold moisture post-baking.	Very nutritious. Easy to cook as a grain (quicker than rice and less likely to go sticky). Distinctive flavour that is not to everyone's liking, with a hint of bitterness, but bland enough to be masked in flavoured breads, cakes or biscuits.
Problems	Prone to rancidity, which makes anything baked with millet taste bitter. The only solution is either to buy from a source that has a quick turnover or to grind the grain yourself and use it quickly.	If too much is used, a soggy, gummy, heavy texture can result.	The flavour, until you get used to it. Not yet widely available and therefore quite expensive.
Cooking notes	Use a small quantity of grains as a top dressing for an interesting appearance and texture. The cooked whole grains (boiled in plenty of water) will disappear when	Don't make potato flour more than 20 per cent of the total flour in either bread or cakes. Avoid in pastry. Mashed potato will provide an easy	Use at up to 15 per cent of flour weight in bread, 10 per cent in biscuits, less in cakes. Used as a flour, quinoa has little binding power. One strategy worth trying in breads is to cook

Name	Millet flour	Potato flour	Quinoa flour
Cooking notes *Cont.*	mixed into a bread or cake dough. Puffed grains can be used in cereal bars – if you don't mind the sensation of eating a bean bag. If using flour, limit it to less than 10 per cent of the flour content of breads. In strong-flavoured cakes, a larger percentage may be okay. Works well as a mixture with twice its weight of gram (chickpea) flour.	substitute in some recipes, but the liquid will need adjusting.	the quinoa grains like rice until they have absorbed as much water as they can, then beat them to a sticky mush that will aid binding and moisture retention. Don't put more than about 10 per cent mush in the dough, though, or it may turn out heavy and sticky.
General assessment	Not a bad ingredient in principle, but often marred by the bitterness caused by rancidity. Only consider using it if you can guarantee its freshness.	In medium quantities, confers whiteness and lightness but no flavour and not much nutrition. Some swear by it, but if it's hard to find or space is limited, don't bother.	Its nutritional excellence and relatively mild flavour make quinoa an exciting proposition for gluten-free baking. We will hear a lot more about quinoa in the next few years.

Name	Rice Flour	Soya Flour	Tapioca Flour
Other names	May simply be called 'rice flour', with no indication of whether it is white or brown	Soy flour	Manioc, cassava (whose meal is known as *gari*)
Description	Milled from the de-husked seeds of *Oryza sativa*. As grain, staple diet of half the world's people. Removal of most of the outer bran layers produces 'semi-pearled' rice. White rice is usually 'polished' with glucose and talc.	Ground de-hulled soya bean (*Glycine max*). Comes as full-fat or low-fat (de-fatted), unheated or heat-treated (to inactivate the amylase and proteinase enzymes that make it a useful baking flour but can also make it indigestible if not properly cooked).	Made by heating the tuberous root of the cassava plant (*Manihot utilissima*), which is then dried into granules (tapioca) or flakes or ground into flour. Tapioca is very low in nutrients.
Nutrition (analysis per 100g)	**Brown** Protein 6.7g Carbohydrate 81.3g Fat 2.8g Fibre 3.8g **White** Protein 7.3g Carbohydrate 85.8g Fat 3.6g Fibre 2.7g	Protein 36.8g Carbohydrate 23.5g Fat 23.5g Fibre 11.9g	Protein 0.4g Carbohydrate 95g Fat 0.1g Fibre – trace
Useful source of	**Brown rice** Vitamin B_1, niacin, magnesium, copper (rich source).	Protein, folate, biotin, copper (good).	Starch!

Name	Rice Flour	Soya Flour	Tapioca Flour
Useful source of *Cont.*	**White rice** Copper.		
Good qualities	Useful base flour for both breads and cakes. White rice has very little flavour, brown a bit more. Brown rice produces a lively sourdough, which can be used to make bread.	Very good source of quality protein. In small quantities (less than 1 per cent) it has a bleaching and 'improving' effect on conventional bread dough. Its high protein and fat content make for an 'egg-substitute' effect in cakes and biscuits.	Useful as a bland base, especially for cakes and biscuits where light texture is required. Absorbs a considerable amount of liquid and has a certain binding quality. At moderate levels, imparts a pleasant, chewy texture to breads.
Problems	Main drawback is a tendency to produce a bitter taste, especially if baked products are kept for any length of time. Although apparently finely ground, both white and brown rice flours give a slightly gritty texture when baked.	Cannot be used in large amounts without creating a heavy, unforgiving structure and awful eating quality. In small amounts it doesn't contribute much in the way of flavour.	Nutritional poverty. If it forms more than about 50 per cent of the flour in a plain bread, pastry or biscuit, the baked texture can become rather dusty and a strange background flavour can emerge.
Cooking notes	Has little binding power, so usually needs to be used in combination with, for example, cornflour or	Use at a maximum of 5 per cent of the dough or batter weight. In cakes and biscuits, use the	Use at 5–10 per cent in breads and sponge cakes and up to 40 per cent in pastry or biscuits. If combined

Name	Rice Flour	Soya Flour	Tapioca Flour
Cooking notes *Cont.*	tapioca flour. Will hold more moisture if gelatinised by mixing with boiling water (approx 200g water to 50g rice flour).	heated (not enzyme-active) flour, if you can get it.	with water without other flours, it makes a dough with a curious, mercurial texture which holds a good deal of liquid while retaining a 'self-levelling' quality. This bakes rather strangely, so it is better to mix tapioca with other flours.
General assessment	Relatively cheap and easy to find, rice flour is a useful component in gluten-free baking. White is significantly less nutritious than brown. The gritty texture and tendency to bitterness mean it is best used in combination with other flours.	Despite its famous nutritional profile, soya flour is hard to use well. Better to enjoy this bean in the form of the curds and fermented sauces so popular in Eastern cookery.	A useful filler and thickener whose very poor nutritional qualities and almost complete lack of flavour limit its potential for good baking.

Yeasted Gluten-Free Bread

This is basic yeasted bread that aims to combine reasonable nutritional value with a texture that is not too far from a conventional brown loaf. The linseeds on top help to mask the tendency of most gluten-free doughs to produce a slightly strange white crust.

Makes 1 small loaf

5g	Fresh yeast
225g	Water (30°C)
140g	Corn (maize) flour
60g	Chestnut flour
20g	Gram (chickpea) flour
30g	Manioc (tapioca) flour
10g	Cider vinegar
5g	Sea salt
495g	**Total**
	Linseeds for topping

Dissolve the yeast in the water and mix with all the other ingredients except the linseeds. The dough should be like a smooth, wet cement. You will be able to pour it.

Grease a small bread tin (or use a non-stick one). Tip the dough into the tin. It should come just under two-thirds of the way up the sides. Don't worry about smoothing it out; it will find its own level.

Cover and prove in a warm place. This dough will not hold as much gas as one made with gluten-containing flour. Aim for a 50 per cent increase in volume. Sprinkle linseeds on top of the dough until there is a good, even covering. If you prefer not to use seeds, carefully brush or spray a little olive or sunflower oil over the top.

Bake in a hot oven (210°C) for about 30 minutes. The loaf is done when it begins to shrink away from the sides of the tin.

Starting a Rice Sourdough

To make the Rice, Brazil Nut and Linseed Bread below, you will need to start a rice sourdough. Brown rice flour is full of wild yeasts and can generate a natural leaven or sourdough in 3 or 4 days without difficulty.

Day 1

30g	Brown rice flour
40g	Water (30°C)
70g	**Total**

Mix the flour and water to a paste, cover loosely with a polythene bag and leave in a fairly warm place (around 30°C is ideal). After one day, stir well and refresh as follows:

Day 2

30g	Brown rice flour
40g	Water (30°C)
70g	Starter from Day 1
140g	**Total**

Stir well and cover as before. After one day, refresh again:

Day 3

30g Brown rice flour

40g Water (30°C)

140g Starter from Day 2

210g Total

You should notice some bubbles and the sourdough should have risen up and then fallen back a bit. Add the fresh flour and water, stir well and cover as before. After one more day, refresh again:

Day 4

45g Brown rice flour

50g Water

210g Starter from Day 3

305g Total

After 24 hours you should have a sourdough that smells nicely acidic and shows clear evidence of bubbling (i.e. gas production by the natural yeasts). The 'creation' phase is now complete. From now on, use your 'starter' to make a 'production sourdough' (see below) and then bread in a simple system with the quantities shown.

Rice, Brazil Nut and Linseed Bread

This bread avoids baker's yeast and gets its interesting texture and high nutritional quality from linseeds (rich in omega-3 and omega-6 essential fatty acids) and brazil nuts (the best natural source of selenium). There is evidence that slow sourdough fermentations make micronutrients more available to the human body than fast, high-yeast ones. So if this bread seems to take an age to rise, it may well be worth waiting for.

Carob bean gum (sometimes called locust bean gum or meal) is a flour produced from the seeds of the honey locust tree (*Ceratonia siliqua*). Like guar gum and acacia gum (also known as gum arabic), it is a natural plant-derived product, which has the ability to absorb many times its own weight in water and to produce a slightly rubbery texture. It is useful in small quantities in some gluten-free recipes since it helps hold otherwise crumbly ingredients together. If you cannot get hold of it, replace its weight with extra egg, or just do without it.

Makes 1 small loaf

Soaked linseeds
The day before making the bread, soak some linseeds as follows. If you forget, do them on the day with hot water.

25g	Linseeds
50g	Water (cold)
75g	**Total**

Rinse the seeds in fresh water, drain, then add them to the specified amount of water. Cover and leave to soak overnight at ambient temperature. By the morning the seeds will resemble frogspawn.

Production sourdough
Make a 'production' sourdough 2–3 hours before making the bread, using warm water.

75g   Rice Sourdough Starter (page 316)

70g   Brown rice flour

85g   Water (35°C)

230g Total

Mix everything together, cover and leave in a warm place (as near to 30°C as you can manage). The sourdough is ready when it has risen appreciably. If it has come up and collapsed on itself, it does not matter, but there is no need to leave it until this has happened before proceeding to make the final dough.

Rice, brazil nut and linseed dough

150g Rice Production Sourdough (from above)

20g Corn (maize) flour

10g Buckwheat flour

75g Brown rice flour

20g Manioc (tapioca) flour

10g Carob bean gum (optional)

10g Cider vinegar

50g Brazil nuts, chopped

50g Egg (1 egg)

5g Sea salt

35g Water (30°C)

75g Soaked Linseeds (from above)

510g Total

Sunflower or olive oil for brushing

Mix all the ingredients together into a very soft dough (not quite as wet as the dough for Yeasted Gluten-Free Bread, above). Using wet hands, pick up all the dough in one piece and smooth it as if you were a potter turning a bowl on the wheel. Shape it into a loaf and drop into a greased or non-stick small loaf tin. The mixture should come about two-thirds of the way up the sides of the tin. Cover and prove in a warm place. It may take up to 5 hours, depending on the vigour of the sourdough and the temperature of the kitchen.

When the loaf is fully proved, brush the top very carefully with sunflower or olive oil. This will give an attractive brown finish to the loaf.

Bake in a fairly hot oven (210°C) for about 30 minutes. The loaf is done when it begins to shrink away from the sides of the tin. If you have doubts, insert a skewer into the middle. If it comes out clean, the loaf is ready.

Maintaining your rice starter

Rice sours can be quite volatile – as seen in the ease with which they begin fermenting. If you leave them out at ambient temperature there is some risk that extraneous moulds may form, so the following rules should be observed when keeping a rice sour between uses:

Keeping the starter for 0–1 day
Store at room temperature.

Keeping the starter for 1–15 days
Store in the fridge at 5°C – optional intermediate refreshment before use.

Keeping the starter for over 15 days
Store in the freezer – intermediate refreshment before and after freezing.

Potato and Quinoa Bread

This is another naturally fermented bread made without baker's yeast. It has a smoother texture than the Rice, Brazil Nut and Linseed Bread and uses quinoa, soya and buckwheat flours to boost nutritional quality.

Make a 'production' sourdough 2–3 hours before making the bread, using warm water. The small quantity of chestnut flour adds a nutty flavour but is not essential. If you do not use it, add 15g rice flour.

Makes 1 small loaf

Production sourdough

50g	Rice Sourdough Starter (page 316)
30g	Brown rice flour
15g	Chestnut flour
60g	Water (35°C)
155g	**Total**

Mix everything together, cover and leave in a warm place (as near to 30°C as you can manage). The sourdough is ready when it has risen appreciably. If it has come up and collapsed on itself, it does not matter, but there is no need to leave it until this has happened before proceeding to make the final dough.

Potato and quinoa dough

150g	Production Sourdough (from above)
50g	Potato flour
15g	Buckwheat flour
50g	Quinoa flour

100g Corn (maize) flour

15g Soya flour

10g Olive oil

5g Sea salt

105g Water (30°C)

500g Total

Mix all the ingredients together into a very soft dough, which can be virtually poured into a greased or non-stick tin, filling it about half full. Cover and prove in a warm place. Proof will take up to 5 hours, depending on the vigour of the sourdough and the temperature of the kitchen. The dough should rise to near the top of the tin (if you filled it half full). Just before baking, dust the surface of the dough with rice or buckwheat flour; this helps prevent the formation of an unsightly whitish crust.

Bake in a fairly hot oven (210°C) for about 30 minutes. The loaf is done when it begins to shrink away from the sides of the tin.

A wet dough like this will produce a very open, chewy crumb. Don't expect it to keep soft and rubbery for long, though. If you want to keep it for more than a day or two, it would be best to slice it and freeze it.

Pizza Bases

A bit of lateral thinking is required to produce a dough that will be thin enough for a pizza base and yet not fall to bits as it is being handled.

This recipe can be adapted to make pancakes or wraps to be used for filling and eating cold. For a sweet pancake, add some honey or maple syrup. The trick is to get the right sloppy consistency so that the mixture flows out thinly enough in the frying-pan.

Makes 2 medium pizza bases

5g	Fresh yeast
250g	Water (30°C)
140g	Corn (maize) flour
20g	Buckwheat flour
50g	Brown rice flour
40g	Manioc (tapioca) flour
20g	Chestnut flour
5g	Sea salt
530g	**Total**

Olive oil for brushing

Toppings of your choice, e.g. tomato paste, tomatoes, peppers, anchovies, olives, herbs, mozzarella or similar cheese

Dissolve the yeast in the water and add to the other ingredients. The dough should be very sloppy, like a batter. Leave to stand for 15–30 minutes to allow the yeast to work.

Heat a girdle or frying-pan, brushing with a smear of olive oil if the surface is not non-stick, and ladle in a good dollop of mixture with a swirling action to make a thin, reasonably circular layer of batter. Cook over a high heat for about 3 minutes, then flip over and cook for another minute. The 'pancake' should be cooked but still quite soft and floppy. If your mixture was too thick, your pizza base will be also.

Turn the pizza base out on to a baking sheet and cook the remaining mixture in the same way. Cover the pizzas with the usual toppings. Bake in a hot oven (220°C) or under a grill for 5–7 minutes, until the cheese is bubbling.

Gluten-free Pastry

The great thing about gluten-free pastry is that there is no gluten to toughen the dough if you overwork it. This means that you can recycle the scraps to your heart's content without the fear that the last tarts or pasties will have the texture of boot leather. However, without any gluten, there is an opposite danger – that the pastry will be so 'short' that it crumbles into dust when baked. That is why this recipe contains a certain amount of gram (chickpea) flour: its high protein content mimics some of the action of gluten (which is also, of course, a protein mix) in wheat pastry.

The base mixture can be turned into sweet or savoury pastry.

Basic pastry mix

60g	Chestnut flour
60g	Gram (chickpea) flour
200g	Manioc (tapioca) flour
40g	Rice flour (brown or white)
130g	Butter
490g	**Total**

Savoury pastry

490g	Basic Pastry Mix (above)
3g	Sea salt
90g	Water (cold)
583g	**Total**

Sweet pastry

490g	Basic Pastry Mix (above)
90g	Light brown sugar
70g	Water (cold)
650g	**Total**

Put all the dry ingredients into a bowl and rub in the butter with your finger-tips. Dissolve the salt or sugar in the water and add to the mixture. Work to a pliable dough.

Roll out and use as for ordinary pastry. It helps to store the pastry in the fridge for an hour or so before using it, but if it gets too cold it will become brittle and crumbly.

Basic Gluten-free Cake

Cake making is probably one of the easier areas of gluten-free baking. As with pastry, the absence of gluten is an advantage when trying to create a melt-in-the-mouth texture. However, there is a grittiness in some gluten-free flours that can produce a rather harsh cake crumb. The following is a basic Madeira-type mixture, which produces a cake that few people can detect as being made with gluten-free ingredients. Ground almonds are expensive but they really transform a sponge and give it a remarkably moist crumb and good keeping qualities.

Makes 2 small cakes

90g	Sunflower oil
200g	Raw cane sugar
180g	Egg (4 medium)
5g	Gluten-free baking powder

2g   Sea salt (optional)

35g   Manioc (tapioca) flour

40g   Rice flour

15g   Gram (chickpea) flour

15g   Buckwheat flour

90g   Ground almonds

672g   Total

Beat the oil with the sugar and then add the eggs. Mix until frothy. Stir the baking powder and salt (if using) into the flours and ground almonds, then add to the liquid mix. Mix thoroughly. The batter will be very sloppy and pourable.

Prepare two 12.5cm diameter cake tins, or small loaf tins or paper cases, either by lining them with baking parchment or by greasing and flouring them. Deposit half the batter in each tin or case. (The mixture can also be used for fairy cakes or in American muffin tins or cases. Aim to fill whatever case you are using just over half full.)

Bake in a moderate oven (170°C) for about 30 minutes. Insert a skewer to check that the cakes are done; if it comes out clean, all is well.

Ginger Cake

This is an example of a simple adaptation of the Basic Gluten-free Cake mix given above. Other additions could involve lemon or orange zest, dried fruits, honey (to replace some or all of the sugar) and/or nuts. Just take care not to overload the sponge with extra ingredients, otherwise it may collapse into a rather dense and soggy mixture.

672g Gluten-free Cake Mix (from above)

  5g Ground ginger

 70g Crystallised stem ginger, finely chopped

747g Total

Stir the ground ginger into the flours before they are added to the liquid mixture. Toss the stem ginger in a little rice flour until it is coated, then fold it gently into the batter at the end of mixing.

Bake in the same way as the basic cake.

Luxury Chocolate Cake

For a long time chocolate almond cake was the only gluten-free product we sold at the bakery. It was never promoted as gluten-free and it was only when people began to ask whether we made anything suitable for coeliacs that we realised this was all we could offer them. But even though it was a completely indulgent product (and one that you wouldn't want to eat every day), it set the standard for all our later gluten-free baking: it was delicious in its own right and no one noticed that it was made without gluten.

Use the best-quality, highest cocoa-solids chocolate you can find or afford. Green & Black's Maya Gold (which carries the Fairtrade mark) would add a subtle hint of orange.

Makes 1 large or 2 small cakes

The cake mix

100g Butter

100g Raw cane sugar

100g Egg (2 eggs)

100g Ground almonds

100g Dark chocolate

500g Total

The ganache

100g Dark chocolate

60g Whipping cream

160g Total

Toasted blanched almonds, to decorate

Cream the butter and sugar together until fluffy and light. Separate the eggs. Add the yolks to the butter and sugar mixture and beat well. Stir in the ground almonds.

Melt the chocolate in a bain-marie or a bowl set over a pan of hot water. Fold it into the almond mixture. Whisk the egg whites until they form soft peaks and then, with a clean large metal spoon, fold them carefully into the chocolate mixture, trying to retain as much air as possible.

Turn the mixture into a greased and floured (or baking-parchment-lined) 20cm cake tin or 2 small cake tins or paper cases. Bake in a moderate oven (170°C) for 30–40 minutes. Don't expect this cake to rise very much; it is moist and close textured. Turn it carefully out of the tin(s) and cool on a wire rack.

To make the ganache, melt the chocolate in a bain-marie or in a bowl set over a pan of hot water. Scald the cream in a saucepan – i.e. bring it just up to boiling point and then remove it from the heat. Pour it immediately into the melted chocolate. Beat the mixture vigorously with a whisk until it is thoroughly mixed and glossy. Using a palette knife, spread it quickly over the top of the cooled cake (and the sides, if desired); it should still be sufficiently liquid to settle into a shiny, smooth coating with no knife marks, but it won't affect the flavour if this doesn't happen. When the ganache has set, decorate with toasted almonds.

CHAPTER THIRTEEN GROWING OLD GRACEFULLY

'When you die, all the bread
you ever wasted is weighed.
If it is heavier than you, hell
is your destination.'

RUSSIAN PROVERB

Few things compare with freshly baked bread. Like freshly picked vegetables or fruit, it has a vitality that is all the more compelling for being transitory. Like fresh air, we recognise and savour it, but we cannot bottle it. If we could, it would be instantly recognisable as not the real thing.

For supermarkets, freshness is a double-edged sword. They waft the word around their stores like a purifying censer: freshly baked, fresh today, freshly squeezed, oven fresh, sealed-in freshness, farm fresh, fresh tasting ... it seems that no product or process, however banal or deceptive ('farm fresh' eggs, for example, are laid by hens kept in battery cages), can fail to benefit from an association with freshness. But in reality freshness is a big problem for supermarkets and their suppliers. Global sourcing, centralised distribution and nationwide reach make it all but impossible to have anything on the shelves in less than 24 hours from when it was picked, baked or cooked. Compare this to the neighbourhood artisan baker who sells all his bread within a few hours of it leaving the oven.

Our culture has been corrupted by freshness, by the delusion that things are only any good if they are fresh and by the lie that they actually *are* fresh, when very often they are merely in a state of chemically suspended animation. So, after some words about the way bread ages, I suggest that we should reject the contemporary cult of permanent youthfulness, rediscover the creativity of thrift and relish bread's dignified decline towards the dust whither we too are bound.

How bread goes stale (or doesn't)

Starch crystallisation

When bread cools down after baking, the starch begins to 'retrograde', or to move from a gel to a crystalline state. The speed at which this happens is dependent on the temperature and humidity at which the bread is stored. Although our palates experience old bread as being 'dry', it is not so much the loss of moisture from the crumb, which is relatively insignificant, as the feeling of denseness in the particles that makes it harder to chew the bread and causes us to describe it as 'stale'. Bread stales most rapidly at +5°C, so it should never be stored in the refrigerator. At -5°C, staling stops, so freezing is a good way of suspending the ageing of bread. However, to freeze and thaw bread, it must be passed twice through its temperature of maximum staling and this is estimated to add the equivalent of a day's worth of staling at room temperature.

Enzymes to keep bread 'fresh'

Enzymes are proteins, found widely in nature, which speed up metabolic reactions, i.e. the conversion of chemical compounds in biological organisms. Enzymes extracted from animal, plant, fungal or bacterial sources are used in the chemical, pharmaceutical and food industries for the production of everything from washing powder to beer and cheese. Many are produced by genetic engineering.

Such enzymes are extensively used in the bakery industry to make dough more pliable or stretchy (to make more puffed-up loaves, croissants etc) and to keep bread soft after baking, thereby extending its 'shelf life'. These 'anti-staling' enzymes appear to work by interfering with and slowing down the process of starch retrogradation. This is good for the retailers, who have more time to sell their loaves, and nice for the consumer if he or she likes bread that stays squishy for days on end. But there may be downsides.

Very fresh, and therefore less 'crystalline', bread is generally recognised to be less digestible than older bread. The effect of crumb-softening enzymes is to keep bread artificially 'young' and more gel-like – in other words in a condition that is known to be less digestible. No wonder many people have a gut feeling that modern bread makes them bloated.

Most of the enzymes used in baking are derived from sources that are not normally consumed as food, so modern industrial bread really does represent a mass experiment on whole populations. It would be good if this experiment were being monitored with a fraction of the energy that the food industry devotes to manipulating the national diet.

Natural freshness

There are some natural ways to reduce the rate of bread staling, or the perception of it.

- A very dense texture, even if quite moist, will be perceived as harder to chew and therefore less fresh than a bread with a more open structure, despite the fact that the latter will dry out more quickly.
- The more moisture that is retained in the baked product, the softer it will appear. This explains the good shelf life of 100 per cent rye breads, with their moisture-holding properties. It is also an argument for working as much liquid as possible into the dough at the mixing stage, as well as for baking at a high temperature or in an oven (especially a retained-heat brick oven) that allows the quickest possible transfer of heat throughout the loaf with minimum moisture loss. However, moisture retention does not prevent the hardening of starch, which is the main symptom of staling.
- Fat helps a little, not so much because it is soft as because it improves the retention of fermentation gases in the crumb structure, thereby increasing the perception of softness.
- Some sources suggest that the organic acids (lactic, acetic, butyric etc) generated in a sourdough fermentation have an inhibiting effect on starch retrogradation. This can be seen by making the ciabatta recipe (page 231) either with or without the rye sourdough component. In my experience it keeps significantly longer when made with the sourdough.
- Enzyme-active (diastatic) malt has some effect on starch crystallisation and was widely used before the deployment of novel food enzymes.

Storing bread

It follows from the above that there is not a great deal that can be done to limit the rate of bread staling. Far better, as I shall show, to put the changing character of ageing bread to culinary advantage. But certain strategies are worth considering:

- To limit the rate of starch crystallisation, store bread at 16°C or above and never in the refrigerator.
- To conserve overall moisture, wrap bread in a polythene bag or similar air-tight film. Any moisture escaping from the outside of the loaf will condense inside the bag and a rough equilibrium will develop.
- To conserve a crunchy crust is not possible for more than a few hours under normal circumstances because the greater moisture in the middle of the loaf will inevitably migrate to the edge and soften the crust. If a loaf is left un-wrapped and exposed to the air (at normal humidity), moisture will evaporate from the surface, giving the impression that the original crust is remaining crunchy. However, although it may remain hard, it will, within a day of baking, have lost the particular character of a freshly baked crust.
- If the aim is to retain as much of the freshly baked character of the bread as possible, the best method of storage beyond a day or two is by freezing. Although this adds about a day of staling, it does limit the process more effectively than any other method. It is advisable to slice a loaf before freezing

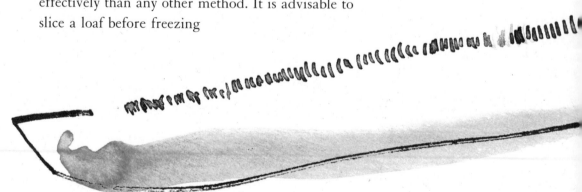

it so that it is then possible to remove individual slices on demand: not only does this speed up defrosting, but it avoids the need to consume a defrosted loaf in its entirety at a time when its rate of staling has already been advanced by freezing.

Reviving old bread

To restore some crunch to a crust that has gone leathery, all that is required is to reheat the surface of the loaf to a depth of a few millimetres. This can be done in a hot oven (200–220°C) in five minutes or so. This is not long enough, however, to soften the starches inside the loaf and so should be considered only as a way of perking up a recently baked loaf that has lost a bit of sparkle, such as a limp baguette or a bloomer that has sweated inside your shopping bag.

To revive the softness of the crumb inside the loaf, it is necessary to ensure that heat penetrates to the middle and thereby changes the starches from the crystalline to the gel state. This takes some time, so the oven must not be so hot that it scorches the crust before the centre of the loaf is warm. For a small (400g) loaf, 12 to 15 minutes at 170°C is about right.

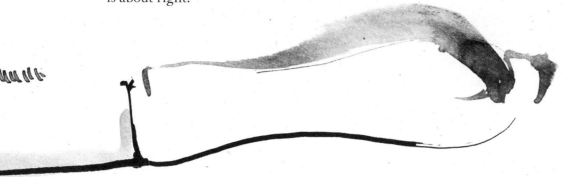

If the loaf that you are trying to refresh seems exceptionally dry, you may need to provide an external source of moisture. Brushing the entire crust with water will create a little steam in the oven as it vaporises. To keep more of this moisture inside the loaf, wrap it in foil after wetting the crust all over. The heat will take a little longer to penetrate to the core. For a crunchy crust, remove the foil for the last few minutes of heating.

Remember that reheating bread will accelerate its subsequent rate of staling. This is why the part-baked 'bake-off' offerings masquerading as 'fresh' bread in supermarkets and forecourts the length and breadth of the land turn pretty much to dust within a day.

Uses for old bread

Among the more perplexing reasons given by one villager for not eating the bread from my bakery was that 'it doesn't fit in the toaster'. Although I interpreted this as a kindly attempt not to give offence, it did indicate the considerable influence that toasting has had on commercial bread production and marketing. In a very real sense, industrial bread is made with domestic toasters in mind. It is therefore rather ironic that so much effort goes into preserving a soft, moist and gummy crumb when exactly the opposite is the *raison d'être* of toast. Toasting a dry slice of bread does two things: it softens the starches in the centre of the slice and it caramelises and partially burns the outer surface. The effect is to boost the caramel flavour, create a contrast between exterior and interior, and to soak up toppings that melt in the residual heat. Toasting a slice of bread whose crumb is already (artificially) soft can cause the collapse of the internal structure into a thin, dense and leathery core with little absorbency. Strong teeth are needed to tear mouthfuls from such stuff.

Be that as it may, toast is the first and most obvious way of using old bread. Then there are favourites such as summer pudding and bread and butter pudding. These are well enough known not to need recipes from me, but

I would add a couple of comments. Summer pudding uses the absorbency of bread to soak up the rich juices of berries and currants. If the bread used is white and soft, the result can be a slimy mess. Much better to use something dry and with a bit of body, like French Country Bread (see page 182). Bread and butter pudding is a wonderful vehicle for using up rich and flavoured breads such as brioche (page 236), bun loaves (page 258) or even stollen (page 265). We made a version for the Village Bakery restaurant that used a mixture of Borodinsky Bread with raisins in it and French Country Bread. It was quite a hit.

The recipes in this chapter illustrate some of the many ways of using bread as it undergoes the natural process of ageing. If nothing else, they show the extent of our culinary loss if we fall for the notion that the only good bread is fresh bread.

Incidentally, the best collection of recipes using bread that I know of is in Silvija Davidson's excellent book, *Loaf, Crust and Crumb* (published by Michael Joseph in 1995 but now sadly out of print).

Aubergine and Red Pepper Bruschetta

Bruschetta originates from central Italy and is now widely known. It is really no more than toasted bread decorated with typical Italian foods – tomatoes, peppers, herbs, cheeses, anchovies, Parma ham, tuna, etc. The toast is often rubbed with garlic and always doused in a fair bit of olive oil. Outside Italy an unfortunate practice has arisen of frying the bread in olive oil, which, apart from heating the oil unnecessarily, makes the whole thing too greasy. It is precisely the balance between dry toast and patches of oil that gives the base of a bruschetta its character.

Italians do not often melt the cheese on a bruschetta, but I must admit to shoving mine under the grill for a few moments just before serving. If you are not going to eat your bruschetta immediately, do not melt the cheese.

There must also be a balance between bread and topping – for example, delicate salads or bland cheese such as mozzarella would be outfaced by too hearty a base. On the other hand, the sharpness of anchovies or the dense fattiness of salami needs more robust support than plain white toast.

The recipe below combines some of my favourite flavours with the bread that, of all the ones in this book, makes the most wonderful toast – naturally leavened *pain de campagne*, or French Country Bread.

Makes 2 bruschette, enough for a light meal

1 small	Aubergine
50g	Olive oil
1 medium	Onion, very thinly sliced into rings
1 medium	Red pepper, seeded and thinly sliced into rings
2 large slices	French Country Bread (page 182)
1 large clove	Garlic
100g	Jutland Blue cheese (or similar)
	Salt and pepper to taste

Cut the aubergine lengthwise into thin strips. Brush these with a little of the olive oil on both sides and sear them on a griddle or under a grill. The aim is to soften and colour them without burning.

Put the remaining olive oil in a frying-pan. Add the onion and heat gently. Put a lid on the pan to sweat the onion. Add the red pepper and cook gently for a further 10 minutes or so until the pepper has softened.

Cut 2 thick slices of French Country Bread and toast them under a grill, colouring them on one side rather more than the other. Peel and squash the garlic clove and rub it all over the less toasted side of the bread. Then tip the onion and pepper on to the garlic side of the toast and spread evenly, taking care to make use of all the olive oil.

Ruck the aubergine slices into little folds and arrange them over the onion and pepper mixture, all along the top of the bruschetta. Cut the cheese into shavings, or crumble it on top of the aubergines. Season with a little salt and pepper if desired. Flash under the grill for a minute, immediately before serving so that the cheese is just beginning to melt.

I have only once dined in an officers' mess. At sixth-form college I trained in the Inshore Rescue Boat service and was sent with a fellow student to Poole Harbour to see how the Royal Navy did things. After a cold day at sea, we scrubbed up as best we could and were treated to silver service in an almost deserted dining room. I was about to tuck into the soup when the immaculately dressed orderly removed the lid from a silver dish and proffered it with a gesture somewhere between a flourish and a challenge. I surveyed the dish and saw what looked like a pile of greasy wood chippings. I had absolutely no idea what to do with them, but would rather have died than appear ignorant. Spooning a few on to my side plate, I noticed a naval lip curl, but nothing was said. Years later, when a friend served soup with croûtons in it, I realised what I had done and re-lived the embarrassment all over again. I am including the following recipe as part of a continuing personal struggle with croûton-induced feelings of social inadequacy.

Green Salad with Croûtons

Croûtons are small squares of toasted or dried bread. Their crunch and dryness are a foil for softer, wetter textures. As with bruschetta, there is no need to fry them in oil. The most they need is a little drizzle.

Choose a light bread without any vegetable bits in it to make croûtons. The Altamura Bread on page 222 is ideal. A wholemeal loaf, such as Basic Bread (see page 141), has more body.

Dried croûtons can be cooled and stored in an airtight bag in the freezer.

Makes a good salad for 2

4 slices	Altamura Bread (page 222)
4 cloves	Garlic
2	Plum tomatoes
150g	Mixed green leaves
50g	Blue cheese (Jutland Blue or Roquefort)
20g	Olive oil
5g	Cider or raspberry vinegar

Arrange the slices of bread on a baking tray in an oven heated to no more than 130°C. The object is to dry the bread without it taking any extra colour. Turn the slices over from time to time to make sure that they dry out evenly. It may take up to an hour if the bread is fairly moist.

As soon as the dried bread is out of the oven, peel and squash the garlic cloves and use to rub each slice well. Cut each plum tomato in half and use one half for each slice, rubbing and squeezing gently so that the surface of the bread is slightly moistened. Now cut the bread slices into roughly 1cm croûtons.

Prepare a salad of mixed leaves with whatever you have to hand: rocket, dandelion, lamb's lettuce, land cress, fresh coriander, endive etc. Put these in a large salad bowl and throw the croûtons on top.

Take the blue cheese and pass it through a garlic press or a mouli grater over the salad: fine strands of cheese are the object. Finally, whisk together the oil and vinegar to make a dressing and pour it over the salad. Toss the salad lightly and serve.

Crumbs

One of the most versatile ways of using bread is as crumbs, either fresh or dried. Crumbs work as a much better filler and thickener than floury starches because their particle size opens out the texture of whatever they are in. The recipes below use crumbs in a variety of ways.

I find the coarse side of a handheld cheese grater is the best tool for making fresh crumbs, provided the bread has a certain firmness to it. This way, some of the crusts (providing they are not too dark) can be grated as well. Rubbing crumbs in the fingers tends to produce rather uneven results with all but the driest bread. You can, of course, use a food processor for this job.

At the Village Bakery, we needed vast quantities of breadcrumbs for the thousands of Christmas puddings that we made each year. I used to cut left-over wholemeal loaves in half lengthways and set them out on trays next to the wood-fired oven. In a couple of days they would be bone dry and we crumbed them with our commercial heavy-duty vegetable grater, which screamed like a banshee and wore out blades with some regularity.

Stuffing

Stuffing recipes almost always call for fresh breadcrumbs but I think that this advice needs to be qualified. For one thing, as I have repeated *ad nauseam*, the crumb-softening enzymes used in much modern bread keep it so squishy for so many days that any attempt to turn it into crumbs is more likely to end up with soggy pellets, like the ones we used as ammunition for elastic-band catapults during boring lessons at school.

Assuming that nobody who has tolerated the rants on this subject so far is likely to use anything other than the best artisan (and preferably their own) bread for crumbs, I still think it wise to recommend making 'fresh' crumbs from bread that is two or three days' old. At this age there need be no fear that it will be too dry and any hardness of the starches will vanish when the crumbs are mixed with milk or egg and subjected to the heat of cooking.

Simple Shallot and Parsley Stuffing

Crumbs made from Arkatena Bread will add a hint of fennel to Silvija Davidson's recipe, which is recommended for roast meat, poultry or vegetables (e.g. peppers).

150g	Arkatena Bread (page 190) or other
150g	Shallots or onions, finely chopped
50g	Unsalted butter
1 small bunch	Parsley, finely chopped
a pinch	Nutmeg, grated
	A little beaten egg (or milk), to bind
	Salt and pepper to taste

Make the bread into crumbs. Sauté the shallots or onions in the butter until soft and translucent. Add the breadcrumbs, parsley, nutmeg and some seasoning. Stir in just enough egg or milk to bind.

Fishcakes

This recipe uses both fresh and dried breadcrumbs. The fresh ones add body to the soft inside of the fishcakes, while the dried ones provide a contrasting crunch on the outside. I suggest the light but tangy French Country Bread for the middle and the more substantial Basic Bread for the outside, but other breads would work just as well.

To some extent, your choice of fish will determine the flavour of these cakes. In these days of over fishing and problems with commercial fish farming, try to choose organic or sustainably managed sources of fish. Graig Farm (see page 353) supplies an interesting range by mail order, some of which are caught off the island of St Helena. Fishcakes are a good way of disguising the flavours of fish like herring and mackerel, which are not to everyone's taste.

Makes 6 large fishcakes

100g	Wholemeal bread, sliced
120g	French Country Bread (page 182), 1–2 days old
170g	Fish fillet (cod, herring or mackerel etc)
30g	Smoked salmon, finely chopped (optional)
50g	Spring onion or red onion, finely chopped
1 heaped tablespoon	Fresh herbs, finely chopped
150g	Potato, mashed
2g	Nutmeg, grated
	Salt and pepper to taste
	Beaten egg, for dipping
	Olive oil for drizzling

Dry the wholemeal bread slices by leaving them in a warm place for a few days or by toasting them in a very low oven (130°C) until they are completely crisp. Grate them into crumbs either by hand or in a food processor.

Make the French Country Bread into crumbs.

Remove any skin or bones from the raw fish and chop it into small pieces. Then mix everything together except the wholemeal breadcrumbs and the beaten egg, seasoning with a little salt and pepper if desired. Work the mixture with your hands until it comes together.

Pour the beaten egg into a shallow bowl. Set out the dry wholemeal breadcrumbs in another bowl.

Shape the mixture into 6 fishcakes, dip them in the egg and then press them firmly into the dried wholemeal crumbs. Make sure the cakes are well covered.

Drizzle a little olive oil over both sides of each fishcake and cook them on a griddle, under a grill, in a frying-pan or in an ovenproof dish at 180°C for about 10 minutes, turning them halfway through cooking.

Charlotte Russe

Generally credited to the famous French chef Antonin Carême – one-time chef to Tsar Alexander I – and probably dedicated to Queen Charlotte, Princess Royal and eldest daughter of King George III, this delicious apple pudding is known in Russia by the charming diminutive *Sharlotka*. It is another breadcrumb recipe, but this time some of the crumbs are fried in butter. Some recipes for Charlotte call for slices of bread or, effectively, cake (in the form of 'ladies' fingers') to line the mould. However, with the rye bread specified in Russian recipes, I think that a lining of crumbs makes for a more delicate pudding.

Russian recipes call for 'black bread', which just means an ordinary rye bread. I suggest using Borodinsky crumbs because of their malty coriander flavour. But one can have too much of a good thing, so it is probably best to remove the bottom crust where the whole coriander seeds are lodged. A plain rye bread would be a perfectly acceptable substitute.

Makes 1 plump Sharlotka

300g   Borodinsky Bread (page 168), at least 4 days old

150g   Butter

  2g   Ground cloves

  5g   Ground cinnamon

150g   Raw cane sugar

150g   White wine

6 medium   Apples (cookers)

50g Ground almonds

50g Currants or raisins

Grate the Borodinsky bread to make crumbs. Use a little of the butter to grease a large pudding basin or mould, about 1.5 litres in capacity. Dust this thoroughly with some of the breadcrumbs, making sure that there are no blind spots. If the apple mix seeps through, Sharlotka may be reluctant to come out of her shell.

Fry the remaining breadcrumbs with the spices and 50g of the sugar in the rest of the butter. When they have caramelised slightly, remove them from the heat and pour on 100g of the white wine.

Peel, core and finely slice the apples. Mix with the rest of the sugar, the almonds, the currants or raisins and the rest of the white wine.

Put a layer of the breadcrumb mix in the bottom of the mould, followed by a layer of the apple mix, and so on, finishing with a layer of breadcrumb mix. Bake in a slow oven (150°C) for about an hour. Turn the mould upside down on to a serving dish and hope for the best. Serve warm with cream or crème-fraîche.

In the early days of the Village Bakery, we used to make ice cream. It was a good way of using gluts of soft fruit from the smallholding and surplus milk from Rosie, Tansy and Samantha (don't ask), our house cows – until, that is, food hygiene regulations required us to invest in expensive equipment for real-time temperature monitoring, at which point we gave up. This was bad news for one regular customer, who was so fond of Brown Bread Ice Cream that he lamented its demise in a long ode in the style of the infamous Scottish 'poet', William McGonagall. Sadly, the text of this supreme piece of doggerel has been lost, which may come as some relief to the customer, who went on to become a Very Important Person and is now Master of an Oxford college.

Brown Bread Ice Cream

The surprising thing about the breadcrumbs in this recipe, which is based on one from *The Village Bakery Cookbook* (1993), by Lis Whitley and Diane Richter, is that they stay crunchy even after being mixed with the liquid custard. The trick is to caramelise them with some sugar, after which they become brittle and almost impervious to softening.

The function of the breadcrumbs is mostly textural, so the choice of bread is not that important, though I can't imagine olive bread working too well. But something like Borodinsky, which has bags of flavour and a certain sweetness, is worth trying.

Makes enough for 6 portions

85g	Wholemeal bread, sliced
50g	Butter
75g	Raw cane sugar
400g	Egg (8 eggs)
75g	Caster sugar
500g	Whole milk or single cream
1	Vanilla pod

Dry the wholemeal bread slices by leaving them in a warm place for a few days or by toasting them in a very low oven (130°C) until they are completely crisp. Grate them into crumbs either by hand or in a food processor. Fry these with the butter until they are crisp. Add the raw cane sugar and continue to heat, stirring regularly, until the mixture caramelises. Leave to cool and, if necessary, break it up into fine crumbs.

Separate the eggs and beat the yolks with the caster sugar until thick and creamy.

Put the milk or cream into a saucepan with the vanilla pod and bring to the boil. Remove the pod, pour the milk on to the egg yolks and whisk thoroughly. Heat this mixture in a double boiler, or in a bowl placed over a pan of gently simmering water, stirring constantly until it is thick enough to coat the back of a wooden spoon. Remove from the heat, strain through a fine sieve and leave to cool completely.

Stir the caramelised breadcrumbs into the cold custard. Whip the egg whites until they are stiff and fold them into the mixture. Pour it into a plastic container and put it in the freezer. Remove it once or twice during the freezing process and give it a stir to stop ice crystals forming.

You could also churn this recipe in an ice-cream machine. Make the mixture up as described and follow the manufacturer's instructions.

Finally, as some reward for having accompanied me this far, may I offer you a drink?

'It seems,' opines Elena Molokhovets in Chapter 46 ('Kvas, Beer, Mead') of her *Gift to Young Housewives*[1], 'that our Russian kvas has all the qualities necessary to be considered not only one of the healthiest and most nutritious drinks, but also one which has healing properties, especially for consumption [tuberculosis].'

Although this sounds like just another example of Russian exceptionalism and self-congratulation, modern research into the beneficial effects of lactic acid bacteria (see page 38) should make us pause before hastening to judgement.

Kvas is a kind of mildly alcoholic small beer, fermented from grains (rye, wheat, buckwheat and barley in the main) and malt. Its name betrays its provenance, since the Russian for sourdough or leaven is *zakvaska*. It has been a favourite drink of the peasantry since medieval times. One feels that William Cobbett would have approved of it as an everyday drink for farming folk.

With its slightly bready flavour and lactic undertones, kvas is something of an acquired taste for Western Europeans. The nearest comparison would be with a bottle-conditioned, cloudy and yeasty wheat beer.

Kvas is a double dose of fermentation, since the main ingredient of the brew is bread, which has itself already been fermented. I leave you with this modest example and celebration of the self-renewing process at the heart of breadmaking.

Kvas

The Russian recipe calls simply for rye bread. It will come as no surprise that I suggest using Borodinsky, but any 100 per cent rye bread will do.

I recommend sourdough instead of the yeast specified in the recipe. It seems to me that, if we are to believe the claims for kvas' healing properties, we should aim for a slow fermentation with plenty of opportunity for the development of lactic acid bacteria.

The function of the raisins is to provide a source of sugar, which creates a secondary fermentation in the bottle. Unless you are an experienced home brewer, equipped with champagne corks and wires, it might be sensible to use plastic screw-top bottles for your kvas. You will be able to see if excessive pressure is building up inside them and if they do explode, there will be only mess, not injury.

Makes 5 litres of kvas

The day before

Prepare a Rye Production Sourdough (page 165)

The kvas mixture

450g Borodinsky (or other rye bread)

4.5 litres Water

300g Molasses (or treacle)

150g Rye Production Sourdough (above)

2 per bottle Raisins

Cut the Borodinsky into small pieces and dry them out thoroughly, either in a warm, dry place over a few days or in a very low oven (130°C). Put them in a bucket of at least 5 litres capacity. Boil the water and pour it over the bread rusks. Cover and leave until the temperature has dropped to about 35°C. Pour the mixture through a fine sieve or a piece of muslin into another bucket. Press the crumby sludge very gently to release the last of the liquid but do not squeeze it hard or too much sediment will fall in.

Add the molasses to the warm liquid and mix thoroughly. Then add the prepared rye sourdough, mix well, cover and leave for 12 hours in a warm place (as near to 30°C as you can).

In the morning, strain and pour into sterilised bottles, adding 2 raisins to each bottle. Seal tightly and move to a cool place.

Molokhovets says that the kvas will be ready to drink in 2 days. I would keep an eye on the bottles. If they start ballooning alarmingly, release some pressure, or just pour and enjoy, provided you don't mind cloudy beer. If, when you unscrew a bottle after a few days, there is no audible release of gas, the bottle fermentation has probably not got going. Give the bottle a bit of a shake and bring it into a warmer place to kickstart the fermentation.

Once it has acquired its modest fizz, kvas is best served chilled. It can also be used as the liquid for making soups such as *borshch* and *shchi*.

RESOURCES

Some of the specialist ingredients and equipment mentioned in this book are not widely available. Below is a brief list of suppliers and also of a few organisations concerned with the relationship between food and health.

Ingredients

ORGANIC FLOUR BY MAIL ORDER

The Watermill, Little Salkeld, Penrith, Cumbria CA10 1NN
Tel: 01768 881523
www.organicmill.co.uk

Shipton Mill, Long Newnton, Tetbury, Gloucestershire GL8 8RP
Tel: 01666 505050
www.shipton-mill.com
Wide range of flours, including ciabatta flour, semolina, rice flour, kibbled rye, Kamut flour, spelt flour and chestnut flour.

Doves Farm Foods Ltd, Salisbury Road, Hungerford, Berkshire RG17 0RF
www.dovesfarm-organic.co.uk
Wide range of flours, including gluten-free blends and rice, buckwheat and gram flours. Mail order through third parties only, with links from the Doves Farm website.

FWP Matthews Ltd, Station Road, Shipton-under-Wychwood,
Chipping Norton, Oxfordshire OX7 6BH
Tel: 01993 830342
www.fwpmatthews.co.uk
Also supplies a range of French flours.

Bacheldre Watermill, Churchstoke, Montgomery, Powys SY15 6TE
Tel: 01588 620489
www.bacheldremill.co.uk

Goodness Direct, South March, Daventry, Northamptonshire NN11 4PH
Tel: 0871 871 6611
www.goodnessdirect.co.uk
Wide range of small packs of speciality and gluten-free flours, plus other ingredients.

SEA SALT

Anglesey Sea Salt Company (Halen Môn Salt), Brynsiencyn,
Anglesey LL61 6TQ
Tel: 01248 430871
www.seasalt.co.uk
Although salt is a 'non-agricultural' ingredient under the terms of the EU Organic Regulation, this salt has been certified by the Soil Association as being derived from clean sea water and processed without additives.

The Low Sodium Sea Salt Company Ltd, 101–103 Palace Road, Bromley,
Kent BR1 3JZ
Tel: 020 8402 6079
www.soloseasalt.com

HOPS

The Organic Herb Trading Company, Milverton, Somerset TA4 1NF
Tel: 01823 401205
www.organicherbtrading.co.uk

ORGANIC AND SUSTAINABLY CAUGHT FISH

Graig Farm Organics, Dolau, Llandrindod Wells, Powys LD1 5TL
Tel: 01597 851655
www.graigfarm.co.uk

DIASTATIC MALT FLOUR

It is worth trying your local home-brewing supplier for this, but the following is a mail-order source:
www.art-of-brewing.co.uk

Equipment

WOOD-FIRED BRICK OVENS

Alf Armstrong, Forno Bravo UK, Ivy Cottage, Quebec, Kirkoswald, Penrith, Cumbria CA10 1DQ
Tel: 07989 410528
www.fornobravo.com
Alf supplies and builds a range of wood-fired brick ovens, from domestic to commercial.

PANNETONS/PROVING BASKETS

Creeds (Southern) Ltd, New Street, Waddesdon, Aylesbury,
Buckinghamshire HP18 0LR
Tel: 0870 350 9000
www.creeds.uk.com
Small range of linen-lined proving baskets. Creeds also supplies other bakery equipment such as thermometers, plastic scrapers, dough marking knives and professional weighing scales.

Dough Boys Bakeries Ltd, 79a Hargwyne Street, London SW9 9RH
Tel: 020 7274 6100
www.breadsetcetera.com
Wide range of bread proving baskets made from bent wood – typically used for Continental rye breads.

DIGITAL SCALES

www.ourweigh.co.uk

PIZZA STONES AND OVEN LINERS

Probably the cheapest ceramic stone for baking 'sole' breads and pizzas is a large, unglazed quarry tile (or two) from your local tile shop. Purpose-made offerings are available from:

Professional Cookware Direct
www.cookware.co.uk

The Hearth Kitchen Company (USA)
www.hearthkitchen.com
Interesting ceramic liner designed to make an ordinary domestic oven perform more like a brick one.

Armorica, 19 Rams Walk, Petersfield, Hampshire GU32 3JA
Tel: 08456 017262
www.armorica.co.uk

PANETTONE CASES

Reynards (UK) Ltd, Greengate, Middleton, Manchester M24 1RU
Tel: 0161 653 7700
www.reynards.com
This is a wholesaler, so you will be asked to buy a large number of cases.

Organisations

The Soil Association, 40–56 Victoria Street, Bristol BS1 6BY
Tel: 0117 314 5000
www.soilassociation.org
The UK's leading environmental charity, promoting sustainable, organic farming and championing human health.

The Food Commission, 94 White Lion Street, London N1 9PF
Tel: 020 7837 2250
www.foodcomm.org.uk
Campaigns for safer, healthier food in the UK.

Foods Matter, 5 Lawn Road, London NW3 2XS
Tel: 020 7722 2866
www.foodsmatter.com
Publishes a magazine about food sensitivity problems and solutions.

Slow Food Movement
www.slowfood.com
International organisation whose aim is 'to protect the pleasures of the table from the homogenisation of modern fast food and life.'

Baking Courses

'As to the act of making bread,
it would be shocking indeed,
if that had to be taught by the means of books.'
WILLIAM COBBETT, *Cottage Economy* (1823)

So why not try a hands-on class with the author of this book? Bread Matters Ltd runs baking courses at the Village Bakery, Melmerby, in the unspoilt Eden Valley near the Lake District.

For further details, visit www.breadmatters.com or write to:

Bread Matters Ltd, The Tower House, Melmerby, Penrith, Cumbria CA10 1HE

NOTES

CHAPTER 1

1. Biagini, R. E., MacKenzie, B. A., Sammons, D. L., Smith, J. P., Striley, C. A., Robertson, S. K., Snawder, J. E. *Evaluation of the prevalence of anti-wheat, anti-flour dust, and anti-alpha-amylase specific IgE antibodies in US blood donors*. Ann Allergy Asthma Immunol. 2004 June; 92(6):649–53. This study found wheat-sensitive antibodies in 3.6 per cent of a large unselected group of blood donors. In terms of the UK population, this would mean that about two million people have some form of wheat intolerance.

2. Constituents of Chorleywood Bread Process loaf: Cauvain, S. and Young, L. (2000). *Baking Problems Solved*. Cambridge: Woodhead. National Association of Master Bakers (1996) *The Master Bakers' Book of Breadmaking*. Ware: NAMB.

3. Dupuis, B. (1997). *The chemistry and toxicology of potassium bromate*. Cereals Food World, 42, 171–183.

4. Gerrard, J. & Sutton, K. (2005). *Addition of transglutaminase to cereal products may generate the epitope responsible for coeliac disease*. Trends in Food Science & Technology 16 (2005) 510–512. Malandain, H. (2005). *Transglutaminases: a meeting point for wheat allergy, coeliac disease and food safety*. Eur Ann Allergy Clin Immunol. 2005; 37:397–403.

5. Moreno-Ancillo, A. et al (2004). *Bread eating induced oral angioedema due to alpha-amylase allergy*. J Investig Allergol Clin Immunol. 2004;14(4):346–7. An earlier study, part-funded by two major enzyme manufacturers, had concluded that people sensitised to Aspergillus species fungi were unlikely to react to alpha-amylase and hemicellulase (derived from Aspergillus) enzymes ingested from baked bread. See:

Cullinan et al (1997). *Clinical responses to ingested alpha-amylase and hemicellulase in persons sensitized to Aspergillus fumigatus.* Allergy. 1997;52:346–349.

6. Sander, I., Raulf-Heimsoth, M., Van Kampen, V., Baur, X. (2000). *Is fungal alpha-amylase in bread an allergen?* Clin Exp Allergy. 2000 Apr;30(4):560–5.

7. Graham, R. D., Welch, R. M. and Bouis, H. E. (2001). *Addressing micronutrient malnutrition through enhancing the nutritional quality of staple foods: principles, perspectives and knowledge gaps.* Advances in Agronomy, 70:77–142.

8. INRA (2002). *The nutritional value of bread can be much improved.* http://w3.inra.fr/presse/fev02/gb/nb2.htm

9. Schroeder, H. (1971). *Losses of vitamins and trace minerals resulting from processing and preservation of foods.* Am J Clin Nutr. 1971 May;24(5):562–73.

10. Chaurand, M. et al (2005). *Influence du type de mouture (cylindres vs meules) sur les teneurs en minéraux des différentes fractions du grain de blé en cultures conventionelles et biologiques.* Industries des Céréales. 2005:142.

11. Fredriksson, H. et al (2004). *Fermentation reduces free asparagine in dough and acrylamide content in bread.* Cereal Chem. 81(5):650–653.

12. Batifoulier, F., Verny, M-A., Chanliaud, E., Rémésy, C. and Demigné, C. (2005). *Effect of different breadmaking methods on thiamine, riboflavin and pyridoxine contents of wheat bread.* Journal of Cereal Science 42 (2005) 101–108.

CHAPTER 2

1. Link between excessive calcium and prostate cancer: http://www.nutraingredients.com/news/ng.asp?id=63908

2. Zhou W. et al (2005). *Dietary iron, zinc, and calcium and the risk of lung cancer.* Epidemiology. 2005 Nov;16(6):772–9.

3. Lindenmeier, M. and T. Hoffmann (2004). *Influence of baking conditions and precursor supplementation on the amounts of the antioxidant pronyl-L-lysine in bakery products.* J Agric Food Chem. 2004,52(2):350–4.

4. Katina, K. et al (2005). *Potential of sourdough for healthier cereal products.* Trends in Food Science & Technology 16 (2005) 104–112.

5. Lopez, H. et al (2003). *Making bread with sourdough improves mineral bioavailability from reconstituted whole wheat flour in rats.* Nutrition. 2003 June;19(6):524–530.

6. Leenhardt, F. et al (2005). *Moderate decrease of pH by sourdough fermentation is sufficient to reduce phytate content of whole wheat flour through endogenous phytase activity.* J Agric Food Chem. 2005;53:98–102.

7. Rosenquist, H. and Å. Hansen (1998). *The antimicrobial effect of organic acids, sour dough and nisin against Bacillus subtilis and B. licheniformis isolated from wheat bread.* Journal of Applied Microbiology. 1998;85:621–631.

8. Sockett, P. N. (1991). *Food poisoning outbreaks associated with manufactured foods in England and Wales: 1980–89.* Communicable Disease Report 1, R105–R109.

9. Pepe, O. et al (2003). *Rope-producing strains of* Bacillus spp. *from wheat bread and strategy for their control by lactic acid bacteria.* Appl Environ Microbiol. 2003 April; 69(4):2321–2329.

10. Di Cagno, R. et al (2002). *Proteolysis by sourdough lactic acid bacteria: effects on wheat flour protein fractions and gliadin peptides involved in human cereal intolerance.* Appl Environ Microbiol. 2002 February; 68(2):623–633.

11. Kobayashi, M. et al (2004). *Degradation of wheat allergen in Japanese soy sauce.* Int J Mol Med. 2004 Jun;13(6): 821–7.

12. Mittag, D. et al (2005). *Immunoglobulin E-reactivity of wheat-allergic subjects (baker's asthma, food allergy, wheat-dependent, exercise-induced anaphylaxis) to wheat protein fractions with different solubility and digestibility.* Mol Nutr Food Res. 2004 Oct;48(5):380–9.

13. Di Cagno, R. et al (2004). *Sourdough bread made from wheat and non-toxic flours and started with selected lactobacilli is tolerated in coeliac sprue patients.* Appl Environ Microbiol. 2004 Feb;70(2):1088–96.

14. Stapledon, G. (1964,1968) *Human Ecology.* Haughley: the Soil Association, 215.

15. Quoted in Wrench, G. (1938). *The wheel of health.* London: C. W. Daniel.

16. Chungui Lu et al. (2005). *Markedly different gene expression in wheat grown with organic or inorganic fertilizer.* Proc R Soc B (2005) 272:1901–1908.

17. Soil Association (2001). *Organic farming, food quality and human health: a review of the evidence.* Bristol: Soil Association. See also: *Does Organic Food Have an 'Extra Quality'?* Elm Farm Research Centre, www.efrc.com

CHAPTER 3

1. William Morris, quoted in Stapledon, G. (1964, 1968). *Human Ecology*. Haughley: Soil Association, 217.

2. Breadmakers: see http://www.esure.com/news_item.jsp?nId=16808

CHAPTER 4

1. High-protein wheat from the Black Isle: personal communication from Michael Marriage of Doves Farm.

2. See the website of the Coeliac Society UK, http://www.coeliac.co.uk

3. Stallknecht, G. F., Gilbertson, K. M. and Ranney, J. E. (1996). *Alternative wheat cereals as food grains: einkorn, emmer, spelt, kamut, and triticale*. http://www.hort. purdue.edu/newcrop/proceedings1996/v3-156.html

4. Gänzle, M. et al (1998). *Modelling of growth of* Lactobacillus sanfranciscensis *and* Candida milleri *in response to process parameters of sourdough fermentation*. Appl Environ Microbiol. 1998 July; 64(7):2616–2623.

5. Cauvain, S and Young, L. (2001). *Baking Problems Solved*. Cambridge: Woodhead, 66.

6. Organic v. non-organic yeast production; see http://www.bioreal.ch/english/comparison.html

CHAPTER 5

1. Waterproof: Molokhovets, E. (1904). *Podarok Molodym Khozyaikam ili sredstvo k umen'sheniyu raskhodov v domashnem khozyaistve* (A Gift to Young Housewives or A Means of Reducing Household Expenses). St Petersburg: Klobukov, paragraph 3687 (my translation). An edited and annotated English translation of the 1897 edition is available as Toomre, J. (1998). *Classic Russian Cooking: Elena Molokhovets' A Gift to Young Housewives*. Bloomington: Indiana University Press.

2. Clarke, C. and Arendt, E. (2005). *A review of the application of sourdough technology to wheat breads*. Advances in Food & Nutrition, 39, 138–161.

3. Doris Grant's no-time dough. Grant, D. (1973). *Your Daily Food*. London: Faber & Faber, 79.

CHAPTER 9

1. Monopolies Commission: quoted in BSSRS (1978). *Our daily bread: who makes the dough?* London: BSSRS.

2. The crustless loaf: see The British Baker, 29.7.05.

CHAPTER 11

1. Gerrard, J. & Sutton, K. (2005). *Addition of transglutaminase to cereal products may generate the epitope responsible for coeliac disease.* Trends in Food Science and Technology 16 (2005) 510–512.

CHAPTER 12

1. Food Standards Agency (2002) McCance & Widdowson's *The Composition of Foods*, 6th summary edition. Cambridge: Royal Society of Chemistry. Bender, D. & Bender, A. (1999). *Benders' Dictionary of Nutrition and Food Technology*, Seventh edition. Cambridge: Woodhead Publishing.

CHAPTER 13

1. Elena Molokhovets: see notes to Chapter 5.

INDEX